Releasing
the

Within

by Gail Carr Feldman, Ph.D.,
and Katherine A. Gleason

ALPHA

A Pearson Education Company

International Standard Book Number: 0-02-864405-0
Library of Congress Catalog Card Number: 2002110189

04   03   02   8   7   6   5   4   3   2   1

Interpretation of the printing code: The rightmost number of the first series of numbers is the year of the book's printing; the rightmost number of the second series of numbers is the number of the book's printing. For example, a printing code of 02-1 shows that the first printing occurred in 2002.

Printed in the United States of America

For marketing and publicity, please call: 317-581-3722

The publisher offers discounts on this book when ordered in quantity for bulk purchases and special sales.

For sales within the United States, please contact the following: Corporate and Government Sales, 1-800-382-3419 or corpsales@pearsontechgroup.com

Outside the United States, please contact the following: International Sales, 317-581-3793 or international@pearsontechgroup.com

Publisher: Marie Butler-Knight
Product Manager: Phil Kitchel
Managing Editor: Jennifer Chisholm
Acquisitions Editor: Randy Ladenheim-Gil
Book Producer: Lee Ann Chearney/Amaranth
Development Editor: Lynn Northrup
Production Editor: Katherin Bidwell
Copy Editor: Jan Zunkel

Cover Designer: Charis Santillie
Book Designer: Trina Wurst
Illustrator: Wendy Frost
Creative Director: Robin Lasek
Indexer: Ginny Bess
Layout/Proofreading: Angela Calvert, Mary Hunt

Releasing
the

Within

*We dedicate this book to the Goddesses. Thank you for
your inspiration, courage, devotion, strength, knowledge,
wisdom, power, patience, and, of course, tenacity!
May your examples champion us on a path of wonder,
spiritual growth, and self-enlightenment.*

Contents

Introduction

My grandmother was a powerful example of Goddess energy. She was a Christian Scientist who, despite the odds against her, survived the influenza epidemic of 1918. She later became a Transcendentalist and taught me to believe in the essential unity of all creation and the innate goodness of human beings. My mother inherited my grandmother's courage and independence. An only child, she had two daughters. I had two daughters, and my sister had four daughters. Times are changing, though, as my sister now has six, yes, six grandsons! So, this powerful Goddess energy of caring and compassion, as well as dedicated delight in life, is now being imparted to this next generation of males. (My first grandchild will be born during the production of this book, but at the time of this writing, I don't know the gender!)

My oldest daughter, Niki, is a massage instructor, body-worker, and yoga teacher; and my youngest, Megan, is a foreign correspondent, most recently stationed in Guatemala. As my girls grew up, our many shared experiences revealed our sacred contract to learn from each other in this lifetime. We know we have traveled together before. It is quite humbling to become aware that your child is in many ways a wiser soul than you.

The potent impact that recognizing the Goddess within can have not only strengthens the self and promotes recognition of your own divinity, but it strengthens your love bonds with family, friends, and all other people. You are gifted by the presence of other people in your life, and you, in turn, are a gift to others. Because of this powerful impact, I was excited to participate in writing this book and helping to expand awareness of the feminine influence. And just to be clear that we're not leaving out the male influence, my husband of 34 years (even though we are now divorced) would be the first to attribute great growth and inner peace to the rather consistent emphasis on spirituality and feminine or maternal values in our family.

As a social worker and then a clinical psychologist for over 30 years, I have witnessed the importance of the inner life—exploring the unconscious, overcoming crisis and trauma, self-responsibility for dissolving defenses, and claiming and asserting love over neurotic impulses. The spiritual comes into my work more and more, as everyone, but especially women, looks for greater meaning in life and ways to understand stressful events. I believe the cycles of birth and death, loss and gain, and the necessary grief that the Goddess stories describe, teach that earth-time is a stage on which people act out the dramas of growth in a highly adventurous journey. And there is always spiritual or supernatural guidance along the way. The feminine archetypes or Goddesses remind you to look within and know that you have all the resources required to live a rich and abundant life, and that you can facilitate others in their growth and healing.

In this book, you will find the stories of a variety of Goddesses drawn from many cultures worldwide. In the present day, humankind is blessed with all the opportunities that an expanding global awareness can bring. We know that you will enjoy this wonderfully rich tapestry of world cultures. We hope that you will see, feel, and experience the great contributions that every culture can make to your own personal life journey. As you learn about a variety of traditions, you will also come to value the culture that you yourself are a part of and participate in building.

In addition to the Goddess stories, each chapter contains questions and essays designed to help you explore yourself and your own Goddess nature in a fun and lively way. To deepen your own exploration, we have included exercises at the end of each chapter. You can do these alone or try them with friends or family members who are interested in personal growth. We hope that this book will inspire your awareness and help you to map your way along the path to your own unique inner Goddess.

Celebrate the divine being *you are!*

—Gail Carr Feldman, Ph.D.

Acknowledgments

I would like to thank the women in my family: my great-grandmother Brodie, my grandmother "Nanna," my mother (with her totally unique name) Videlle Dolphe, and my sister Judy. It took many years into my adult life before I recognized their intelligence, wisdom, and persistent love. My community of women friends, from childhood on, has been the mainstay of my mental health and happiness. Karen, Maggie, Gwen, Marcia, Diane, Kathy, and Barbara—the Goddess is present in every one of you. Thank you for your many blessings. And from the moment they were born, I knew that my daughters, Nicole and Megan, were filled with sacred energy. Along the way, I learned so much from our spiritual bond. I now see them as the full-grown Goddesses they are, and I am grateful.

—GF

An enormous thank you to Lee Ann Chearney at Amaranth for her vision, humor, and total Goddess-like fabulousness. This book never would have happened without her. I also need to thank Gail for her insight and voluminous knowledge. Thanks also to Michael Thomas Ford, who knows his mythology and is in touch with his Goddess self, and to Doug Rose for being himself. Thanks, too, to the staff at Alpha Books for their devotion to releasing the Goddess! I also want to thank my teachers: Carol Fox Prescott, who taught me about the breath; Beth Rosen; Peter Rizzo, Cliff Schuman, Annie Piper, and everyone else at Bhava Yoga Center; and the felines, past and present—Fred, Black Kitty, Friendly and all the kittens, Lucy, Woofie, Bruno, and, of course, Elphaba.

—KAG

Part 1

Celebrate Spirituality

In Part 1, you take a look at Goddesses through the lens of world culture and religion, history, the ages and stages of feminine life, the reproductive cycle, and more to understand the Goddess Force and how to use it in your own life. Drawing on Goddesses from a variety of human experience, we'll bring the ancient out of the past and into the present in a timeless appreciation of the resonance of profound spiritual awareness. Speaking women to women, we encourage you on a path of self-exploration to access and release your own unique Goddess within, whoever she may be! We hope you will enjoy the confidence and well-being that comes with Goddess discovery and self-enlightenment.

Chapter 1

Goddesses, Spirituality, and You

Have you noticed how many amazing women are all around you? From the classroom, to the boardroom, in stadiums and in congress, in doctors' offices and judges' chambers, on TV and in the movies, powerful, smart, sexy women are everywhere, doing everything. Think about your child's daycare provider or your local loan officer. Consider Doris Fisher, co-founder of The Gap chain of stores; Jackie Joyner Kersee, Olympic gold medal heptathlete; Former First Lady and now Senator Hillary Clinton; pioneering journalist Barbara Walters; or Oscar winner comedian Whoopi Goldberg. What do all these women have in common? They know who they really are, and knowing that, they have tapped into their true divine natures.

You can tap into your divine nature and release your inner Goddess, too. Yes, you! Even if you are not young or beautiful, even if you are less successful than you think you should be, even if you have no special skills, you can explore yourself and find the divine within. You don't need to spend years in study, nor must you commit yourself to a specific religion or faith. You can begin to release your inner Goddess right now. In fact, just by picking up this book, you have already begun!

You want to be the best that you can be—physically, emotionally, and spiritually. You try to cook healthful meals for yourself or for your family. You go to the gym and work out (or at least you plan to), or maybe you get your exercise tossing a ball around with your kids or pushing a vacuum cleaner. You try to get enough rest and make sure that your children do, too. You try to break bad habits and cultivate good ones. You contemplate your feelings, analyze them, and strive for better relationships with your friends, partners, family, and co-workers. Perhaps you read books about spirituality and holistic lifestyles, attend seminars, yoga classes, study groups, or church.

Regardless of where you are in relation to your goals, you can use this book to help you access the best that is inside you. We see these higher qualities that exist in all of us as the Goddess Force, the current of feminine energy that has existed throughout time. Come and learn about your true self by learning about Goddesses, and unleash the Goddess Force in your life!

Picture the Goddess Force

What do you conceive the Goddess force to be? Maybe you see the Goddess Force as the love and energy of a powerful deity, the Divine feminine aspect of God. You may think of the Goddess as a warm and nurturing natural support. You may feel the Goddess force when the wind blows or when a ray of sunshine slices through a bank of clouds. The Goddess Force may manifest itself as music or art. Or you may see the Goddess force in the face of the Virgin Mary or an icon of Saint Barbara. You may feel the Goddess force in the flow of love welling up inside for your children or others dear to you. But you don't have to believe in a Goddess (or a God) to begin to reach your best self and release your personal Goddess Force. And you don't have to be a woman to recognize the Goddess Force, either.

> 66 Art! Who comprehends her? With whom can one consult concerning this great goddess?
>
> —Ludwig van Beethoven, composer (1810)

You can think of the Goddesses in this book as metaphors for the various aspects of the female psyche and personality—pieces of yourself.

Or you can look at the Goddesses as powerful symbols, or what psychotherapist Carl Gustav Jung (1875–1961) called archetypes—images, patterns, situations, or metaphors that appear in the cultures of all of humankind. These archetypes connect us to the collective unconscious—the pool of myths and symbols that are understood the world over and throughout time.

Popular movies are full of archetypes. In *The Wizard of Oz*, as in many fairytales, Dorothy, the Persona or Hero, is on a quest. On her journey, she meets many archetypes—the Great Mother in Glinda the Good Witch; the Animus and Anima, the male and female spirits of the human psyche in the Scarecrow, the Tin Man, and the Cowardly Lion; the Trickster in the Wizard; and Darkness in the Wicked Witch of the West. All of these archetypes are a part of Dorothy (and they are a part of you, too!). So while Dorothy completes her quest, she learns about herself, and this knowledge enables her to go home. An understanding of archetypes and how you relate to them in your day-to-day life can help you feel connected to others as women, to women from different times and different lands, and to our own best selves.

If you were going to a costume party and had to dress as a Goddess, what would you wear? You might want to dress in a toga and sandals, like a classical Greek or Roman Goddess. You might want to be a more contemporary Goddess and wear a fabulous Vera Wang gown. Or you might go as Lady Godiva, clothed in nothing but your own flowing hair. Your Goddess outfit could reflect the dress of a historical Goddess; it could be based on a fairytale character; it could be made up of all your favorite articles of clothing; or it can be a fantasy outfit that may never exist in reality. Your Goddess outfit might include the following:

- Soft blue suede boots with wings
- A delicately embroidered silk blouse
- A velvet cape
- A fringed suede jacket
- A golden bustier
- A well-worn pair of jeans
- A diamond tiara
- A hardhat
- A pair of broken-in running shoes
- Ruby slippers

Take a minute to think about your Goddess outfit. Or better yet, plan a Goddess costume party. Your Goddess outfit will probably be different from everyone else's. Your Goddess outfit reflects your Inner Goddess, and she is as unique as you are.

Stepping into Goddess Shoes

Does dealing with your sister sometimes feel like a trip to the underworld? Have you ever wished you could send your partner down into the dark regions? Well, you are not alone. The Goddess Inanna, the queen of heaven in the ancient Sumerian tradition, had just those experiences. Her story is a very ancient tale. Because the Sumerians were among the first ancient people to invent writing, their Goddesses are the oldest ones who we know about today. The story of Inanna dates from about 3500 B.C.E.

Imagine this: You have decided to travel to the land of the dead, where your sister reigns as queen. On your descent to this underworld, you pass through seven gates and leave an article of clothing at each one. By the time you reach your sister, you are naked. There you are told that you can only leave the land of the dead if you find a substitute to take your place. You are allowed to return home, but only to find your replacement. Foul-breathed demons follow you. At home, you find that instead of mourning your loss, your partner is celebrating with wine, dancing, and song. Because of this less-than-devoted behavior, you send your partner to the land of the dead in your place.

Not surprisingly, there are a couple other versions of Inanna's tale. In the one above, Inanna eventually agrees that her partner, Dumuzi, God of corn, vegetation, and sheep, can come back to the land of the living for six months out of the year as long as his sister takes his place in the underworld. In another version, while Inanna is still in the underworld, Dumuzi and his sister agree to take her place. In yet another version, Inanna travels to the underworld in search of Dumuzi, who has died. She secures his release for part of the year, but must allow him to return to the underworld every winter.

Throughout history, poets, priestesses, mystics, and ordinary people have found inspiration, wisdom, entertainment, and solace in stories such as the one about Inanna. On one level, you can read her story as an explanation for why the Earth has seasons—winter comes when Dumuzi is gone. You can also look to Inanna as an example of feminine strength and bravery. If she can face her sister, the queen of the dead, then surely you can summon her strength and face yours. In addition to having a fearsome sister, Inanna finds out that she has a less-than-ideal mate. Armed with this knowledge, and with her strength and bravery, she sends the no-good guy away. She has the courage to act. Try on Inanna's powers. If she can do it, then you can, too!

66 Whenever I prepare for a journey, I prepare as though for death. Should I never return, all is in order.

—Katherine Mansfield, short-story writer (1922)

In contemporary times, many people see all Goddesses from all cultures as aspects of one Great Goddess, who embodies the total female energy of the Universe. Thus, Inanna is just one part of the Great Goddess. She is also part of you as a woman and a part of the story of all of our lives. In this book, you will look at various Goddesses and see how their stories and energies relate to you and to the challenges you face in the modern world. In doing so, you will identify the many forms of Goddess energy and begin to open yourself to the sense of power, healing, and connection that comes with an acknowledgement of the spiritual dimension in your life. You will learn about many Goddesses from a variety of cultures, but ultimately this book is about your life and your spirituality. And thus, the most important things you will learn may be about yourself.

Goddesses, Goddesses Everywhere

But who are these Goddesses? The many Goddesses you are about to meet represent the best of different continents, cultures, and various historical periods. Some of these Goddesses are characters whom you would traditionally consider to be Goddesses. They are, or were, part of a religious pantheon, a group or family of deities, who receive the worship of a segment of the human population.

Some of the Goddesses in this book—Snow White and Baba Yaga—come from fairy tales. They may once have been Goddesses in a more traditional sense, but after Goddesses fell out of favor and were replaced by one single God, they were relegated to folk and fairy stories. We will examine these fairytale characters and other Goddesses, and you will see how similar many fairytale characters are to traditional Goddesses. Even if they don't fit a traditional definition of Goddess, and even if no one ever built them temples or prayed for their help, these fairytale characters are still relevant today because they represent feminine archetypes and they have influenced your attitudes about being female.

Do you ever listen to opera? Do you remember the scene in the movie *Moonstruck* when Cher (now there's a Goddess!) and Nicholas Cage have their romantic night at New York City's Metropolitan Opera House? One of the reasons that people love to go to operas is that opera characters are passionate and larger than life. Some of the stories of opera's larger-than-life heroines are based on the stories of historically worshipped Goddesses. Other opera heroines are archetypes just like fairytale characters.

Forget about opera as a dusty, boring, out-of-this-century relic. If you want a quick way to arouse your Goddess passion, try a stormy opera Goddess encounter. Borrow an opera CD from your local library and listen in. The drama and passion of opera can really inspire you when you are cleaning the house, folding the laundry, or chopping vegetables. Opera can also be great when you are feeling sorry for yourself. Sometimes listening to a passionately tragic story can help you release your own woes or maybe just put them in perspective. Hey, no matter what is happening in your life, you've probably got it better than some of these women .... Start exploring opera Goddesses, from Madame Butterfly to Luisa Miller to Violetta, *La Traviata*'s fallen woman, to the infamous Valkyries, the eight wild maidens of Valhalla (see the following table for more). Remember that saying, "The opera isn't over till the fat lady sings!"

Move Over, Maria Callas and Kathleen Battle: Releasing Your Opera Goddess

Opera Goddess	Her Story
Aida (pronounced *ah-EE-duh*) in Giuseppe Verdi's *Aida*, set in Ancient Egypt	Aida, a slave girl who works for the daughter of the king, is caught in a love triangle with her mistress and the leader of the Egyptian army. To top it off, her father is the leader of the opposing army. When her lover is

Opera Goddess	Her Story
	sentenced to death by being sealed in a tomb, she sneaks inside so that she will be with him forever.
Mimi, in Giacomo Puccini's *La Boheme*, set in the Latin Quarter of nineteenth-century Paris	Parisian Mimi, who has consumption, finds true love when she meets her neighbor, the poet Rodolpho. They break up, get back together, and then she dies.
Carmen, in George Bizet's *Carmen*, set in nineteenth-century Seville, Spain	Carmen seduces Jose, even though he has a girlfriend. When a handsome bullfighter pays her attention, she ignores Jose. In a fit of jealousy, Jose kills Carmen and then throws himself on her corpse, sobbing.
Leonore, in Ludwig van Beethoven's *Fidelio*, set in eighteenth-century Spain	Leonore, dressed as a man, rescues her husband from prison. Amazingly, this story has a happy ending.
Susanna, in Wolfgang Amadeus Mozart's *Marriage of Figaro*, set in eighteenth-century Spain (a popular place for operas!)	In this romantic comedy, Susanna is all set to marry Figaro, but her employer, the Count, has his eye on her. Mayhem ensues. There's confusion, cross-dressing, and all sorts of schemes, but it all comes out right in the end.

Another great set of Goddess archetypes are the ones you can find in a deck of Tarot cards. Carl Jung studied the Tarot and found that the pictures on the cards relate to timeless human archetypes of transformation. Besides using Tarot cards for fortune telling, you can use them as the focus of meditation. Meditating on a card can help you identify patterns and archetypes in your own life.

Which Tarot Queen are you? In a Tarot card reading, the Queen cards are often used to represent the woman whose cards are being read, especially if the woman is over 40. Knowing which Queen, or archetype, you most closely identify with can help you to recognize the positive qualities that you already manifest. This knowledge can also help you to pinpoint the areas of your life in which you could make some improvements.

Studying Tarot Queen of Wands, a card that represents ambition, growth, and leadership, you could learn about your own deepest ambition, or you could come to realize that you have always reacted badly to having a female boss. Musing on the imagery of the Queen of Cups, a card of intuition, you could become more aware of your own intuition and the direction that it is pointing you. In contrast, the Queen of Swords represents analytic thought and knowledge of the everyday world. She is a woman of strong character and keen mind. From her, you can learn about your relationship to knowledge, both what you already know and what you have yet to find out. The Queen of Pentacles rules over fertility. She is creative, easy-going, and grounded, a real Earth-Mother type. Studying her image, you could learn about your own mothering qualities or about a mother figure in your life.

Take this quick quiz to see which Tarot Queen you most closely identify with:

1. If I had to be one element, I would be …
   a) Fire   c) Air
   b) Water   d) Earth

2. In my day-to-day life I am most concerned with …
   a) Action or growth
   b) Emotion or intuition
   c) Thought or communication
   d) The physical or material

3. Your best buddy from work wants to set you up on a blind date. You …

a) Say, "Great! Where and when?"

b) Bite your nails, pace, and try to decide what to do.

c) Ask a million questions, and then call everyone you know to see what bits of information you can find about this new person.

d) Shake your head, dig in your heels when your friend tries to persuade you, and ultimately proclaim that blind dates never work out anyhow.

4. Your birthday is coming up. You are most likely to celebrate by …

a) Going out dancing with your friends.

b) Going away on a spiritual retreat.

c) Visiting a museum or attending a cultural event.

d) Inviting friends over and cooking a feast.

If you answered mostly (a)s, you are most closely associated with the Queen of Wands. You are a go-getter with strong leadership skills. You are also passionate, enthusiastic, and motivated. Be careful not to let your healthy aggression and enthusiasm turn into pushiness or arrogance.

If you answered mostly (b)s, you are most closely associated with the Queen of Cups. You are emotional, intuitive, and in touch with creativity and your own heart. You are also a nurturer and are a great help to individuals lucky enough to be your friend. Be careful not to let your sensitive imagination and delicate emotional instrument sweep you away into constant worry and fear.

If you answered mostly (c)s, you are most closely associated with the Queen of Swords. You are a thinker, an observer, and a lover of knowledge. You may also have good organizational skills and know how speak in public and lead a crowd. Be careful not to let gossip, anger at having your ideas misunderstood, or your own preconceived ideas cloud what is really happening in front of you.

If you answered mostly (d)s, you are most closely associated with the Queen of Pentacles. You are practical, full of common sense, and have an encyclopedic knowledge of great cooking and housekeeping tips. You are also a natural in business, taking care of children, and any form of gardening. Beware the tendency to turn moody, sad, or clingy when you are feeling insecure about your finances or material possessions.

Other Goddesses in this book are real historical women—from Joan of Arc to Maya Angelou, Princess Diana, Queen Victoria, and Mother Teresa. You'll be introduced to many, many Goddesses. Some of them you may know; others you might not. In learning about these Goddesses, you will learn about yourself. In the process, you might meet aspects of yourself that you didn't know.

And we will celebrate that knowledge. We will celebrate all that is divine and spiritual about women because, the way we see it, in the end, all women are Goddesses.

How to Use This Book

You move through your daily life. You cook and eat, drink a cup of tea or a double espresso. You sleep and exercise and make love. We're going to explore the Goddess by connecting to her through the things that you do every day. In exploring the actions of your life and connecting them to the divine, you will make your very breath a part of the divine. And when you do that, you release your Goddess within. So, do you love to cook? Do you sleep too much? Do you like to do yoga? Are you quick-tempered? Do you laugh a lot? Cry too much? All your actions are divine. Who are you? Who do you want to be? Where is the Goddess Force that inspires *you?*

While most of the activities we discuss will be familiar to you, other activities—meditation and participating in rituals or ceremonies—may seem more unusual or even exotic. Have fun with the material that is new for you. Work through the book from the beginning, if that feels right. Or skip around. In flipping through the table of contents, you may find yourself drawn to one chapter in particular. Maybe issues of food and eating have been on your mind a lot recently. If so, go ahead and start with Chapter 3 and read about Greedy Woman from Nigeria, Deer Woman from the American Southwest, Eve from Paradise, and the ancient Greeks Demeter and Persephone.

At the end of each chapter, we have presented two exercises that will help you explore the Goddesses and how they relate to the chapter topic. Undertake these with a spirit of adventure. Have fun with them and see what you find out about yourself. You may learn something profound. Or you may find that folding origami cranes, which can be used as a form of Goddess meditation, just does not do it for you. You can work on the exercises alone or you can get together with a group of friends to do them. Some of the exercises call for supplies. We've tried to limit all the things you will need to easily accessible arts and crafts materials, but feel free to make substitutions to fit your budget or time constraints. And don't worry about trying to do a perfect job. Try to focus on the process rather than creating a perfect result.

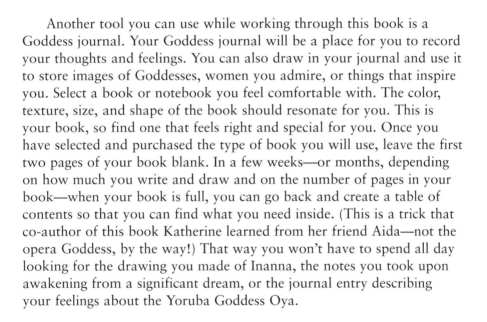

66 I always say, keep a diary and some day it'll keep you.

—Mae West, actress (1937) 99

Another tool you can use while working through this book is a Goddess journal. Your Goddess journal will be a place for you to record your thoughts and feelings. You can also draw in your journal and use it to store images of Goddesses, women you admire, or things that inspire you. Select a book or notebook you feel comfortable with. The color, texture, size, and shape of the book should resonate for you. This is your book, so find one that feels right and special for you. Once you have selected and purchased the type of book you will use, leave the first two pages of your book blank. In a few weeks—or months, depending on how much you write and draw and on the number of pages in your book—when your book is full, you can go back and create a table of contents so that you can find what you need inside. (This is a trick that co-author of this book Katherine learned from her friend Aida—not the opera Goddess, by the way!) That way you won't have to spend all day looking for the drawing you made of Inanna, the notes you took upon awakening from a significant dream, or the journal entry describing your feelings about the Yoruba Goddess Oya.

Goddesses in History

In scholarly circles, debate rages about the history of Goddess worship. Some scholars claim that before Christianity, before the invention of the written word, people worshipped one Great Goddess, the mother of all life. Human culture of that era is thought to have been peace loving, woman centered, earth honoring, and matriarchal. Eventually, patriarchal cultures began to take over, and to bolster male authority, the rulers fragmented the Goddess, broke her down into many smaller and less-important deities, and developed male Gods who were worshipped alongside their divine sisters. For the most part, the Goddesses who we know about today appear to be drawn from the period in history after this fragmentation. The earliest written records describe both Gods and Goddesses who have jurisdiction over various different facets of nature and human life. Ancient Greece, with its culture of male supremacy and its pantheon of Gods and Goddesses, is seen as an example of such a patriarchal culture. The rise of Christianity and monotheism—the worship of one male God and one God only—is described as the suppression of the pagan Goddess (*pagan* meaning people "of the land," who worshipped an Earth Mother Goddess), a denial of the human body and sexuality, and further solidification of male power over women.

> 66 I read the book of Job last night—I don't think God comes well out of it.
>
> —Virginia Woolf, novelist (1922) 99

Other scholars disagree with this scenario. They believe that it is impossible, based on the archeological record, to prove that prehistoric humans worshipped one Great Goddess. They point to evidence suggesting that these prehistoric societies venerated a variety of Gods, such as the figures represented in cave paintings, and Goddesses, such as the statuette known as the Venus of Willendorf. (You'll meet the Venus in Chapter 12.) In this view, the Goddesses are seen as local ones, worshipped only in a specific and narrow geographic area.

In more recent history, women in the United States and Canada began rediscovering Goddesses in the 1970s. Many women who participated in the second wave of feminism began researching the history of religion. These researchers dusted off the stories of a variety of Goddesses from various corners of the globe. For individuals who had been brought up with a knowledge limited to Christianity and Judaism, much of what they discovered about Goddesses was a revelation. They also worked at reclaiming the stories of women from the Judeo-Christian tradition.

Lilith is an example of one Goddess who has been reclaimed by a feminist view of spirituality. Although she does not appear in the Bible as we know it today, scholars have found traces of Lilith in the Old Testament. It is believed, based on information gathered from a text written around 2400 B.C.E., that she was originally a Sumerian storm demon. She also appears in Hebrew Scriptures; in the Talmud, the collection of ancient rabbinical writings that form the basis of traditional Judaism; and in the texts of the Kabala, esoteric mystery teachings based on the Hebrew Scriptures. In rabbinical legend, Lilith was Adam's first wife. She and Adam were created at the same time, and she gave Adam the gift of wisdom before she flew away, leaving him alone in the Garden. In the reclaimed version of her story, Lilith leaves the Garden because she refuses to be subservient to Adam. God then creates Eve as a submissive partner for Adam. In the present day, Lilith is seen to represent the equality of the sexes. In the late 1990s, Canadian singer/songwriter Sarah McLachlan created a hugely successful tour of women musicians called Lilith Fair. Today Lilith stands for wisdom, freedom, courage, pleasure, and sexual passion.

The theories and stories of Goddess cultures that scholars and researchers began to uncover in the 1970s created a lot of excitement, which led to further research in these areas. But these exciting new ideas were not limited to archeologists and historians. Books about the religion of prehistoric peoples, such as Merlin Stone's 1976 volume *When God Was a Woman,* which promoted the one Great Goddess idea, proliferated and began to influence the thinking of women outside academia. One of the most influential books of this period, Starhawk's *The Spiral Dance,* which appeared in 1979 and is still widely read today, further popularized the idea that the Supreme Being hadn't always been male.

In her inspiring book, Starhawk, whose original name was Miriam Simos, drew together the new ideas about Goddess worship, a desire for peace and equality among all peoples, concern for the environment, and an active and determined spirit to make the world a better place. In addition to writing, Starhawk and a number of her friends founded a group in San Francisco called the Reclaiming Collective. The members of this collective, who call themselves witches, view the Earth as a living being. Like other modern-day witches, they see all life on Earth as sacred and interconnected, and they consider it their primary duty in life to protect the Earth and all of her creatures. They see the Goddess as immanent in, or an inherent part of, the Earth's natural cycles of birth, growth, death, decay, and regeneration. Because of their belief in the sacredness of the Earth and their commitment to action, many members of Reclaiming participate in nonviolent protests. For example, members of the Reclaiming community have supported blockades to prevent the clear-cutting of old-growth redwood trees in California. Spirituality, from a Reclaiming perspective, is a fundamental tool for transformation. Personal, societal, and environmental changes are all brought about through the magic of the Goddess.

Many other spiritual traditions evolved out of the recovery of Goddess cultures and women's desires for a more holistic view of life and an active role in the spiritual realm. Some women investigated the Goddesses, their own feelings about their bodies, and the cycles of nature on their own, without following a group or any organized philosophy. Other women chose to investigate their spirituality in the context of Christianity, while still others continued on their spiritual path within Judaism.

Alternatively, instead of remaining within the Judeo-Christian tradition or looking to the past, some women seekers turned to extant traditions in which Goddesses had always been important. These individuals did not want to look to ancient times and prehistory to find their deities. Instead, they may have celebrated the power of Goddesses such as Oya, the Yoruban Goddess of storms, wind, and sudden change. Oya, a powerful deity who originated in West Africa and was brought to the New World with the forced emigration of slavery, is also a warrior, guardian of cemeteries, and the protector of women. She fights— alongside her husband, Shango, the God of Thunder—against injustice. Oya is part of a pantheon of Gods and Goddesses known as the Orisha who are worshipped in Africa, North America, the Caribbean, and Central and South America. She can initiate sudden change, the way a thunderstorm or cyclone can sweep clean everything in its path.

As the winds of historic change blew stronger and interest in women's spirituality grew, slowly some traditional religious institutions began to change as well. Some churches and synagogues started to allow women a larger role in services and even ordained women rabbis and clergy. By the late 1990s, fashionable young people in New York City began to wear images of Goddesses printed on their clothing and handbags. In early 2001, author Isobel Bird began to publish *Circle of Three*, a series of young adult books about three high school girls and their developing relationships with Goddesses. Increasingly more and more people are drawn to Goddess spirituality and relationships with the feminine divine. Many people see this shift in consciousness as a crucial change, the only way we can heal ourselves and the planet and ensure a healthy future for generations to come.

Kali, another Goddess who represents change, comes from India's vibrant, present-day Hindu pantheon. Kali is worshipped in India daily, particularly in Calcutta, which derives its name from the Kalighat, Kali's temple. Kali is the fiercest of warriors. The story goes that she sprang from the Goddess Durga's head during a battle in which the Gods and Goddesses were losing to an evil demon and his army. Kali vanquished the demon's forces and then made herself a necklace of skulls and a girdle of severed arms. Not surprisingly, given her choice of accessories, Kali is also associated with death and destruction. When Kali brings change, she clears the slate of all that is unnecessary so you can start again. (Sometimes the old house has to be completely torn down to build a new house.) We'll take a closer look at Kali in Chapter 9.

Can Goddesses Bring About Change?

Whether the change is sudden, drastic, and caused by outside forces or the restructuring of your life is by choice, your inner Goddess can provide the strength to help you cope. Psychologists say that the first step in any process of change is *awareness*. If, for example, you want to stop biting your nails, you first must become aware of when you bite them. Without this awareness of your own behavior, you have no hope of catching yourself in the act and no hope of making the change. Always be gentle with yourself as you practice awareness. The second step in any process of change is *acceptance*. Telling yourself you are a terrible person after you have just consumed an entire bag of chocolate-chip cookies is like pouring grease on a fire. You just make yourself feel worse, and because you feel bad, you are more likely to binge again to try to relieve yourself from the bad feeling. The third step toward change is *action*. When you connect to the Goddesses, you are joining a tradition of women who have drawn strength from the Goddesses to accept and understand what is and to move into action. You can use this connection to help you change the things that you want to change in your life.

You might call on Demeter to help you to become a better cook or gardener. You might use the energies of Nox to help you sleep. Take inspiration from Artemis or Atalanta to start running again. Or emulate Bastet, the Egyptian goddess of pleasure, and really let yourself go and have a good time. Many women have found that employing spiritual or holistic means is the only way to effect lasting change. Investigating your life through the lens of the many Goddesses presented in this book will enable you to see what is joyful and right about your life. You will celebrate all that is good—your determination, your sense of humor, your heart. You will also see which areas, if any, you would like to improve. Learning about the Goddesses can help you connect to your own Inner Goddess. Connection to your Inner Goddess can help you to create your very best self and release your Goddess within.

Exercise #1: Creating an Altar to Your Inner Goddess

Sacred spaces can be powerful places where you go to inspire and motivate your heart, mind, and soul. Choose a place in your home, indoors or outdoors, to create an altar that celebrates your Inner Goddess. You can use a small table, a knick-knack shelf, an old desk, an upside-down crate, or even a windowsill. You just need a surface that will remain undisturbed by other members of your household, where you can place objects that you associate with your Inner Goddess.

Your altar might hold images of Goddesses that intrigue you; photographs of your grandmothers or your children; sea shells, which are associated with the Yoruban Goddess Yemaya; small stones; feathers; flowers; candles; a particularly beautiful postcard that inspires you. Your altar will evolve over time as a continuously changing work in progress. Add and remove objects as your mood changes and as your views of both yourself and the Goddesses shift. In every chapter, we'll make suggestions for more things you can add to your altar. Think of it as an ongoing project and as a mirror of you and your emerging Goddess nature.

Instant Goddess

Actress Ethel Barrymore said, "You grow up the day you have your first real laugh at yourself." Most Goddesses we know have a great sense of humor. Look in the mirror right now and have a laugh with the Goddess confidante you see there. Take another peek; you've just got a glimpse of your Goddess within!

Exercise #2: Opening Pandora's Box

You will need the following items:

- A white gift box about 6" × 6" × 6"
- Markers, pens, crayons, or colored pencils

- A glue stick
- Scissors
- Old magazines
- Yarn, feathers, beads, cloth scraps, polished stones, and other unique items that inspire you

Greek Goddess Pandora, whose name means "the gift of all," married Epimetheus, Prometheus's brother. As a wedding gift, Zeus sent Pandora to her new husband with a delicate box locked with a golden key and the warning that she must never look inside it. Zeus's gift, though, was far from an act of generosity. Angry at Prometheus for stealing fire, he gave Pandora the box hoping that she would find its secrets irresistible and open it—which, of course, she did. Upon turning the golden key, Pandora unleashed the forces Zeus had placed there: Hunger, Plague, War, and Despair. But also Hope, to light the way back toward enlightenment and the end of suffering.

We all have a face that we present to the world, and an Inner face that sometimes we ourselves don't quite recognize, even if we try to look for it in the mirror of our hearts and souls. Sometimes, looking at ourselves—outside and in—is a bit like opening Pandora's box. We're not sure what will come out, but we hope for the best! In this exercise, you will create a box that shows outwardly the face you present to the world. It can reflect the way you look, dress, act, your work, your family, whatever you show outside. The inside of the box, though, should reflect your inner self, those things you keep in your heart. Include your hopes, your dreams, your wishes.

For example, you might decorate the outside of your box with pictures cut from a magazine of a woman behind a desk or making dinner for her family, or a symmetrical pattern of beads around the edge of the box. This would symbolize you as a career woman or mother, emphasizing the orderly, organized image you present to the world. You might decorate the inside of the box with a wild profusion of beads, feathers, and colorful designs, representing your more carefree inner self.

You may be surprised at what you create. You will be even more surprised if you do this exercise with other women, because you will see how very different each life representation is. Is your box full of color and texture? Is it neat, all corners tight and just so, or ripped and jagged? Is your creation flat or is it three-dimensional? Are the flaps of your box open or closed? (Are you accessible and open to the world or private and solitary?) What images did you use? A calendar? A fine art painting? A highway? A child?

Just after completing your box, write in your Goddess journal about what the experience of creation felt like to you. Place the box on your altar. For one week, look at your box every day for five minutes. Go back and write in your journal again about what the box says about you, now that you've had time to observe and think about it. Have you discovered something new? How different were your impressions in the moment of creation from your impressions after waiting and looking? When we look at ourselves with honesty, it may feel like a Pandora's box that unleashes a fury of emotions, realizations, problems, and challenges. But with the passion and fury come the hope and the dream for enlightenment. Embrace Pandora's box as your "gift of all."

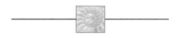

In doing both of these exercises you have started yourself on the Goddess path of self-discovery. You are beginning to learn who you really are. You are like Inanna—brave, strong, and in possession of the courage to act. The actions that you have taken so far have started to release your Goddess. Read on to continue the process and to explore the manifestations of the Goddesses in all the ages and stages of women.

Chapter 2

The Ages and Stages of Women

In your own life, you are the woman on the Tarot's Star card. Notice that the woman in the image is pouring water both into the pool and onto land. Her action represents the connection of the land, or material world, to the world of water, or spirit and emotions. The stars above the woman send her the inspiration of spiritual energy and truth.

Stand in the Star's mythic landscape, and you are a Goddess who evokes a connection between matter and spirit. Place Tarot's Star card on your Goddess altar and meditate upon the feminine divine synthesis of hope and inspiration.

You live in the material world, and yet you have an Inner Goddess, or a spirit, and emotions. You are also connected to the stars and inspired by them. In astrology, your birth chart is a map of the universe at the moment of your birth that describes the kind of inspiration the stars send only to you. An awareness of your unique spirit connection to the heavens above and the earth below can inspire you to realize your own hopes and dreams. A simple way to foster your own feelings of connection to the universe is to look at the sky. When was the last time you stood under a starry night sky and pondered your place in the big picture? Do you feel that you are a Goddess who is part of a divine universe?

66 To stay in one place and watch the seasons come and go is tantamount to constant travel: one is traveling with the earth.

—Marguerite Yourcenar, writer (1980)

Just as everyone else, you are affected by the cycles of nature—spring gives way to summer, which leads to fall and then winter. Every day, with the turning of the Earth, the sun and the moon appear to rise, cross our sky, and then set to rise again the next day. You have seen the visible part of the moon wax (grow bigger), reach fullness, wane, disappear from the sky for a day or two, and then begin to wax again. We are born, we mature, we grow old, we eventually die, and perhaps we are reborn. As a woman, you also experience your own natural cycle of ovulation and menstruation. And you participate in the larger feminine cycle moving from childhood to puberty and menarche and through menopause to what some women have called "cronedom," the wisdom of the mature years.

If you are still menstruating, you probably know where you are in that monthly cycle. (You also probably know what time of day it is and the season!) But do you know where you stand on your unique lifepath, where you are on the curve of the feminine life cycle?

Multiple Goddesses for Multiple Lives

Did you know that over the last 100 years, the average life expectancy has increased by almost 30 years? A woman born in 1900 expected to live to about 45 or so. In 2000, a woman had every chance of living till 75, give or take a few years. By the year 2020, many of us may be living vital lives all the way to 100 or beyond.

This means that you may have 20 or so more years of "quality" time before old age starts to hamper your activities. You have more time than any previous generation to explore yourself, to create yourself. Instead of growing up to be one kind of Goddess—Earth Mother, mystic, domestic queen, mistress of love, athlete, nature girl, warrior, career woman, or what have you—you can take on multiple roles in one life span. In essence, you have the opportunity to live more than one life in one lifetime. (You don't need to wait for reincarnation to experience more than one idea of yourself!) You are blessed with the opportunity to reinvent yourself. And you can reinvent yourself in any way that you desire. Gone are the days when women were limited and confined to the home and the roles of wife and mother (at least that's true here in the United States). Gone are the days when a short life span only allowed you one narrow experience of life. Now, you can be anything you want to be, and then you can change your mind and become someone else!

In the course of your everyday life—shopping for food, going to work or school, feeding the kids, folding laundry—do you remember that your life choices are up to you? Do you remember that you can direct and control your own destiny? Many women become overwhelmed by the business of everyday life and forget, or never realize, that they are the ones who sit in the driver's seat. But once you take the wheel, do you know where you are headed? Knowing your life purpose or purposes can help you to find the way. Between taking out the trash, making dinner, having your car serviced, mowing the lawn, shopping for shoes for the kids, have you considered your reasons for being on this Earth? You may feel that this is an unanswerable question. Or one best left up to the Goddesses (or God). But determining your life purpose can help you to establish your values and help to give you the strength to live by them.

> 66 Like the winds of the sea are the winds of fate,
> As we voyage along through life
> 'Tis the set of the soul
> That decides its goal
> And not the calm or the strife.
>
> —Ella Wheeler Wilcox, poet (1897) 99

If you know what you value in life—in terms of people, things, and abstract concepts—you will have an easier time making decisions. You will also find it easier to get through difficult situations or periods in your life. It can even help with the boredom of an afternoon at the Laundromat! If, for example, you know that your purpose in life is to express love, then every domestic chore becomes less of a burden and more of a sacred act. By caring for the physical needs of family and loved ones, you are not the maid (although sometimes it may feel that way), but the expression both of your Inner Goddess and the love of the universe. Or you may express your love and your Inner Goddess through your career by working hard and being helpful and respectful to your co-workers and clients. When you know your purpose, every action you perform can take on great significance, and your life rises from one of petty details to an experience of the divine.

Do you feel locked into a situation that is making you unhappy? Have you ever considered that your idea of yourself may be your biggest obstacle? The good news is that you can always change your mind. Planning for the future and acting on change are both things that you can start to do today. Start by answering this question: What kind of Goddess are you right now, today? Pick the one you most closely identify with from the following list:

a. Earth Mother

e. Athlete/Nature Girl

b. Mystic

f. Career Woman/Warrior

c. Domestic Queen

g. Creature of Mud and Dust

d. Mistress of Love

Now pick the image that you feel most closely represents you in your present stage of life:

If you picked a), you chose Demeter, the classical Greek Earth Mother. Illustration b) represents Persephone, Demeter's daughter, who spends half her time in the underworld and half as Goddess of spring and thus is in tune with the mystical qualities of life; c) is a picture of Hera, the Greek Domestic Queen. Illustration d) is a picture of Aphrodite, the Greek Goddess of Love. If you picked e), you identified with Artemis, the great Greek Huntress who represents nature and athletic abilities. Illustration f) is of Athena, the Greek Goddess of Wisdom, who is a Warrior, Career Woman, and city dweller. If you chose g), it looks like you're not feeling so great today, huh? Just know that you *will* feel better. Your feelings, your mind, and your life can all change, and starting today, you can make sure that happens.

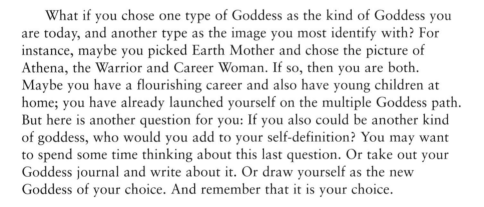

66 Age is something that doesn't matter, unless you are a cheese.

—Billie Burke, actress (1962) **99**

What if you chose one type of Goddess as the kind of Goddess you are today, and another type as the image you most identify with? For instance, maybe you picked Earth Mother and chose the picture of Athena, the Warrior and Career Woman. If so, then you are both. Maybe you have a flourishing career and also have young children at home; you have already launched yourself on the multiple Goddess path. But here is another question for you: If you also could be another kind of goddess, who would you add to your self-definition? You may want to spend some time thinking about this last question. Or take out your Goddess journal and write about it. Or draw yourself as the new Goddess of your choice. And remember that it is your choice.

Happy Birthday, Goddess!

How do you view your own birthday? Do you celebrate? Or do you sulk and hope that no one will notice? This year, why not remember all the Goddesses in attendance at your birth (mythical and real-world) and celebrate the anniversary of this blessed event? You could have a birth Goddess party. As you explore and add to who you are, you may find that you want to celebrate your rebirths—such as the emergence of a new Goddess quality in yourself, learning a new skill, or the start of a new job. Is your destiny set at birth? Or are you on an ever-changing, ever-evolving path? The Fates are always there at important beginnings!

You have probably heard of the Three Fates, the ancient Greek Goddesses of, well, fate. They are also known as the Moirae, which means "allotters." Originally, the Fates were considered to be birth Goddesses. They were present at each human birth where Clotho, the first Fate, began to draw the thread of life for that individual from her spindle. Her sister Lachesis is responsible for measuring the thread and determining how long each life will be. And Atropos, the third sister, who some see as the old moon that rules the past, cuts the thread, thus determining the person's hour of death. Some people believe that the Fates spin, measure, and cut thread for each person at the moment of that person's birth. Others think that the spinning and measuring process is one that goes on throughout the person's life, and that the life ends when the thread is cut. The idea that the Fates represent an unfavorable or preordained destiny, instead of just your lot or portion of life, is a more recent notion that probably developed some time after the fall of the Greek Empire and the rise of Rome.

Try to imagine the Three Fates at your own birth. They were there welcoming you into the world. Or, if you like, think of the three Saami birth Goddesses Sar-akka, Juks-akka, and Uks-akka from Scandinavia. Sar-akka helps to open the womb to let the child out. Her sister Juks-akka helps to ensure that the new child will be successful. The third sister, Uks-akka, welcomes the newborn into the light of day and guards the door to the home, protecting all who pass through. With all these Goddesses in attendance, how could your birth not have been a divine affair?

Remember that the Goddesses were there to welcome you into the world, not to doom you to a life of hardships and disaster. The Fates dole out portions of life in the form of their thread, but they do not say what that life is to contain. Only you can do that. Certainly, you have had events in your life that were out of your control. We have all had accidents. How you respond to accidents, though, is up to you. Staying aware of your life purpose, through bad times and good, can help you to negotiate all the cycles of life and make all your experiences more enjoyable. So, even with the influence of the Three Fates, you still have free will!

Life at the Crossroads Under the Moon

The stars in your astrological birth chart influence you, but so does the moon. Do you know what sign of the zodiac the moon was in at the hour of your birth? Your moon sign can help to explain your emotional nature, your unconscious, and your relationships with other women. The moon has long been associated with women, probably because the moon's cycle from dark to waxing to full, and then waning again, lasts $29^{1}/_{2}$ days, about the same length as most women's menstrual cycles. Do you feel affected by the cycle of the moon's phases? Are you more energetic or emotional or silly during a full moon? If so, you are not alone. Many people report an intensification of feelings at such times. In the journey of life, standing under the emotional pull of the full moon, which path should you take?

Lucina, Diana, and Hecate are three Greco-Roman Goddesses associated with the moon who form a triad. In this grouping, Lucina represents birth, Diana is growth, and Hecate is death. Because Lucina's name actually means "bringer of light," it's not surprising that she was associated with birth, a coming into the light. Lucina is often depicted wearing a veil and holding both a flower and an infant. She has also been associated with the Goddess Juno, the Roman queen Goddess and protector of women.

Diana is Goddess of the moon, night, fertility, and women, as well as of wild animals and hunting. In the Greek tradition, she is known as Artemis. She is often pictured accompanied by hunting dogs or a stag. Her festival, which was celebrated on August 15, is now recognized as the Feast of the Assumption of the Virgin Mary.

Hecate, the death aspect of this grouping, is the Goddess of the crossroads, the moon, particularly when it is dark, and is associated with sorcery. Statues of Hecate, which depict her in triple form, were often placed at crossroads where she was worshipped and said to protect people from evil. Hecate is sometimes depicted with three bodies: that of a young woman, a woman in middle age, and an old woman. She has also been seen as having three heads—dog, horse, and lion (or dog, horse, and boar). She carries a flaming torch and is seen as the link between the visible and invisible worlds. Some people think of Lucina–Diana–Hecate triad as representing the three aspects of Diana. In the sky she is Lucina or Luna, on Earth she is Diana, and in the lower world and at night she is Hecate.

Does facing decisions feel like death to you? Meet Hecate, the Goddess of the crossroads! So why not use the volatile feelings of the full moon or your cranky premenstrual sentiments to help you make decisions? Oftentimes our inability to make a decision is because we are trying to please someone other than ourselves. Or we are listening to our reason and not to our hearts and emotions. As Dr. Christiane Northrup, a physician and writer on women's health, has pointed out, suppressing our feelings, living just for others, and giving our lives away can result in menstrual cycle problems such as PMS, ovarian cysts, and fibroids. And who wants that? Honor the emotion of the full moon and harness its intuitive powers to help you manifest your deepest, fullest hopes and dreams.

66 The moon develops the imagination, as chemicals develop photographic images.

—Sheila Ballantyne, writer (1975) 99

You can learn to make better decisions that honor your nature, emotions, imagination, and spirit. Try to involve your creative brain when making a decision. Draw, paint, or act out in dance the question at hand, instead of relying on words alone. (And do the map-making exercise at the end of this chapter.) Another way to start making better decisions is to remember that Hecate comes with two partners who represent birth and growth. In making a decision, you rule out one life possibility, and that untaken path is like a little death. Maybe a decision you have to make will represent the death of a fantasy. For example, you decide to start saving money toward that car you want instead of counting on a lottery win. After you have faced Hecate and her moonlit crossroads, you can move on to the new birth of choice represented by Lucina and the growth of Diana that comes from moving along a new path.

Have you been putting off an important decision? Resolve to make that decision today so that you can move on and be reborn into Lucina's new light.

A Day in the Life: A Lifetime in Microcosm

The cycle of days may be the most obvious one that you experience because it happens every day. You have probably heard the biblical verse that says "to everything there is a season," which means that there is a right time for every action. Well, there is also a right day and a right time of day. Are you in tune with your own personal rhythm of days? Do you greet each day like the new beginning, the rebirth that it truly is? Or do you stay up too late watching late-night TV and wake in the morning feeling groggy and irritable?

The Zoryi are the three Slavic Goddesses of morning, evening, and midnight. Every morning, Zorya Utrennyaya (which means "aurora of the morning") opens the gates of the palace of the sun so that her father, the sun God, can drive out in his golden chariot drawn by a pair of white horses and begin the daily journey across the sky. In addition to her other duties, Zorya Utrennyaya protects warriors in battle and saves them from death. In the evening, when the sun God returns home, Zorya Vechernyaya (aurora of the evening) closes the gate. In some accounts, the sun God is not male, but is a female Goddess and is the mother of the Zoryi. In this version, the moon God is their father. The third sister, whose name has been lost, has jurisdiction over the dark hours of night. Together, all three sisters are guardians of the world. They watch over the bear who lives confined in the constellation Ursa Major (also known as the Big Dipper) and prevent him from escaping and destroying the world.

Are you a natural night owl? What time of day (or night) do you feel most creative, vibrant, and alive? Can you arrange your schedule so that you can use that time? It may be pretty obvious, but if you are a night owl, you will be better off not working a job that requires you to be somewhere at six in the morning. Conversely, you early birds will be especially miserable working the graveyard shift.

When you do wake up (whenever that is), think of Zorya Utrennyaya. Imagine the energy of the sun Goddess's horses, pawing the ground, snorting, ready to burst through the gate and into the sky. Feel the power that Zorya Utrennyaya holds in her hands. If she felt like it, she could keep the gate closed and the sun inside. But she does not do that. Every day, whether she feels like it or not, she lets the sun shine. (Okay, sometimes it's hidden behind clouds, but it's still up there.) Start each day with her spirit, and let your own light shine.

If dawn is a rebirth, then sunset, or the time you go to bed, is a little death. (Do you avoid going to bed for that reason? If so, take a look at Chapter 5.) Honor Zorya Vechernyaya. She also holds the power of those horses in her hands. She is the link between the visible daytime world and the world of night, the unconscious, and dreams.

Wouldn't it be nice to feel like every day mattered? Well, it does, because a day in your life is a microcosm of your life. Look at each and every day as if it were a life, your life. Have you done what you wanted and needed to do with your life today? Make sure that you do one thing every day that makes you feel like it really *is* your life. Now is the right time for you to act. Take one small action toward a goal, or meditate, or pray, or cook something really fabulous. That way, what you do counts. That way, each and every day counts.

The Ultimate Triple Goddess: Maiden, Mother, Crone

The Triple Goddess is a powerful archetype. She represents both the monthly cyclical nature of woman and the female life cycle. She is the moment before ovulation, pregnancy, and menstruation. She is also a virginal and prepubescent girl, a mother, and a post-menopausal woman. And she is all of these at the same time. She tells you that you, too, contain all the ages of woman within you. No matter what your actual age, you are also young, adult, and mature. You possess the innocence, energy, and vitality of the Maiden; the fertility, creativity, and power of the Mother; and the wisdom, compassion, and fearlessness of the Crone.

Today, the roles of Maiden, Mother, and Crone have new, evolving meaning. In a world changed by contraception and the Pill, high-technology fertility procedures such as in-vitro fertilization (IVF), and estrogen hormone replacement therapy (HRT), the line between women's ages and stages is blurring and changing. Want to postpone or delay childbearing and extend maidenhood? Use contraception to manipulate or control your menstrual cycle (if chastity is an outmoded Goddess concept for you—for some women, it is still a valid choice). Do you desire motherhood above all other Goddess roles? Enhance your fertility with high-tech treatment that makes motherhood well into women's 40s a commonplace social trend (at least in this country!). Are you eager to age with grace and vitality? Explore the medical advances that encourage healthy aging—from HRT to proper nutrition and exercise protocols.

 The Triple Goddess embodies three ages of women. She is the Maiden, the Mother, and the Crone. Some people see her as three aspects of one larger feminine energy. She represents the waxing, full, and waning moon. She is creator, protector, and destroyer; birth, growth, and death; the earth, sky, and underworld. Sometimes the Triple Goddess appears with three different names—Lucina, Diana, and Hecate, for example. Other times, she is known under the same name with different aspects of her womanhood emphasized. Hera, the Greek Goddess of women and the queen of the Greek pantheon, had three temples in the city of Stymphalus, Greece. One honored her as Maiden, one as Mother, and one as Crone. Like the moon, or your period, her nature is cyclical. She continuously moves from one stage to the next and then begins the cycle all over again. The Triple Goddess is found in most every culture from India's Bhavani, the Giver of Existence, to the Celtic Brigid, known as the High One, to the Triple Pussa, a Chinese Buddhist Goddess associated with Kwan Yin, the Goddess of mercy.

How does the word *crone* strike you? Do you picture an ancient, stooped-over woman dressed in black and leaning on a cane? Since the 1970s, many women have tried to reclaim the word crone and purge it of its negative connotations. In the same way, women have worked to discard the negativity associated with menopause. Some women even have croning ceremonies, celebrations of their entry into the wisdom of post-menopausal life. If menopause is a little death, it is only a death of biological fertility. Recent scientific research suggests that even though your ovaries will stop producing eggs, they and your uterus will continue to secret hormones, chemicals, and certain beneficial lipids. So, there is certainly life after menopause!

66 Even as a girl whose menopause was decades away, I found comfort in the idea that when it happened, it was all part of an optimal design. The thought of it linked me to my mythical ancestors, those dusty, lanky, demimonde women striding across the veldt, their brains expanding with every step.

—Natalie Angier, science writer (1999)

If all goes well, you have a good shot at living to be 100-plus years old. That means you will have 40 some years of life after you have reached menopause. It is no longer the case that women hit menopause or the magic number 60 and are considered old, over the hill, defunct. If you think 60 is old, think again! Think of a fabulous older woman whom you admire. As of this writing in 2002, actress and human rights crusader Bea Arthur (of TV's *Maude* and *Golden Girls* fame) is performing her one-woman show on Broadway, and she is about to celebrate her seventy-sixth birthday. Argentine singer and political activist Mercedes Sosa is on tour of North America at age 67. And the writer, poet, and activist Maya Angelou, at the age of 73, is bringing her poetry into the mainstream, creating her own line of Hallmark products to pen more great inspirational words for women.

Learn from these women. Know that you have been given a gift of 20 or even 30 years of good, active living. Use your gift. Explore your options. Learn about yourself and grow. Let yourself be as many different Goddesses as you like. The Goddesses are all inside you. All you have to do is let them grow, change, be reborn, and flourish in as many ways and for as many days as you chose.

Exercise #1: Make Your Life Map

Do you know where you are? Do you know where you're going? Making a life map is one way to help you find out.

You will need a large sheet of paper and a clear surface on which to work. You will also need whichever of these items appeals to you:

- Colored pens and pencils
- Crayons
- Images from magazines
- Postcards
- Photographs
- A glue stick
- Yarn or string
- Sand or pebbles

Starting in the middle of your paper, draw or collage an image to represent you in the present moment. Don't worry if you're not much of an artist. Your representation of yourself does not have to actually look like you. You can use a symbol or a Goddess, or you can draw something abstract that captures your unique nature.

Now put down three or four life events on the path that have led you to where you are now. You may want to make an image to represent your high school or college graduation, your marriage, a divorce, moving to a new home, a promotion at work, the birth of children, the adoption of a pet, meeting a significant friend, an illness, or reading a life-changing book. Your events may not line up in a neat line. Your road probably has forks, and it may even have switchbacks and hairpin turns. If you want, mark the crossroads with an image of Hecate to remind you that the Goddess has watched over your past decisions, or guided you in some way. Let the images from your past help you to see your future. Looking at your past can help you to know who you are and where you are; without that knowledge, it can be hard to know where you are going.

Now draw roads leading away from where you are in the present. If you are on the verge of making a big decision, you may want to draw just two roads—one to represent "yes," the other "no." Put Hecate in the middle as the place where the two roads cross. Try drawing both alternatives and see which one is more appealing. Ask Hecate for help, if you need it. If you feel you have multiple paths in front of you, go ahead and draw many branches in your road. What would you most like to be, do, or get? Imagine what is up ahead. Is the path you are thinking of taking leading you closer to or farther from your real desires? Draw the road to whatever it is that you do want. Is the road straight or curvy? Are there obstacles in your path? Can you draw a bridge or a ladder to help you climb over those barriers? Imagine yourself walking along the path to your goal and reaching it.

If you don't know what you want, let the significant images from your past guide you. What have you done in the past that made you the happiest? Are there elements of that joy in your life today? Can you move a little closer to those kinds of experiences?

When you're done with your map, place it on the wall over your Goddess altar. Take a look at it every day for a week to remind yourself of who you are and where you are going.

 Instant Goddess

Songwriter and musician Carole King wrote a beautiful song called "Child of Mine." For us, this song expresses the beauty of the parent/child relationship. What song moves you and your daughter, or you and your mother, or you and your inner child, to joy? Sing that song together tonight with love.

Exercise #2: A Show of Hands

Your family and its cycles are a microcosm of the universe, too. A record of the changes and evolutions of the women in your family is fun to make; it helps you to feel connected to one another and to the generations to come.

To start, you will need some female members of your extended family. These could be your grandmother, mother, aunt, female cousins, or your daughters. You will also need a sheet of heavy paper and some finger paint.

You may also want to use the following:

- Colored pens and pencils
- Photographs
- Crayons
- A glue stick

Arrange the sheet of paper on a flat surface. Taking turns, have each woman coat her hand with finger paint and make a handprint on the sheet. Write the date on the page and add the names of the women. If you like, each person can add a written message. Or add collage elements such as photographs, ticket stubs, or the program from a significant event.

You can repeat this activity throughout the years. You probably will not want to do it every year. Select special years that mark life passages. You could focus on significant birthdays such as 21, 30, 40, 65, and 80. Or you could make a hand-print page to honor events such as a graduation or marriage.

If you do make hand printing a part of your celebration of life's milestones, you will want to get a scrapbook to keep them in. As your book of hands grows, you will be able to see how the hands and lives of all the women involved have grown, changed, and evolved with experience and age. You will see how together you have grown as a family of women. As each woman passes on, as we all must eventually, another will come in and you will be able to see, in your own family, how the cycle of life continues. Your hand scrapbook will become a multigenerational family record and an heirloom to maintain and pass down from generation to generation.

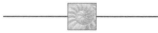

Have you decided to walk the Goddess path? Have the previous exercises moved you forward and helped you acknowledge the Goddess aspects of all the cycles in your life? Can you see that no matter what your age or stage in life, you are divine? At every age, you carry within you the Maiden, the Mother, and the Crone. Feel all parts of that triple self and know your Goddess nature. Read on and discover how to release your Goddess in all her infinite variety.

Your Goddess in Her Infinite Variety

"Age cannot wither her, nor custom stale her infinite variety," so wrote Shakespeare about the Egyptian queen Cleopatra. In Part 2, you start to explore your own Goddess qualities and strengths as you quest to incorporate a greater spirituality into your life every day. You will learn to release the Goddess of infinite variety that lies within your own special and sacred self—in chapters exploring food and nourishment; drink, the river of life; sleep, your inner rejuvenation and source of prophecy; exercise, movement in harmony; play, enjoying life; sex, the sensually spiritual; strength, your centering power; plus creativity, fertility, and imagination. You may be surprised to find that your Goddess qualities express themselves in your normal everyday experiences, habits, and practices. You are divine!

Chapter 3

Food: Nourishing Energy

Your feelings about food, eating, and your appetites may be pretty volatile and complex. Are you someone who obsesses about food? Do you constantly think about your next meal or snack? Or do you feel that food and eating are just a bother, a distraction from your real interests? Do you ever resent that you have to eat? Your feelings about food probably lie somewhere between these two extremes. You may have learned some of your attitudes toward food from your own mother. And you may have trained yourself to develop a fondness for salads or an antipathy toward snacking.

Of course, North American society is saturated with images of food and ideas about it. There is no end to doctors and companies pitching special diets—no fat, low fat, low carb, high protein. If you are like most women in our society, you probably think you should be thinner. At one time or another, you may even have wished that you did not have an appetite at all, that you never felt hungry.

Hunger: The Desire to Be Full

What is physical hunger, really? It is your body's signal that it needs food. Your body uses the food you eat to maintain your muscles, organs, heart, and brain—all of you! The food you eat keeps you alive. When it comes right down to it, food is fuel. It provides the energy you need whether you are active or not. Instead of detaching from your hunger and treating it as something to be suppressed, denied, or ignored, we ask you to embrace your hunger as the healthy desire for vitality, a desire for life itself. You may have been taught to think that hunger is a bad thing and that with the first pang it must immediately be satisfied. In the times of the Goddesses, hunger was simply a signal to begin gathering and preparing food. Hunger helped humankind to anticipate and fully enjoy each nutritious meal.

You may believe that food is somehow antithetical to the spiritual life. Many people equate spirituality with renunciation or asceticism. Giving up food is seen as spiritual, but enjoying food is not. But having your proverbial cake and eating it, too, can be a spiritual experience. Even the process of healthy fasting, which many people do for physical cleansing and heightened spiritual awareness, is not a process of deprivation. Fasting explores hunger in both a physical and spiritual way, and always leads you back to nourishment and healthy, mindful eating. Proper nutrition and a holistic attitude toward food can aid you on your spiritual path and help you to access and understand your Goddess hunger and desire.

66 Only the dead fail to reach out with both hands.

—Christine de Pisan (1405) 99

Most of the time, do you feel comfortable with your hunger for food? What about your hunger for power, sex, or love? Do you feel that your hungers are dirty little secrets that you must hide? Or do you enjoy and celebrate your desires? You've probably heard someone describe a good student as an individual with a real hunger for knowledge. In this context, hunger is seen as a good thing. The student has drive and a passion to learn. So, what's wrong with your hunger? Hunger is a quest, a primal force of life. Eat life!

On one level, you can read Greedy Woman's story as a cautionary tale. Very simply, when people are greedy, bad things happen to all of humankind. But there is more to Greedy Woman's story than that. Try to imagine what life would be like if Greedy Woman had not taken "too much." The sky would have stayed close to the earth and people would not have to learn, grow, and evolve. At first glance, you might think that idea is appealing. But without the need to work, to secure food, clothing, and shelter, human life would be very different from how you know it today.

Greedy Woman, the Goddess associated with agriculture in the tradition of the Bini people of Nigeria, has certainly been painted with a negative brush; just look at her name! Her story, though, reveals much about women, hunger, and desire. According to the story, at the very beginning of human existence, people did not have to work. They lazed around, and whenever they were hungry, they reached up and cut off a piece of the sky to eat. One day, Greedy Woman cut off an enormous piece of sky. She ate and ate, but she could not finish it. Although her story does not say so, maybe she was in a bad mood that day. Or maybe her eyes were just bigger than her stomach. Greedy Woman ate some more from her piece of sky. She even enlisted the help of neighbors. The whole village worked on trying to finish the piece of sky that Greedy Woman had cut from the heavens. Finally, the entire village felt stuffed to maximum capacity, and they gave up, and threw away what was left of the chunk of sky. Their wasteful action angered the sky and it moved far away from the earth so that people could no longer reach up and cut off pieces to eat. From that day forward, people have had to work for their food. To touch the sky again and ingest its wonder and mysteries, humankind would need to embark on a path of striving and discovery.

Without the need to work, humankind never would have developed agriculture. Without agriculture, humans would never have built cities or roads. There probably wouldn't be books, magazines, or newspapers. Striving and trying to accomplish are part of what makes human beings human. So, we must give Greedy Woman her due. Let's celebrate Greedy Woman and her hunger. Greedy Woman made it possible for us to reach for the sky. And she taught us that we must consider the balance between having too much, nothing, and what's just right. Your hunger, like Greedy Woman's, is a part of the cycle of nature from which all life springs.

Repeat this affirmation written by African American author, television personality, and, we think, contemporary Goddess, Iyanla Vanzant, to acknowledge and celebrate your Goddess hunger—as Iyanla says, "the divine power within you." Place a symbol of one of your life's passions on your Goddess altar—whether that is for healthy food, travel, sports, art, music, your family, clothes, whatever!—and revel in your desire to explore it to the fullest.

I Am filled with good. I Am filled with light. I Am filled with faith. I Am filled with the truth of my being, which is enduring, dynamic, and divine.

Greedy Woman can also remind you to take reasonable portions of food. Eating one piece of cake is fine, even if it's not the most nutritious choice. But eating an entire cake—well, that's quite another thing! Many women ignore portion sizes, especially when enjoying prepared foods that are billed as low fat or no fat. Certainly, a pint of fat-free frozen dessert has fewer calories than a pint of regular ice cream, but even so, the fat-free variety packs a heavy wallop of empty calories.

Nature's Abundance: Germination, Incubation, Growth, and Harvest

As a woman, like it or not, you are probably responsible for most of the meal planning, grocery shopping, and food preparation in your household. But how often do we think about where our food comes from, how it is grown or harvested, and how that food travels from the fields or the ranch or the factory to feed your family at the dinner table? In a twenty-first-century world of prepared and processed foods, most of us are quite removed from the natural balance of lean and abundance that comes with the fluctuations of weather and the seasonal cycle. After all, in many urban markets you can get just about anything year round, right? Seasons lose their meaning. And food from a box, bag, or can holds little connection to the rich black earth that nurtures and grows that food. Chocolate doughnuts do not grow in Kansas fields!

Reconnecting to the natural cycle of barrenness, germination, incubation, growth, and harvest can help you explore a larger cycle of desire, hunger, grief, joy, and abundance. Without food, we starve. Throughout history, many of the world's cultures have developed stories to explain the cycle of the seasons, to connect our human natures to the natural workings of the Earth, our planet. Believing in these narratives enabled people to imbue the Earth with a human divinity. Today, we can still learn from these accounts. The story of Demeter and Persephone reminds us of the natural cycle of life and death, the strong human bond between mother and daughter, and the creative urge that sparks abundance and brings barren fields to glorious bounty. After exploring their story, you may not be so eager to accept mass-produced, processed foods, or to put just anything in your mouth!

You have probably heard of Demeter, the ancient Greek Goddess of the harvest. Demeter's story, which dates from the seventh or eighth century B.C.E., bears some similarity to the story of Inanna that you read about in Chapter 1. One day, Demeter's only daughter, Persephone, the Goddess of spring and seed corn, vanishes. Distraught, Demeter searches the world, seeking her beloved daughter. Finally, she learns that Persephone has been abducted by Hades, the God of the underworld, and that he intends to keep her in the land of the dead as his queen.

Demeter falls into a grief so intense that all the crops whither. Seeds that have begun to sprout shrivel and die. Nothing can grow. Eventually, Demeter's fellow Gods and Goddesses begin to worry that all of humankind will starve. One by one they arrive to talk to her, to convince her to release her fertile powers and allow the earth to grow green again, but to no avail. Zeus, ruler of the pantheon, decides that Hades has to let Persephone go. Reluctantly, Hades agrees, but before Persephone leaves, he offers her a pomegranate. The young woman breaks off a few of the sweet red seeds and eats them.

The joyful reunion between mother and daughter is darkened only when Demeter learns that Persephone has eaten in the underworld. She knows that this means Persephone will have to return to the land of the dead. But she is cheered by the knowledge that Persephone only ate a few seeds and therefore will only have to spend a few months every year away from Demeter. The cycle of Demeter's grief and joy produces the seasons on Earth. Persephone's movement from the darkness of the underworld to the lightness of the heavens reassures us that autumn and winter are passing times of inner reflection and that spring will return to blossom into the full fruits of summer.

Inanna's story merges Persephone and Demeter into one all-powerful Goddess endowed with a fierce self-determination. Unlike Persephone, Inanna *chooses* to explore the underworld and then negotiates her own release, without the aid of a parent. Inanna creates the seasons through her own curiosity, maturation, and power.

You may not feel that you've got the time to shop for food, much less to cook meals from scratch using fresh ingredients. Where in your busy schedule of work reports and meetings, chauffeuring the kids to school and piano lessons or hockey practice, housekeeping, trips to the gym, and a few stolen minutes with your spouse or partner do you find the time to cook? Who wants dinner in a box, but what else can you do?

Change comes one Goddess at a time, and yes, we mean you! The only way we, as a culture, can return to a more wholesome and healthy way of eating is to make the time and effort to return to natural foods, grown and harvested in a natural, earth-enhancing way. Be your own Erin Brockovich! Insist on a healthy environment to produce healthy food and clean water to nurture healthy families. Take a look at what you eat and decide whether you could be making better choices. When you eat natural foods, you ingest more vitamins, minerals, and other nutrients that make you strong and vital.

Connecting to the natural cycle, a manifestation of Demeter's grief and joy through her close emotional bond to her daughter, Persephone, helps you to connect your Goddess nature to the earth. Remember, it was women who invented agriculture and domesticated animals 10,000 years ago while the men were out hunting. Eating locally grown food can help you feel more connected to your environment and to nature. Check out all the fruits and vegetables at your local health-food store. Or stop by a farm stand or farmer's market. By reconnecting to the natural cycles of harvest and planting and to the comparative barrenness of winter, you can connect to the everyday experiences of people who live in less industrialized nations, and you can connect to your ancestors to whom the cycle of crops and weather were central.

 Food is an important part of a balanced diet.

—Fran Lebowitz, U.S. writer (1978)

Buying organic produce is another way to feel more connected to Demeter, the earth Goddess, and the earth. Organic fruits and vegetables have been grown without synthetic fertilizers and pesticides. These chemicals can leave a residue on foods and can build up in the body, causing fatigue and illness. Many pesticides, in addition to killing insects, also damage wild birds, other small animals, and the farmers who use them. In many areas, the use of synthetic fertilizers has depleted the soil, making it impossible to grow anything without adding tons more fertilizer. These fertilizers also run off into lakes and streams, causing an explosion of plant growth that can choke off the life of native fish. Organic farming avoids these chemicals. The soil is built up with natural compost—rotting vegetable matter—and insect populations are controlled by means of other, less damaging insects. Organic farming helps to protect the health of the consumer, the farmer, and wildlife. Supporting organic farmers is one small, everyday way that you can honor Demeter, the earth, and all of her creatures. You may say that organic foods are more expensive than other foods, but what price can you put on your health and well-being? Invest in your body, your health, and your family's health.

You can also honor the earth and avoid chemical residues by eating lower on the food chain. If you eat a lot of meat, consider that the cow from which the meat comes was fed hormones and antibiotics to help it gain weight fast. The cow was also fed a diet of grains that had been treated with pesticides and synthetic fertilizers. When you eat the cow, you are also eating all the chemicals that the cow has eaten. Some studies from the early 1980s suggest that animal fats, including the fat found in meats and dairy products, carry a concentration of pesticides. Investigators at the Environmental Defense Fund measured the level of pesticides found in women's breast milk and found that the more animal fats a woman consumed, the more pesticides in her milk. If you must eat meat, consider animals that have been given free range and have been raised organically without the aid of hormones, antibiotics, and pesticides. The same goes for dairy products.

Many doctors advise that North Americans need to eat a diet lower in fat and cholesterol and higher in fiber. Eating a vegetarian diet does just those things. You may also want to consider moving to a more plant-based diet on humanitarian grounds. Animals used as food are rarely treated well. On factory farms, young chickens have their beaks cut off so that they cannot peck each other. They are crammed together in huge cages and rarely get to scratch actual earth or see the sun. Like cows, chickens, too, are filled with hormones and antibiotics. They live short, miserable lives.

Many people believe that when you eat the meat of an animal, you not only ingest its flesh, but you consume all its suffering, its sorrow, anger, and frustration, too. Keep in mind that you are but one of the earth's creatures. Honor the other animals of the earth. If you buy meat, buy organic and free-range. Then at least you will know that the animal you are eating had a bit of a healthy life before it ended up on your table.

How self-aware are you about what you eat? Your food choices have an impact on every creature on the planet. When you buy organic produce, you spare the environment from the destructive forces of pesticides and soil erosion. When you choose a strict vegetarian diet, you spare an animal's life. Remember the adage: You are what you eat.

Ingesting Knowledge

You have probably read about the impact that the media has on your body image as a woman. Your whole life, you have been surrounded by images of beautiful and impossibly thin models and actresses—from 1960s superstar Twiggy to Naomi Campbell, from 1940s screen legend Lauren Bacall to Gwyneth Paltrow and Halle Berry. How do you feel about the way you look? When was the last time you really looked at your body?

The food we nourish our bodies with becomes a part of our bodies, our selves. Nowhere is this more present than in the story of Adam and Eve. Eve ingests fruit from the tree of knowledge, which leads to self-awareness.

Eve and the apple! Eve tasted the forbidden fruit from the tree of knowledge and got Adam to do the same. After they had eaten from the apple, they saw that they were naked and felt embarrassed. Adam and Eve tried to cover themselves, and were expelled from paradise, the Garden of Eden, by God. No wonder women have issues with food! Ever since that time, women's appetites—for food, knowledge, sex, or power, to name a few—have often been viewed negatively and have engendered feelings of self-consciousness.

You may feel that you are too fat. You may have trouble seeing your body for what it really is. Many women think that they have to lose weight when they really don't. Some women do need to lose weight but convince themselves that excess weight is healthy (Greedy Woman didn't do so well with this point of view ...). Others still see themselves as little girls well after they have grown out of that phase. Regardless of your size, or how big you think you are, your body is special and unique.

Take a look around at the gym or the mall or wherever you go. Notice how many different body types you see—tall, short, lithe, athletic, buxom, pear-shaped. See the particular beauty of each type. Check out the women in paintings from earlier eras before thin was so very in; make a trip to your city's local art museum and look at the bodies of the women in the paintings. The lovely rounded arms of the Comtesse D'Haussonville in Jean Auguste Dominique Ingres's (1780–1867) portrait of her are a far cry from the sinewy limbs of today's iron-pumping stars. And what about the voluptuous women Peter Paul Rubens (1577–1640) painted during the Renaissance? Remember the many faces and shapes of real beauty that artists have explored, and the real beauty of the contemporary women that you see all around you, the next time you sit down with a copy of *Vogue* and start to feel that your body is all wrong.

> 66 Food and I had always been in battle and had reached a stale-mate at about 10 pounds more than I really wanted to weigh. To hold that line I had to count calories and feel guilty about what I shouldn't eat. But when I started to learn about food, appreciating the incredible variety I hadn't known before and eating more unprocessed foods, I stopped battling. My appetite began to change. I stopped counting calories. I stopped feeling guilty. I had just one rule: If I was hungry, I would eat; if I wasn't hungry, I would say no.
>
> —Frances Moore Lappé, writer (1982) 99

Your body is special. Your body is what enables you to experience life—its pleasures and pains, tastes, sights, and smells. Your body supports and nurtures your mind, heart, and spirit. So, you need to nurture it, too. No matter what the media says to tempt you into excess—either starving yourself or stuffing yourself—*you* are in control. You control what you eat and how you look. You can achieve balance, health, and a return to the Edenic sense of wholeness by being active and eating right.

When you feel your best, you don't need to worry so much about how you look because you know you look good. A healthful diet, one of moderation and not extremes, will both engender and feed your healthy appetite. In achieving balance, you will achieve a beautiful body image that is individual and oh-so-you. Only one Goddess can look like you, and that's you!

Mindful Eating, Goddess Style

Unfortunately, you may, at one point or another, use food for reasons other than satisfying your hunger. Have you ever eaten an entire bag of chips after a stressful day? Or stuffed half a cake into your mouth before you could really think about what you were doing? Do you know why you do these things? Often such behavior is not simply the result of hunger. And it's not greed, either. Sometimes food becomes a substitute for emotion. Let's say your difficult boss got really furious over a technicality. Do you blow up and vent your feelings? Probably not. Or do you air your ire in a calm but authoritative manner? You probably don't do that either. Most women hold their anger inside, but it leaks out in the form of binge eating or in other self-destructive behaviors.

Think about the last time you ate in a way that you knew you shouldn't have. Could you have been angry or depressed about some event, situation, or another person's behavior? Next time you notice that you are veering toward a binge, try thinking of Kali, the Hindu Goddess of destruction and resurrection. See if you can channel your anger into a constructive project. Maybe you'll want to take your rugs out into the yard and beat them. Or clean out that cabinet under the kitchen sink. Or update your resumé and send it out. (You can read more about Kali and the creative uses of anger in Chapter 9.)

Anger is just one emotion, and it is one that you may try to stuff down inside you with food. But maybe you overeat when you're bored, or when you experience stress or anxiety. You blanket your unease with food and give yourself an illusion of calm. You could be overeating from habit. Or you may use food as a way to try to feel love. In many ways, food is love. You probably cook for the people you love. You prepare special meals and maybe even a cake for their birthdays. If you are overeating, however, and probably not ever feeling satisfied, then you need to find another way to be loving toward yourself. One way to love yourself is to pay attention and focus your awareness on yourself and your actions.

> 66 There is a communion of more than our bodies when bread is broken and wine is drunk. And that is my answer when people ask me: Why do you write about hunger, and not wars or love?
>
> —M.F.K. Fisher, U.S. food writer (1954) 99

Mindful eating, eating with awareness, can be very nurturing and can play an important part in your spiritual life. Mindful eating will also help you to leave the table feeling more satisfied. How do you take your meals? Do you grab a bite and eat in the car? Do you eat out of a pot while standing in the kitchen? Do you sprawl in front of the television, eyes glued to the screen, and scoop food into your mouth? Or do you set the table, put on relaxing music, sit down, and take a deep breath, before you dig in? If you are like most people, you probably eat in a rush. Or you eat while parked in front of the TV. Heightening your awareness to how you eat can help you to feel the Goddess qualities of your food, and a connection to the Goddess qualities of your meal will help you to connect to the power of the Goddess within you.

The Zuni Goddess Deer Woman knew the best way for her to eat a meal. She ate standing up. She'd nibble at the new buds of a bush, graze on some flowers, or peel the bark from a tree. She was a deer, after all. Unfortunately, her husband, a human man, did not like her lack of table manners. He wanted her to act more like him. One day, he criticized her eating habits. She knew that the way she ate was important to her health. She couldn't eat the way her husband did, so she packed up her things, and she left him. Maybe Deer Woman's reaction was a little extreme, but don't you admire her instinct for self-preservation?

The principles of mindful eating are pretty simple. While you eat, you want to try to be aware of your own experience. You want to be conscious of your total experience with the food that you are eating, and that means you want to be aware both of what you are eating and how you are eating it. What does chewing feel like? How does the food taste? What is the sensation of the food as it moves from your mouth to your throat and down?

If you eat in front of the television, turn it off. If you live with other people, you may encounter some initial resistance to this idea, but think of Deer Woman, and turn the set off anyway. You may want to explore mindful eating when you are alone at first, and after you have gained insight, you can use your experience to improve your family's eating habits as well. First, put on some calming music. Set the table. Dim the lights, if you like, or light candles. Food deserves your respect; without it you would die. So, treat a meal like the sacred, life-giving occasion that it is. Before you begin to eat, sit down. Place your feet flat on the floor and take a few deep breaths. Close your eyes and inhale the aroma of the food. Open your eyes and look at the meal you are about to enjoy. Take another deep breath and let it out slowly. Then raise your fork. Try to take small bites. Chew your food thoroughly and note all the sensations your food gives you.

You may want to chew with your eyes closed so that you can better focus on your sense of taste. Notice the way the food feels in your mouth. Notice the way the flavors change as you chew. See if the food tastes different to different parts of your tongue. Once you have chewed well, swallow. Pay attention to the flavor of the food after you have swallowed it. Take another deep breath; then take another bite. Continue to eat slowly and chew well. Try to keep your attention focused on what you are doing—chewing, tasting, swallowing. If you find that your mind has wandered and you are thinking about a problem from your workday or a phone call you need to make, then gently bring you mind back to the present moment. To do this, take a deep breath and let it out slowly. If you have a lot of trouble keeping your focus on your actions, you may want to talk to yourself about what you are doing. Tell yourself, "I am chewing. I am chewing spinach." Describe the taste of the spinach, or whatever you're eating, to yourself.

Make a commitment to yourself to practice mindful eating during at least one meal every day for a week. If you want to turn your mindful meal into more of a ritual, light a candle and thank Amaterasu, the Japanese Goddess of the sun, for allowing her light to shine and helping plants to grow. Thank Demeter, the Goddess of the harvest, and her daughter Persephone for the nourishing fruits, grains, and vegetables you are about to consume. If you have chosen to eat animal flesh, take the time to thank the animal from which that meat comes. Then give thanks to the cook who prepared the meal. (If you are the cook, you may be tempted to skip this step. Don't! You deserve thanks, too!)

66 What really matters is not how much or how often we cook, but how deeply we pay attention when we do cook. Many of us are used to thinking that fixing a meal is something to rush through so that we can get to the more important stuff. When we realize that cooking is itself an important—even sacred—act, perhaps we will no longer resent the time we spend in the kitchen.

—Cait Johnson, writer (2001) 99

You can bring your new awareness to the preparation of food, as well. Everyone knows that a home-cooked meal tastes better because it's cooked with love. Make sure that you provide that ingredient when you cook. Remember that frozen lasagna heated in the microwave prepared with love tastes better than the same meal prepared with resentment. But try to honor Demeter by using fresh and, if possible, organic produce. If you feel resentful when it comes time to cook, acknowledge Greedy Woman's hunger and try to thank her, because without her we would have discovered neither cooking nor the wonderful creativity that art has inspired, nor your favorite dish!

When you cook, imagine the loving (and sometimes kooky) energy of Julia Child, that Goddess of television cooking shows who sprang to prominence in the early 1960s. Remember the love and attention that Frenchwoman Babette, in the Danish movie *Babette's Feast,* devoted to every culinary detail. Be inspired by Martha Stewart's gorgeous, stylish creations. Or relive the passion of author Laura Esquivel's heroine Tita in *Like Water for Chocolate.* Keep in mind that all of Tita's emotions infused her cooking—after one of her tears falls into the cake batter she is mixing, everyone who tastes the cake is struck with her desire and frustrated longing. Try to pass along your best. In the same way Demeter has given you her love and nurturance, cook a little and spread your love.

Exercise #1: Get to Know Your Apples

In the story of Eve and Adam, the apple represents knowledge. Apples also represent love and are associated with Aphrodite, the ancient Greek Goddess of love. Start your love affair with apples by going to visit an orchard, farm stand, or natural-food store.

Take your Goddess journal with you. If you are able to visit an orchard, spend a few moments sketching one of the apple trees. Then examine all of the apples for sale. How many different varieties of apples can you find? Ask if any of the apples are specific to your geographic region. If so, pick out one of that kind and select two more varieties that are new to you. So, instead of buying the usual McIntosh, Red Delicious, or maybe Granny Smith, you will be bringing home three new potential apple friends.

Write down the names of these new varieties in your journal, and take your apples home. When you get home, place one example of each variety of apple you have purchased on the table. One by one, examine each apple. Turn to a clean page in your journal for each apple, note the apple's name, and answer the following questions, which will help you to connect in a holistic way, using all of your senses, to the fruit before you.

1. What does the apple smell like? Does this smell remind you of anything? Write a few words or sentences about your associations.

2. What does the apple feel like? Describe the texture of the skin. What about the apple's weight and temperature? Again, make note of any associations you have in connection with touching this apple.

3. Look at the apple closely. Is there anything unusual about its shape or color? Describe the apple's color, or try drawing the apple. Write down any thoughts or memories the sight of this apple provokes.

4. If this apple had a sound, what would it be? Try saying the name of the variety out loud a few times. Do you think the name suits this apple? If not, come up with a name that sounds better. Say that name out loud.

Now, you are going to need some quiet alone time. Select one apple, wash it gently in cool water, and wipe it dry. With your apple in hand and journal nearby, sit down in a comfortable chair. Place your feet flat on the floor and take a few deep breaths. If you have drawn a picture of an apple tree, look at it. Get the image firmly in your mind and close your eyes. If you don't have such a picture, close your eyes and imagine a tree.

Imagine that your apple is growing on the tree. Cradle the apple in your hands and imagine Demeter's nurturing energy. See this energy as a glowing green ball, moving from the earth, into the roots of the tree, up the tree's trunk, along the branches, and into your apple. (The green is the color of the heart chakra. It represents growth and healing.) Hold the image of this loving energy in your mind and breathe deeply for a few minutes. Feel how this circuit of energy connects you, through the apple and the tree, to the earth. Know that embracing this energy moves you into your Goddess power and enables you to make healthy choices about the food that you place in your body. When you feel ready, slowly open your eyes. Look at your apple.

Find the page in your journal for the right variety of apple and write about your experience. Then answer this question: Does the apple seem different from the way it did before you imagined it as part of the cycle of Demeter's love? Or does it appear the same?

Gaze at the apple again and breathe deeply. See the nourishing energy within the apple. When you feel ready, take a medium-size bite from the apple. Breathe, take your time, but take a bite. Notice the sound when your teeth break through the skin. Pay attention to the feel of the apple on your teeth, tongue, and lips. Chew this first bite slowly. Feel the way the pulp releases its juice as you chew. Notice that different parts of your tongue are sensitive to different flavors. Imagine the nourishing energy of the apple, slipping down your throat as you swallow. Imagine that energy—a green healing light—traveling from your stomach, through your blood, to your heart. Feel how the apple nourishes you. Feel how the apple connects you to the earth. You may feel emotional doing this part of the exercise. Or you may feel bored or silly. Do it anyway. Write about your feelings, or draw them, in your journal.

When you're done, answer these last questions (you may want to take another bite first!):

1. How does the apple taste? Is the apple juicy or dry? Is it sweet, sour, bitter, or a combination? Does the apple taste the way you thought it would or does it taste better?

2. Have your feelings about the apple changed? And what about your feelings about apples in general?

If you have the time now, answer the first four questions for the two other varieties of apples that you bought. Or save those questions for later. You may want to wait a few days and go through the entire process again with the remaining apple varieties.

 Instant Goddess

We've all got a recipe we've been longing to try, but never have the time. Perhaps you want to bake bread from scratch. Or learn how to make that lovely Polish cookie your grandmother painstakingly baked for every holiday, but nobody makes anymore. Or do that Ratatouille recipe with all fresh veggies from the local farmer's market. Today's the day. Get cooking, Goddess!

Exercise #2: Plant and Harvest

Have you ever grown your own food? Even if you live in a small apartment, you can try growing something edible. A small pot of home-grown herbs looks great and makes a nice addition to any dish you may want to cook.

You can find a pot, potting soil, and a packet of seeds at many hardware or houeware stores. Chives, basil, or thyme can all be grown indoors without too much trouble. Or buy a commercially prepared herb kit that comes with everything you need in one box. If you live in a very dark apartment, you may want to consider getting a plant light as well. These lightbulbs, unlike the ones you use in your reading lamp, produce full spectrum light that mimics real sunlight. You should be able to find a small one for around five dollars. Of course, if you can grow your herbs outside on a patio or deck in warm weather so they can get natural sunlight, so much the better.

In addition to a pot, potting soil, and a packet of seeds, you'll want a small plastic bag, a container full of water, and some old newspaper. Once you have assembled all your materials, find some quiet time and a clear surface on which to work. Spread the newspaper over your working surface.

Open your bag of potting soil. Smell the aroma of the earth. Sift the soil through your fingers. Try not to worry about making a mess. The newspaper you put down should catch any loose dirt.

Scoop soil into your pot until it is almost full. You want the soil level to be about an inch below the top edge of your pot. If you have purchased a kit, follow the directions for planting that came with it.

Take out your seeds. Hold a few of them in your hand. Examine them. Close your eyes, take a deep breath, and imagine them growing. Imagine roots pushing out from the center of one seed. Then a stem begins to unfurl. It pushes through the dirt, searching for the light. Feel the live, growing energy of the seed's potential. That is Persephone's energy. Know that it is in the seed, and that it is in you, too.

Sprinkle the seeds over the surface of the soil. Cover the seeds with about a quarter inch more soil. Envision Persephone in the underworld, waiting to spring forth into the light.

Saturate the pot with water. Place the plastic bag over the top of the pot to lock in the moisture and place the pot in a warm, sunny spot. Or put the pot under a grow light. If you are using a light, make sure that the lightbulb is not so close to the plastic as to cause it to burn.

After about a week, depending on the kind of herb you have planted, you should start to see shoots emerging. Once the shoots appear, you can remove the plastic bag. Make sure to frequently check the pot for water. It's easy for little plants to dry out outside or in a hot, sunny window.

Your herbs will take a few weeks to mature. When they're ready, pick a sprig. Examine the leaves. Crush some leaves between your fingers and smell their aroma. Add some fresh herbs to your next bowl of soup. Or sprinkle them on cooked vegetables. Enjoy your herbs however you see fit, and know that you planted them, grew them, and get to reap their rewards.

These exercises and the issues that you have read about in this chapter help you toward the self-knowledge and balance that is a part of the Goddess path. You are like Greedy Woman with her zest for life, Demeter and Persephone with the powerful love of a woman for her daughter or for her own inner child, Eve in her quest for knowledge, and Deer Woman in that you know what you need. You can let go of self-consciousness and guilt, live in the cycles of nature, and act with compassion toward yourself and others.

Now you are ready to move on to the next chapter where you will drink from the well of wisdom and meet Turtle Woman, the Native American Goddess, who is the creator of life; the women who perform the ancient Japanese tea ceremony; Hathor, the Egyptian Goddess of blood and wine; and Cerridwen, the Celtic Goddess of potions.

Drink: The River of Life

Water, do you love it or hate it? Do you find it tasteless and boring to drink? Or refreshing and cleansing? Do you even drink water at all? Do you like getting wet? Do you spend a long time in the shower or bath? Or do you jump in, do your washing, and jump out? And what about swimming? Which do you like best—pools, lakes, or rivers? Do you love the ocean or do you find it frightening? In many, many cultures the world over, water is considered sacred. Water is seen both as a crucial life-giving element and as the source of life itself.

Emerging from the Primordial Ooze

Did you know that 70 percent of the Earth's surface is covered with water? And did you know that your body is made up of about 60 percent water? Infants contain even more water—about 73 percent—and a human embryo in the womb is 80 percent water. Maybe these figures are not so surprising. In many ways, we do come from water. During pregnancy, the womb holds a small sea of water in the form of amniotic fluid. We are born from that water.

We all come from the Goddess.
And to her we shall return,
Like a drop of rain,
Flowing to the ocean.

—Zsuzsanna Budapest, spiritual teacher/writer (1971) 99

From the perspective of evolutionary biology, the first creatures on Earth appeared in the water hundreds of millions of years ago. Scientists describe this water as a primordial ooze—a soup of water, amino acids, and other nutrients—from which the first living cells formed. And creation stories from cultures around the globe recognize the existence of water before there was earth.

Turtle Woman, the creator Goddess of the Arapaho people of the North American plains, is very old. Before the world existed, she dove into the primordial waters. She swam and she swam, some say for an entire day and a night. Some say for even longer. She was under water for so long that she almost died. Eventually, she found some mud. With all four feet, she scooped up the mud and brought it to the surface with her. From the mud she created the world.

Why did Turtle Woman create world? Maybe she was bored with water alone. Maybe she was feeling creative. Maybe she was just tired of being wet. We don't know for sure. Whatever her reasons, her actions made life on earth possible. In some ways, Turtle Woman exemplifies our human position in relation to water. We need it to live and to create other lives, whether those lives are babies, plants, or animals. And yet, water can kill us by depriving us of air. Have you ever felt that you were faced with a soupy sea? Or that you were drowning? In literature and in life, many female Goddesses have chosen the path of drowning, from *Hamlet*'s Ophelia to Kate Chopin's Edna in *The Awakening* and, in life, the brilliant novelist Virginia Woolf. Maybe looking at your desk makes you feel like drowning. Maybe it is walking into the bedrooms of your children. Or facing a kitchen sink full of dirty dishes. With the strength of Turtle Woman, you can rise from the primordial ooze and you can create dry land, an oasis of order forged from chaos.

Although water can be deadly, just a few days without water will also kill you. The primacy of water is recognized in probably every culture of the world. There are water Goddesses, rain Goddesses, river Goddesses, and Goddesses of lakes and streams. Emergence from water is seen as a birth. Water is the giver of life. In Russia to this day, people refer to the river Volga as Mother Volga, and in many ways she is a mother. In the form of water, she provides for her people. She helps them to grow crops, and she yields fish. Did you know that a number of other Native American traditions describe a woman, or two women, as the original creator? These women use their powers to transform a soupy sea into a habitable world, populated with animals and people. A number of different tribes tell the story of the Goddesses of the Eastern and Western Oceans. One day, these two Goddesses met on a rainbow that formed a bridge over the primordial waters. Together they focused their minds, and land appeared. Then they made birds, animals, and, finally, people.

Here is a quick look at some of the world's huge number of Goddesses who are associated with water. Some of these Goddesses try to help people, some of them are a lot less than helpful, and some of them can behave either way, depending on their moods.

A Fountain of Water Goddesses

Goddess	People/Region	Action(s)
Abuk, represented by a snake	Dinka/Sudan	She feeds people by helping corn to grow.
Baba Yaga, a crone	Slavic/Russia	She rules over rainfall and the flow of cow's milk. She guards the Water of Life and Death.
Bà Ngu, Dolphin Goddess	Annam/Indonesia	She rescues sailors.
Iguanuptigili	Cuna/Central America	She causes floods.
Nitat Unarabe	Ainu/Japan	She lives in marshes and populates the world with demons.
Nuskwalsikanda	Bella Coola/ U.S. Northwest	She causes streams and rivers to flow.

continues

A Fountain of Water Goddesses   (continued)

Goddess	People/Region	Action(s)
Omau-u Wuhti, Thunder Kachina	Hopi/U.S. Southwest	She brings rain.
Pharmaceia, a nymph	Ancient Greece	She watches over a poisonous and magical stream.
Russalki, beautiful nymphs	Slavic/Russia	They rule over all fertility, tempt and drown men.
Sag, lion's body with a bird's head	Ancient Egypt	She withholds rain and causes droughts.
Siren	Ancient Greece	Half-bird and half-woman, she lures sailors to their deaths with her sweet song.

And as we've said, water is also associated with death. Oya and Oshun, jealous sister Goddesses in the Yoruba tradition from Nigeria, drown people on occasion. Among her many titles, Oya is Goddess of the Niger River. It is said that if you mention sister Oshun's name while crossing the Niger, Oya will drown you, and if you pronounce Oya's name when crossing the Oshun River, Oshun will take you down into the watery deep from which you will not return. (Learn more about Oya in Chapter 9.) The Aboriginal people of Queensland, Australia, tell stories about female water spirits who are the slaves of Bunyip, an angry and malevolent being, bent on human destruction. The lovely water spirits tempt men with their songs, seduce them with their stunning beauty, and cause them to wade into the dark waters where they drown. In the Ancient Greek tradition, the waters of the underworld, the rivers Acheron, Cocytus, Phlegethon, Styx, and Lethe, form the border between the world of the living and the world of the dead. In India, the sacred river Ganges, a pilgrimage site for hundreds of thousands of Hindus, is also the place where people come to die to be released from the cycle of reincarnation. So, we have water both at the very beginnings of life and at the very end.

 A woman's vows I write upon the waves.

—Sophocles, 495–406 B.C.E.

Think about where you live and how much water there is around you. Is water abundant or scarce? Is your environment wet or dry? How do you feel about your closeness to water? Where you choose to live can say a lot about who you are. Proximity to water is a powerful (and ancient) consideration in choosing where to settle; no place on earth is habitable without water. Is there enough water in your world?

Ritual Drinks and Drinking Rituals

Because water and other liquids are so important to human life, it's not surprising that we have many rituals associated with water and drinking. Have you ever participated in a water ritual? Maybe you were baptized into the Christian faith. Maybe you have toasted the bride and groom at a Jewish wedding. Maybe you have served tea at a formal event. By using liquid in a ritual context, we acknowledge the sacred nature of our origins in the primordial ooze. The beverage becomes a sacred connection between you and your fellow drinkers and between you and the divine.

The Japanese sencha-do tea ceremony is a formalized ritual for the sharing of tea. This form of the ceremony became popular in the eighteenth century and was adopted by the chief priestess of the Daisho-ji women's temple in Kyoto. The sencha-do, which has its roots in Buddhist tradition, has been practiced by women from this temple ever since. We consider the high priestess, and her long line of followers who perform the ceremony, to be Goddesses. In enacting the tea ceremony, the Tea Goddesses exemplify four principles of Japanese philosophy: harmony, respect, purity, and tranquility.

There are many steps to the sencha-do ceremony. Briefly, the hostess places the cups on the tray, rinses them with water, and wipes them dry with a special cloth. Then she warms the teapot by swishing hot water into it. She also pours hot water into the cups at this time. She dries the teapot and wipes the bamboo tea-measuring scoop with a piece of silk. Then she is ready to add the tea leaves to the pot and pour in hot water. When the tea has steeped, she pours the warming water from the cups out and pours the tea in. Then she places each cup on a saucer and hands the tray to her assistant who serves the guests. After the first cup of tea, the guests bow their heads in thanks and eat a small sweet, such as a red bean paste cake. Then the second cup of tea is served. Other forms of the Japanese tea ceremony are even longer and more complicated. In the simplified sencha-do ceremony, there are even rules about the placement of the teacups on the tray. The tearoom is also specially cleaned and decorated for the ceremony. All these rules and traditions help to make the ceremony a sacred occasion of harmony, respect, purity, tranquility, and yes, tea.

You can use a tea ceremony to greet guests. The ceremony is a way to communicate with your guests in a calm and positive way. It is also a form of meditation and a great way to relax. Have you been out running around all day? Try performing your own little tea ceremony just for you. Find a quiet space, indoors or out, prepare a pot of tea and drink it mindfully, focusing on all of your senses. Performing a tea ceremony, even in very simplified form, will relax you. It will also link you to an ancient tradition and to the whole lineage of Goddesses who have performed the ceremony before you. With the tea ceremony, your relaxation time will become a sacred time for you.

Did you know that tea is the world's most popular beverage? Green tea is the tea used in the tea ceremony. Green tea is made from tea leaves that have been dried but not fermented. (The leaves of black teas get their color from the fermentation process.) In addition to a small amount of caffeine, green tea has been shown to contain many healthful nutrients, including the antioxidant vitamins A, C, and E. Green tea also contains catechin, a substance that may help fight the growth of certain tumors, relieve allergy symptoms, prevent tooth decay, and inhibit the rise of blood serum cholesterol. No wonder people love their tea!

Does the tea ceremony sound like something you would like to try? Or do you worry about the caffeine? Green tea does contain caffeine, but it has much less caffeine than other teas, and it has a lot less caffeine than coffee or caffeinated sodas. Many people feel that the health benefits of green tea outweigh the caffeine content.

Are you addicted to caffeine? Do you get a headache if you haven't had your morning coffee fix? Many women in North America consume too much caffeine. In fact, the average North American consumes about 28 gallons of coffee and 32 gallons of caffeinated sodas a year. Besides making you jittery, caffeine can cause premenstrual breast soreness and cysts, and may impact fertility, if consumed in excessive amounts. Because caffeine is a diuretic, if you drink a lot of coffee or soda, you can end up dehydrated. Dehydration can make you feel tired, listless, and unfocused. It can also cut you off from the Goddess quality of intuition and make it harder for you to visualize. A lack of water can cause an imbalance in the sixth chakra, an energy center in the body that is the seat of intuition and visions. (To learn more about the chakras, turn to Chapter 6.) The solution? Cut down on caffeine and make sure that you drink plenty of water, too.

> 66 Coffee: We can get it anywhere, and get as loaded as we like on it, until such teeth-chattering, eye-bulging, nonsense-gibbering time as we may be classified unable to operate heavy machinery.
>
> —Joan Frank, journalist (1991) 99

Many women avoid drinking water. Some say it tastes bad. If you are used to drinking sugary sodas or ones full of artificial sweeteners, water will taste kind of bland and, well, watery to you. Just as an experiment, give up soda for a week. Drink water and see if you get used to it. Maybe the tap water in your city tastes really chemical and bad? Try a bottle of spring water. In the past, people always drank beverages in which the water had been boiled—such as tea, coffee, or bottled sodas—because fresh, unboiled water was full of bacteria and other pathogens that could make you sick. For the same reason, people in historical times drank a staggering amount of beer and wine. In North America today, we are surrounded by healthful sources of water. No longer can you cry, "water, water everywhere, but not a drop to drink."

It Goes Right to Her Head

Despite all their health benefits, are tea and water still not your "cup of tea"? What about wine and beer? Certainly you know about all the negative effects of alcohol. Of course, alcohol has been used for ritual and religious purposes for centuries and centuries.

In the following story, a Goddess gets drunk and beer saves humankind. As you have probably noticed, Goddesses are not always very well behaved. They have strong passions—for sex, power, or blood—and sometimes they act out. In this case, beer soothed the savage beast in the form of Hathor. Do you use alcohol to tame your beast? When you come home with frayed nerves from a day at work, from shopping, or from carting the kids around, is the first thing that you want when you step in the door a beer or a glass of wine? Have you ever considered that maybe instead of reaching for that drink you could try meditating, putting on some soothing music, or making a cup of herbal tea?

 Hathor, the Egyptian Queen of Heaven, is associated with beauty, love, pleasure, motherhood, destruction, and the underworld. Typically, she is depicted as a woman with a cow's head or as a cow, because the sky and heavens were thought to be an enormous cow that hovered over the earth. She is often seen as a human wearing a sun-disk flanked by cow's horns on her head. Once she took the form of a lion to help the sun god Ra put down a rebellion among his human followers. She fought so fiercely and with such relish that Ra became afraid. He was sure that she would kill all of humankind. To stop her, he mixed the red juice of a pomegranate with beer and had it poured around the land. The puddles of red beer resembled blood, and Hathor in her bloodlust lapped them up. She became so drunk that she could not continue her slaughter, and humankind was saved. The same story is told of Sekhmet, the Lion Goddess, daughter of Ra and Goddess of fire, hunting, war, and justice, to name a few of her aspects.

In North America, over the last 150 years the relationship between women and alcohol has shifted dramatically. In the early 1900s, Carry Nation (1846–1911) spearheaded the campaign for temperance—abstention from alcohol—by means of her ax. Nation was famous, or infamous, for smashing casks of beer. She once said that a factory in Pittsburgh was making personalized hatchets for her. They were to be emblazoned with the words "Carry Nation's Loving Home Defenders. Smash the Saloon and build up the home." Early feminists in their quest for the vote and a larger social role for women saw the drinking of alcohol by men as a destructive act that kept women in impoverished, powerless situations at home. Because few women worked outside the home, it was crucial that working men brought home their paychecks after a week at work and did not squander all their money in bars, as many men did!

Carry Nation and other temperance crusaders helped to pave the way for the Prohibition Act, a law that made it illegal to sell alcohol in the United States. In contrast, today on college campuses nationwide, the incident of binge drinking is rising to alarming levels among young women. Keeping pace glass for glass with male classmates can be a dangerous way to express female power, as Hathor's example proves. While we don't recommend a return to prohibition, moderation with alcohol is a smart, liberated choice for women.

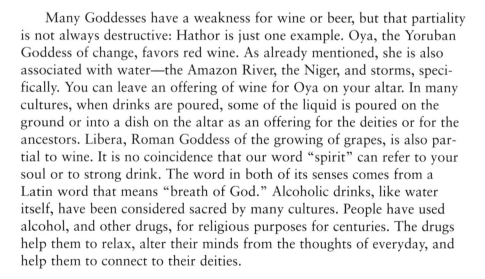

> I was one of those who was very happy when the original prohibition amendment passed; I thought innocently that a law in this country would automatically be complied with, and my own observation led me to feel rather ardently that the less strong liquor anyone consumed the better it was. During prohibition I observed the law meticulously, but I came gradually to see that laws are only observed with the consent of the individuals concerned and a moral change still depends on the individual and not on the passage of any law.
>
> —Eleanor Roosevelt (1939)

Many Goddesses have a weakness for wine or beer, but that partiality is not always destructive: Hathor is just one example. Oya, the Yoruban Goddess of change, favors red wine. As already mentioned, she is also associated with water—the Amazon River, the Niger, and storms, specifically. You can leave an offering of wine for Oya on your altar. In many cultures, when drinks are poured, some of the liquid is poured on the ground or into a dish on the altar as an offering for the deities or for the ancestors. Libera, Roman Goddess of the growing of grapes, is also partial to wine. It is no coincidence that our word "spirit" can refer to your soul or to strong drink. The word in both of its senses comes from a Latin word that means "breath of God." Alcoholic drinks, like water itself, have been considered sacred by many cultures. People have used alcohol, and other drugs, for religious purposes for centuries. The drugs help them to relax, alter their minds from the thoughts of everyday, and help them to connect to their deities.

Making a Magic Potion

Have you ever wanted to make wine or beer? Do you wish that you could brew the perfect cup of coffee? Do you covet the chai recipe your best friend has been using and keeping secret? As a child, did you mix up "potions," using spices from your mother's kitchen, perfume, mud, sand, leaves, and whatever else you could get your hands on? Women (and girls) have concocted brews since time immemorial. In fact, there is even a Finnish Goddess, Osmotar, who is credited with being the first person ever to make beer.

Cerridwen, the Celtic Goddess of wisdom, poetry, and grain, is also associated with magic and creativity. In addition to these attributes, she is a destroyer Goddess and a shape-shifter—she is able to change her physical form at will. She was known as the White Lady of Inspiration and Death. She lives at the bottom of a lake. The story goes that Cerridwen had two children—a very beautiful girl and a boy who was just plain ugly. To compensate her son for his lack of good looks, Cerridwen put together a magic potion that would confer all the knowledge in the world to the drinker. She figured that if her son was not going to be handsome, at least he could be the smartest boy ever. The potion had to simmer for a year and a day, so she hired a boy named Gwion Bach to stir the brew. Gwion stirred and stirred for an entire year. When the potion was ready, three drops of the bubbling brew splashed on Gwion's finger. Automatically he put his finger in his mouth; the brew was hot. Suddenly he possessed all knowledge. In one version of the story, the cauldron then cracked in two, leaving none of the precious potion for Cerridwen's poor ugly son, and Gwion, fearing Cerridwen's wrath, ran away. In another version, Gwion lifted up the cauldron and tried to make off with it and its brew. In both versions of the story, Cerridwen chased after him. To escape her, he turned himself into a hare, and Cerridwen changed into a greyhound. He changed into a fish, and she transformed herself into an otter. He morphed into a songbird, and she became a hawk. Finally, he turned himself into a kernel of corn, and she changed into a chicken and ate him. After nine months, she gave birth. Some say her new baby was none other than Gwion himself. Because she was still mad at him, she put him in a little boat on the lake, and he was soon adopted by a prince. The infant Gwion grew up to be Taliesin, a famous Celtic bard and poet.

Some of Cerridwen's story may seem pretty weird. She does swallow a boy in the form of a piece of corn and then give birth to him. But, just like you do every day, Cerridwen makes magic by cooking. Do you have a special recipe that you keep secret? Maybe you whip up a special dish (or drink) for your family or loved ones when they are feeling down. Or maybe you concoct a festive punch to celebrate special occasions. The stories of our culture are full of potions, both natural and magical. In *The Wizard of Oz*, Dorothy and her friends are put to sleep by the Wicked Witch of the West with a potion of poppies. ("Poppies, poppies; that will make them sleep!") And then Glinda, the Good Witch of the North, awakens them with snow—water in a cool and cleansing form.

> The voice of the sea speaks to the soul. The touch of the sea is sensuous, enfolding the body in its soft, close embrace.
>
> —Kate Chopin, writer (1899)

In many ways, tea and coffee are both potions. You drink them to feel alert. Or you drink them to relax. Herbal teas, such as chamomile, will help you sleep. Other teas may help improve your memory, brighten your mood, curb your appetite, or alleviate menstrual cramps. There is probably an herb that can be drunk in tea form that may help you deal with whatever ails you. Some herbal teas are delicious, and others taste less than wonderful. But at least they don't sound as disgusting as the potion that Achaea, a Greco-Roman Goddess of the earth and fate, drinks to help her foretell the future. Pure bull's blood—imagine that!

Exercise #1: Fire Burn and Cauldron Bubble

Haven't you always wanted to make a magic potion? Well, now is your chance! The witches in *Macbeth* chanted over their cauldron full of bubbling brew, but that doesn't mean that you have to. And neither do you have to add eye of newt or toe of frog!

You can mix up your own magical potion, using any ingredients that you see fit. If you have a juicer, dust it off and use it to create your own brand of healthful magic. The following table presents some common foods, the qualities or things they attract, and the Goddess(es) associated with them.

Food	Will Bring You ...	Goddess(es)
Almonds	Knowledge, money	Athena
Apples	Love	Aphrodite
Avocado	Sexual love	Venus/Freya

continues

continued

Food	Will Bring You ...	Goddess(es)
Banana	Fertility, strength, money	Ix Chel
Blackberries	Protection, wealth, health	Brigid
Carrot	Fertility, sexual love	Freya/Pele
Celery	Psychic power, mental acuity	Hecate
Cucumber	Virtue, health, fertility	Artemis
Ginger	Strength, vitality	Morrigan
Grapes	Fertility, mental acuity, strength	Oya
Honey	Beauty, love, sensuality	Oshun
Lemon	Purity, mental clarity	Amaterasu
Oranges	Luck, prosperity	Oshun
Pomegranates	Psychic powers	Persephone
Strawberries	Compassion, love, luck	Kwan Yin/Demeter
Watermelon	Nurturance, fertility, sisterhood	Yemaya

You could make a potion to attract love by mixing apple, carrot, and grape juice. Or you could put apple and banana into a blender to make a love/fertility smoothie. Add milk, soy milk, yogurt, or orange juice. If you are studying for a big test, you may want to try celery juice with lemon. Add some ginger for an extra burst of energy and stamina. While preparing your potion, think about the Goddess qualities you would like to develop in yourself. Imagine yourself as having those qualities. (Because—you know what?—you really do. You just have to let them out.) If you are working with love, see yourself as Aphrodite, Venus, Freya, or Pele. If you are working to boost your mental powers, think of yourself as the bright sun Goddess, Ameratsu. Surely she must see all and know all. Sit with your drink in a calm and quiet place. Drink it mindfully, and enjoy!

When you're done, write your potion recipe in your Goddess journal and, on the same page, draw a picture of the Goddess you would like to have manifest in your life. Place a token for that Goddess on your altar so that you can look at it every day until you feel her Goddess stirrings within you. After a few days, you may want to make some notes on the results of your potion experiment. Did you feel more attractive after you drank your potion? Did other people notice your sparkle? And how did you do on that big test?

Instant Goddess

Do you like to swim, body-surf ocean waves, fish off a small-town pier, or just take a walk on a beach or along a riverbank? Make like Turtle Woman and bask in the creative energy of the water's edge. Sunbathing is a fine alternative, too (don't forget the sunblock ... and a large, refreshing bottle of pure mineral water)!

Exercise #2: Clean—Inside and Out

Taking a shower may clean and refresh your body, but what about your mind? A ritual bath can be very healing and grounding. It's also a great way to relieve physical aches and pains, dissolve stress, or loosen up the congestion of a cold.

You will need the following:

- A clean tub
- Candles
- Essential oil, bath oil, or bubble bath

You may also want these:

- Your favorite incense
- Relaxing music

Make sure you will have some uninterrupted quiet time. Unplug the phone and turn off the TV. Fill your clean tub with warm water. Add a few drops of essential oil, bath oil, or your bubble bath. Once the tub is full, light your candles and place them by the side of the tub. Light your incense, if you are using it.

If you are using one, make sure that you have placed your CD/tape player in a dry place where it will not get splashed. Be extra sure that you are dry, and turn on your music or a recording of ocean sounds.

Before you step into the tub, say this:

Water, cleanse me; cleanse my body and my mind.

Get into the water and relax. Try this relaxation technique. Starting with your toes, imagine stress, worry, negativity, aches, and pain seeping out and into the water where they dissolve. Move up to your ankles and see all the tension pour out of them, and then, in turn, your calves, knees, thighs, hips, buttocks, abdomen, back, chest, shoulders, upper arms, elbows, forearms, wrists, and fingers. Imagine all the tension in your neck leaving you and melting into the water. Finally, imagine all your stress and tension leaving your head. Have you ever watched the sunset over the water? Think of that kind of beautiful melting.

> In a woman washing her clothes among rocks in the sea, D.H. Lawrence sees the very goddess Aphrodite. I sense this great feminine spirit when I lift my young daughter, wrapped in towels and dripping with mythic water, from the bathtub, or glimpse my wife stepping from the shower. These are not mere aesthetic moments, if there is such a thing, but full and serious revelations of divinity, the spirit of the material world.
>
> —Thomas Moore, psychotherapist and author (2002)

Allow yourself to feel nourished, nurtured, and supported by the water. If you are really relaxed, do your arms float a bit? And what about your feet? Can you imagine floating in a calm sea, completely held and rocked by the movement of the water? Absorb the nurturing energy from this water and soak in it for as long as you can. You deserve it! If the water temperature gets too low, add a little more hot water, and enjoy your time with the element of water.

As you prepare to leave your bath, imagine that the water has replaced all of your tension with strength and creativity. You are Turtle Woman coming up from the primordial ooze, ready to create the world anew. And you yourself are new, too. Before you stand up, say these words:

I am cleansed, renewed, and full of water's power.

Get up slowly and let yourself feel your emergence into the air as a rebirth. Picture Aphrodite, the Greek Goddess of love and beauty, rising for the first time from the foam of the sea.

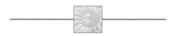

Did you enjoy making your magic potion? Creating it, did you feel connected to Cerridwen? And how was drinking your potion? Did it taste good? Did it help you to feel another facet of your Inner Goddess?

And how was it being Turtle Woman and arising from the primordial ooze? Did you feel grounded and strong, the way you really are? The tea ceremony, like many other rituals, is also a source of strength. Hathor's story may seem negative, but we all need to tame and balance our destructive and constructive energies. The shadow self must be acknowledged and appropriately controlled, knowing that without darkness, there can be no light.

Have a glass of water before you go on to the next chapter. Feel better? Now you're ready to learn about Nox, the mother of Morpheus; the enduring Sleeping Beauty; the Goddess properties of sleep and dreams from the Djanggawul, who from dreams create reality; and Halcyone, from whose story comes the famous expression "halcyon days."

Chapter 5

Sleep: Inner Rejuvenation

Do you love to sleep? Or do you hate the idea that you may be missing something during your hours of repose? Do you sleep at night? Or during the day? Do you wake up refreshed and ready to take on new challenges? Maybe you have insomnia and hardly sleep at all. If you do sleep, do you rest deeply or sleep fitfully? Do you remember your dreams upon awakening? Are they interesting and entertaining or do they seem strange and disturbing? Or do you find them just plain silly?

Whether you acknowledge it or not, sleeping and dreaming are an important part of your life. Getting enough sleep will help you to feel calm, centered, and in touch with your Goddess self. Too little sleep can leave you cranky and irritable. Lack of sleep can hamper your abilities at work, reduce your patience with your family and friends, and even contribute to your chances of having an accident.

Sleep, Sweet Sleep

Do you know how much sleep you need? You have probably heard that adults need eight hours of sleep every night. Maybe you don't sleep that much. For some women, eight hours is the right amount. Other women find they need more, while some need less. If you tend to fall asleep while reading, attending a meeting, a movie, or a performance, then you probably are sleep deprived. Here is another way to tell whether you are getting enough sleep: If you don't have to get up in the morning, do you sleep many more hours than you do on a school or work morning? Say you get up at seven every weekday and go to bed at midnight for a total of seven hours of sleep per night. On the weekend, if you go to bed at the same time, but wake up at 10 or 11, then those seven hours of snooze time you have been allowing yourself during the week are probably not enough for you.

> **66** Blessed be sleep! We are all young then; we are all happy. Then our dead are living.
>
> —Fanny Fern, writer (1870) **99**

Do your children resist or fight you when you tell them it's bedtime? Do you remember how you reacted as a child to the idea that you had to go to bed? Were you afraid of the dark? Or afraid to be alone in your room? Did you insist that an adult make sure that the closet door was closed and that there were no monsters or other creatures hiding under your bed? Did you make them leave the light on?

Well before Zeus, Hera, Athena, and the nine other Greek deities of Mount Olympus attained their thrones, Nox, the ancient Greek Goddess of the night, emerged from the primordial chaos. She existed as a great black bird before the earth was formed. Eventually she laid an egg, and Love hatched from inside it. One half of the eggshell became Gaia, the earth, and the other half became Uranus, the heavens. Gaia and Uranus ultimately became the grandparents of Zeus. Nox is also the mother of Hypnos, the God of sleep. Some say she is also the mother of Morpheus, the God of dreams, but others say that Morpheus is the son of Hypnos, and that Nox is his grandmother.

Imagine Nox. She is the mother of love and sleep. She is also the night. Her darkness is a loving presence in which to sleep. You may have been conditioned to think of the night and darkness as empty, scary, or evil, but try to let in this new idea: Night and darkness are the beginning, and they are filled with Nox's enveloping love. When you go to bed tonight, look at the darkness in your room as a deeply nurturing force. All new life comes from darkness and in the proper time grows toward the light. Seeds sprout underground in the darkness of the rich, moist soil. Flowering bulbs need several months of darkness if they are going to produce blooms. Your own creative ideas emerge from the dark depths of the unconscious. And you need about eight hours of loving darkness and sleep every night to grow to your best and brightest self.

Do you get enough sleep? Are you sleepy right now? A 2002 poll conducted by the National Sleep Foundation found that 47 million American adults are not getting their own minimum amount of sleep on a nightly basis. Of course, you have a multitude of things to do, and sleeping may not be at the top of your list, but consider this: Scientists have found that people who don't get enough sleep are more likely to feel stressed, angry, and dissatisfied with life.

Even Goddesses sleep. The Sleeping Goddess of Malta is a prime example. Although archeologists are not absolutely sure of her function, they agree that her statue, which dates from about 3500 B.C.E. and was found in an underground temple called the Hypogeum, depicts a woman comfortably asleep. So, make like the Sleeping Goddess of Malta and schedule yourself enough sleep time. Give yourself time to recharge your batteries and absorb Nox's dark love. Let Nox's son Hypnos do his job and see to it that people sleep. To sleep well, your bedroom should be dark, quiet, and cool. Sleep researchers recommend a bedroom temperature between 60 and 65 degrees. And, of course, your bed needs to be comfortable for you. Remember that Nox is the mother of all love. Getting enough rest will improve your mood and help you to be a mother of love, too.

> ❝ How do people go to sleep? I'm afraid I've lost the knack. I might try busting myself smartly over the temple with the night-light. I might repeat to myself, slowly and soothingly, a list of quotations beautiful from minds profound; if I can remember any of the damn things.
>
> —Dorothy Parker, writer (1942)

Beauty Sleep

Maybe your nightly sleep is interrupted by your partner, your children, or your pets. Perhaps noisy neighbors, passing cars, or garbage trucks wake you regularly. Maybe you wake up in the middle of the night for no reason at all. Or maybe you have a hard time falling asleep, and toss and turn all night.

After many years of trying, the king and the queen finally gave birth to a child—a little girl. Overjoyed, they asked all the fairies in the kingdom to be the girl's godmothers. They held a feast and invited all seven fairies. But an eighth fairy showed up and, even though she was seated at the table, she was angry. When it came time for the fairies to give the young princess their gifts, the youngest fairy held back. She was worried that the old forgotten fairy would give the princess an unlucky gift. The first fairy gave the princess beauty; the second, wit; the third, wonderful grace; the fourth, the ability to dance; the fifth, a gorgeous singing voice; and the sixth, the talent to play all kinds of music perfectly. Then the old forgotten fairy came forward to give her gift. She said that the princess would, at the age of 16, prick her hand with a spindle and die of the wound. The guests were all stunned and began to cry. The young fairy spoke up and reassured them. Although she could not undo the old fairy's spell, she was able to make it less severe. The spindle prick would not kill the young princess but would put her into a deep sleep that would last 100 years. At the end of this time period, the princess would be awakened by a handsome prince. And the young fairy's words came to pass. Despite the ban that the king had placed on spindles, the princess did prick her finger and fall into an enchanted sleep. At the end of her 100-year rest, a prince found her castle in the woods. Captivated by this sleeping beauty, her glowing skin, and radiant health, he awakened her. After 100 years, Sleeping Beauty woke up to a world that was new to her, and she started a grown-up life for herself with her prince.

Do you sleep an enchanted sleep the way Sleeping Beauty did? Do you get your beauty rest and wake up feeling refreshed? Or do you suffer from insomnia? Sleep researchers estimate that more than 100 million Americans fail to get a good night's sleep on a regular basis. That means that there are a lot of sleepy people out there. Doctors at Brigham and Women's Hospital's Sleep HealthCenter in Boston have come up with 10 rules to help you get a good night's sleep:

1. If you don't fall asleep within 20 minutes, get out of bed and do something relaxing, such as reading, and then get back into bed and try to fall asleep again.

2. Avoid housework, paying bills, work, or any stimulating activity within two hours of your bedtime.

3. Avoid napping because it may interfere with your ability to fall asleep at night.

4. Avoid alcohol within five hours of your bedtime. Alcohol can cause nighttime awakenings.

5. Avoid caffeine after noon. That means no tea, coffee, caffeinated soda, or chocolate. They can cause shallow sleep and make it easy for you to wake during the night.

6. Make sure your bedroom is quiet, safe, and relaxing. Turn your clock away from the bed so that you are not tempted to look at it frequently and count out how much time is left till morning.

7. Go to bed at the same time every night and get up at the same time every morning.

8. Schedule a time for yourself to worry about problems, and resolve them before your bedtime, so that you can get into bed with a clear mind.

9. Exercising every day can help you to sleep at night. But make sure to schedule your workouts at least four hours before your bedtime.

10. Avoid going to bed on an empty stomach or on a full one. Hunger can keep you awake and so can a belly full of food.

 A dream is to look at the night and see things.

—Ruth Krauss, children's book writer (1952)

If you suffer from insomnia, try these tips and see whether your sleep improves. You may also want to try practicing a relaxation technique like the one detailed in the ritual bath exercise in Chapter 4. Or use your own imagery or meditation technique before you go to bed as a way of developing a sacred pre-sleep ritual. Cast a spell on yourself to sleep deeply and peacefully all night. Use your capacity for self-suggestion to direct and allow yourself to float into the state of sleep.

When you wake up in the morning, you should feel refreshed, recharged, even reborn. Waking up is a rebirth. You are entering a new day, full of new life possibilities and opportunities. You don't want to miss out because you feel too tired. What if Sleeping Beauty had not been able to sleep? Can you imagine how terrible she would have felt after 100 years of lying in bed awake? Instead of meeting her prince with joy and curiosity, she probably would have snapped his head off. Don't turn yourself into a crabby beauty! You need rest, and you deserve rest. Try to make sure you get it. You don't want to sleep for 100 years, the way Sleeping Beauty did, but to look, feel, and be your best, you need the inner rejuvenation that only sleep can provide.

Creative Dreaming

Everybody dreams. You may not remember your nighttime dreams but you do have them, and you have them every night. Throughout history, people have been fascinated by dreams, and humankind has come up with a variety of ways of looking at dreams. Dreams have been seen as communications from ancestors or as a way of seeing into the future or the past. They have been described as representations of our secret wishes and desires. Dreams can also be a means by which you connect to the collective unconscious, the pool of mythic images and archetypes common to all people that we mentioned in Chapter 1. Our word *dream* comes from an Old English word that means "joy, gladness, and music." In that sense, your dreams are a way to keep you happy and entertained while you sleep. The normal sleep cycle, including the rapid eye movement (REM) of dreaming, balances the system both physiologically and emotionally. Dreams contain vivid images and metaphors that provide significant information about your drives, wishes, and fears. Paying attention to your dreams can help you to learn and grow both emotionally and spiritually. No matter how mundane they may seem to you at first glance, your dreams are a testament to the amazing Goddess-like power of creativity that lies within you.

Dreamtime is the ancient time in which deities traveled over the countryside creating people, plants, sacred places, and the rules of living. The Dreamtime is both very old and present today. It is considered the source of all life. Ancestors, such as the Djanggawul, left the Dreamings, or sacred knowledge, at special places in the landscape. The Dreaming encompasses a tribe's spiritual history and the story of the tribe's creation. The Dreaming is also the process by which the tribe and the world around it were created. Every Aboriginal person carries a part of the original Dreaming inside herself.

The Djanggawul are fertility and creator Goddesses from the tradition of the Aborigine people of Australia. The two sisters are known as the Dreamtime Daughters of the Sun. Their names are either Miralaid and Bildjiwararoju or Djanggau and Djunkgao. In some stories, they also have a brother. Before people were on the land, the Djanggawul sisters arrived in Arnhem Land in North Eastern Australia by boat. They carried their sacred objects with them and used them to create wells, plants, and animals. The sisters gave birth to the first people, the ancestors of the Aborigines of Arnhem Land. The Djanggawul sisters also gave the people their Dreamings, the sacred knowledge of their clan.

66 Throw your dreams into space like a kite, and you do not know what it will bring back, a new life, a new friend, a new love, a new country.

—Anais Nin, writer (1931) **99**

In the story of the Djanggawul, dreams really do create reality. You can create the world of your dreams, too. If you want to, that is! You probably have dreams—nighttime ones and day dreams—that you would like to see manifest in reality. Know that if you can imagine it, you can make it happen. Imagining the thing that you want is the first step toward getting it. There are many popular books on the subject of creative visualization, the process of imagining yourself reaching your goals as an aid to attaining them. Look for books by Shakti Gawain, a real Goddess in the field of creative visualization; Sonia Choquette's book *Your Heart's Desire*, or Barbara Sher's and Anne Gottlieb's *Wishcraft*.

You may not realize it, but you probably use creative visualization every day. Let's say you're on your way home from work and you begin to think about dinner. You imagine what food you have at home. Could you put together the things you have at home into a meal? Or do you need to stop on the way home and buy something to make the meal work? Or maybe you imagine yourself finishing a big project at work, and you allow the good feeling that image brings to help you push on with your work.

You don't have to be able to conjure up Technicolor images in your mind to use creative visualization. Sometimes when you use creative visualization, what you imagine will be a vague picture of what you want. Sometimes it will be more of a feeling. You can use real images to help you with your creative visualization. Pin a picture of the beach where you would like to vacation over your desk. Let the picture help you to imagine that you are at that beach. Let your imaginings help you to work hard to earn the money to afford the vacation to actually go to that beach. Sales executives often use the power of images to help motivate their sales force. If you know you could win a new car if you work hard, and you see an image of the car you could win, you will work harder than you would without being able to see the car. What image will you display as inspiration to help you manifest your dreams?

In Your Dreams

Of course, your dreams and the events they contain are not always things that you would want to have happen in real life. Sometimes your dreams can provide you with information about yourself, your emotions, and your life situation. Even the most boring dream (or the most strange) can contain interesting and valuable information for you. Your dreams can help you get in touch with your Goddess by clarifying your picture of a most central character—you!

Halcyone's story may seem a bit melodramatic, but it has endured for a long time. The best source for this story is the *Metamorphoses* by the Roman poet Ovid (43 B.C.E.–17 C.E.). One way to understand Halcyone's story is to look at it as if it were a dream. The winds of change blow through Halcyone's life, carry away her husband, and leave her grief-stricken. If all parts of the dream are also parts of Halcyone, then her husband's death represents the death of a part of her self. This death would indicate that she is leaving one stage of life for a new one. And indeed, she is reborn as a soaring bird, a being that embodies Haclyone's new strength and powers.

In the following story, Halcyone learns the truth from her nighttime dream. You can learn from your dreams, too, and the knowledge you discover can help bring you greater acceptance of the changes in your life. We do hope that what you learn is not news as bad as Halcyone's, but if it is, know that transformation and rebirth will inevitably follow.

Halcyone, also known as Alcyone, was the daughter of the King of the Winds. As a young woman, she married Ceyx, the King of Thessaly and son of the Day Star. Halcyone and Ceyx were completely devoted to each other. So much so that when Ceyx planned to take trip across the ocean to consult an oracle, Halcyone grew worried. She did not want him to go because, as the princess of the Winds and her father's daughter, she understood just how dangerous such a sea voyage could be. The Winds were under her father's command, but they were not always completely under his control despite his best efforts.

When Halcyone saw that she could not dissuade Ceyx, she asked to go with him. But Ceyx, aware of the dangers, could not bear the thought that he would bring the one he loved into harm's way. He insisted that she remain behind, promised to return quickly, and set off in his ship. Halcyone waved to him from the shore and stood watching as his boat disappeared over the horizon.

As night fell, a storm broke out on the ocean, but Halcyone, unaware of the peril that faced her Ceyx, slept peacefully. His boat was tossed, flooded, and then smashed. He and his crew drowned. Halcyone continued to count each day until her lover's return. She busied herself in weaving a new robe for herself and one for Ceyx. And she prayed to Juno, Queen of the Gods, for Ceyx's safe return.

Juno was moved by Halcyone's devotion and felt that she should know the truth. She sent her messenger Iris to the home of Hypnos, the God of Sleep, to ask him to send Halcyone a dream that would let her know what had happened to poor Ceyx. Iris hurried to Hypnos's house and, after several tries, shook the God awake. Hypnos then woke his son Morpheus, the God of Dreams, and Morpheus flew toward Halcyone and transformed himself into the image of Ceyx. He appeared in Halcyone's dream as her departed husband and told her how he had died. In her sleep, Halcyone cried out to him, and her cry awoke her. Once awake, she knew the truth: Her Ceyx was dead.

In the morning, she went to the pier from which he had departed. Far, far out on the water, she saw something bobbing toward shore. As the object drew closer, she knew it was the body of her dead husband. She leapt from the shore, but instead of dropping down into the water, she skimmed the surface, and she flew to greet her husband's body. She tried to hug him with her wings, and he seemed to respond. The Goddess Juno was kind. She saw to it that Ceyx, too, was transformed into a bird. Every year when the two love birds nest, Halcyone's father restrains the winds, and the waters of the sea are calm and placid. These days of perfect peace, which usually occur around the time of the winter solstice, are named after Halcyone and are commonly known as halcyon days.

Do you know what your dreams mean? Are you curious about them? People have been fascinated with dream interpretations since the beginning of time. Although they had existed as early as the ninth century, books of dream symbolism became popular in the nineteenth century. Books such as these gave definitions for the images that might turn up in your dreams. Dreaming of the color green was said to mean the dreamer was envious. A dream in which cows appeared was said to bring bad luck. And eating grapes in a dream was supposed to foretell rain. In the present day, some people still look at images from dreams as universal symbols that mean the same thing no matter who the dreamer is. Most people believe that dream images have a more personal meaning. A car in your dream will have a different meaning than a car in your best friend's dream, while a car in the dream of a 10-year-old girl in India will have yet another significance.

Sigmund Freud (1856–1939), the pioneer of psychoanalysis, called dreams the "royal road to the unconscious." Freud believed that your dreams represent a compromise between your unconscious wishes that may be too intense and primitive to acknowledge or express openly and your sense of what is right and proper. Carl Jung saw dreams as a doorway into the collective unconscious and its archetypes.

One current school of thought describes everything in your dream— from other people to insects to those weird flying toasters—as a part of you, the dreamer. If you dream about flying toasters, you can ask yourself, "How am I like that flying toaster?" Try writing about how you are like an image from your dream in your Goddess journal (or start a dream journal, which we'll talk about in a moment). Pretend that you are the object from your dream and describe yourself. Describe what you, as the object, are doing in the dream. Let's look at our hypothetical flying toaster example. You might write something like this:

I am a toaster. I am shiny and sort of old-fashioned looking. I am flying. I cannot see the ground. Toasters are not supposed to fly. And yet I am a toaster, and I am flying. I am doing the impossible! Toasters are supposed to toast bread. That is what they are made for. I am not toasting bread. I am not doing what I was made for.

If you wrote this, you could very reasonably conclude that you need to start looking for a new job where you could use your natural skills and talents and really soar by doing what you were made to do instead of toiling at a job that asks you to do the impossible.

You can also look at your dream as microcosm of your life. How does your dream mirror the way that you live in the world? Do you dream about rocketing down the highway in a car, but feel unsure of your destination? If so, maybe your life feels like that—one gigantic rush to some unknown place. Maybe your dream is giving you a hint that you should slow down, or to stop at the rest stop on the highway, admire the view, and take a few deep breaths.

However you choose to interpret your dreams, they can let you see a side of your own story that you usually sleep through. Being aware of your dreams can be entertaining. It can also help you to stay in touch with your true wishes, desires, and your Goddess self.

> 66 Why does one feel so different at night? Why is it so exciting to be awake when everybody else is asleep? Late—it is very late! And yet every moment you feel more and more wakeful, as though you were slowly, almost with every breath, waking up into a new, wonderful, far more thrilling and exciting world than the daylight one. And what is this queer sensation that you're a conspirator? Lightly, stealthily you move about your room. You take something off the dressing-table and put it down again without a sound. And everything, even the bed-post, knows you, responds, shares your secret ....
>
> —Katherine Mansfield, writer (1922) 99

Exercise #1: Your Dream Space

Is your bed comfortable? Does it give you the proper support—physically, emotionally, and spiritually? Could you spend 100 years in your bed? Imagine your perfect bed. Get out your journal and write about your dream bed.

- What color are the sheets on your dream bed? Are they smooth and silky? Or do you like to sleep on snuggly flannels or T-shirt sheets?
- Does your dream bed have lots of plump feather pillows? Or do you prefer to lay your head on a firmer surface? Would you really like a body pillow to rest against as you sleep? And what about eye pillows?
- Does your dream bedroom have a scent? Does it have its own sound?

Draw a picture of your ideal Goddess bedroom. Make it as lush and luxurious as you like. Or keep it simple, if that's what appeals to you. Place the image of your ideal dream space on your altar.

If your dream bed and bedroom don't match the one that you sleep in, go ahead and take some steps toward making your dream a reality. There are many actions you can take to turn your bedroom into your very own dream space.

Look at your bed itself. Is the mattress worn and lumpy? A mattress is a major investment, but keep in mind that your sleep is precious, too. It's also worth it to invest in good-quality pillows and bedding. A white noise machine can help block out bothersome sounds. Ear plugs can also insulate you from noise, and for some people they become a signal telling the brain that it's time to shut out the world and go to sleep. And a little incense or an essential oil diffuser can help to create a relaxing mood. There are many items—from the small and inexpensive to the costly—that can help you get the rest you crave, and these things can help you feel like the Goddess that you truly are.

Make a commitment to your Goddess. This week, take one small step toward creating your dream bedroom and give your self the gift of sleep. Worried that your spouse or partner won't go along with this bedroom makeover? You may find your partner more enthusiastic than you suspect once he or she sees you looking toward the night hours as a source of pleasure and refreshment; who knows where this may lead you both?

 Instant Goddess

Try yoga corpse pose: Lie on your back with your arms extended at your sides, palms up, and your legs stretched out with your feet relaxed and falling outward. Take a deep breath in, a deep breath out. Let the breath travel through your whole body. Imagine the Egyptian Goddess of magic, love, and death, Isis, breathing life into your body. Relax into sleep with the rhythm of the breath of life!

Exercise #2: Dream a Little Dream

Investigating your dreams can be fun and most illuminating. To start, you will need to remember a dream. The best way to do this is to begin keeping a dream journal. Before you go to bed, place paper, or your Goddess journal, and a pen on your nightstand. As you fall asleep, tell yourself that you will remember your dreams. If you wake up during the night, write down whatever you remember about your dream. Or draw an image from your dream that has stuck with you.

In the morning, lie quietly in bed for a moment. Before you do anything else, take your dream journal and start writing. Your impressions of your dream may be vague, but put down whatever little thing you can. When you start, you may just be able to remember a feeling, a sense of physical space, or a color. Often just putting down your vague impressions helps you to remember more concrete details, and then one detail leads to another and another, and pretty soon you have remembered a big chunk of your dream.

Sometimes fragments of dreams may come to you as you go about your day. Seeing the photocopy machine at work may remind you that you dreamed about the machine spewing out endless copies of a blank page. Take a moment to jot down some notes on what you have remembered.

If you record your dreams regularly, you will develop the habit of remembering them. Once you are remembering your dreams, you can begin to use them to get answers to questions you have been contemplating. To do this, write down a question you have. Maybe you are thinking of taking a new position at work, but are not sure if it's right for you. You could write "Should I take the new job?" in your dream journal before you go to sleep. In the morning, write down your dream. Put down every little detail. Then read over what you have written. Can you find an answer in your dream? Your dream will probably not come out and shout "yes!" but it may give you clues about your subconscious desires and anxieties about the job.

After you have been recording your dreams for a while, you will have a nice collection of your own dream images, and you can start compiling an index of your own dream symbols. Do you dream about trains frequently? Or do your dreams feature staircases, public restrooms, or traffic jams? Your dream index will help you to see the meaning of your dreams on your terms. And understanding your dreams will help you become more authentic and complete with all your dreamy Goddess qualities.

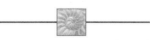

Making yourself comfortable in your bed and bedroom will help you sleep well. A night of good, healthy sleep will help you feel more alert and powerful. And, from your dreams, you can learn more about what you need and desire for a whole and healthy life. Ah, to sleep, to dream …. Plan to pay a little more attention to your need for shut-eye. Nox loves to see you sleeping! If you are comfortable and sleeping well, you will be reborn each morning, full of the beauty of Goddess energy and ready to turn your dreams into reality.

Do you feel rested? If so, you are ready to move on to the next chapter. There you will join the great Goddess dance and meet the ancient Greek Goddess Atalanta, the embodiment of pure feminine athleticism; Uzume, the Japanese Goddess of mirth and dancing; the Red Shoes from the fairy tale of that name; and Kundalini, the Hindu mother Goddess and source of all physical power.

Chapter 6

Exercise: Moving in Harmony

Does just hearing the word *exercise* make you curl up into a whining ball on the couch? Were you humiliated as a child or teenager in gym class? Or are you a marathon runner, cyclist, gymnast, and avid hiker all rolled into one buff and toned body? Maybe you used to work out or dance or swim, but have gotten too busy, too distracted, and stopped.

Certainly you have heard about the benefits of exercise. You understand that the body is an energetic system designed to move. If you don't exercise regularly, you have probably, at one time or another, made a plan to start. You may feel guilty that you haven't started a routine because you know you should. If you do exercise, you may feel that you should work harder or that you should be even more toned than you already are. But "shoulds" do not make you feel better. In fact, your sinking feeling that you should start running or swimming or practicing yoga or training harder just may be one of the things that is keeping you from your Goddess-given right to enjoy the movement of your physical body.

We live in an extremely goal-oriented, perfection-driven society. Sometimes fixating on a goal—in this case, six-pack abs and buns of steel—can stop you in your tracks. If you know you will never develop the "perfect" physique, run a three-minute mile, or be an Olympic gymnast, why bother?

But regular exercise is not just about muscle definition and weight control. Yes, physical activity will make you stronger, but the benefits of a regular exercise practice go beyond the mere physical. The sense of well-being that comes from a regular physical practice—be it yoga, jogging, kayaking, dancing, or plain old walking—can help you to appreciate the body that you have, with all its strengths, weaknesses, and remarkable capacity for regeneration. And appreciating your own unique body is part of recognizing and releasing your Goddess self.

My grandmother started walking five miles a day when she was 60—she's 97 today and we don't know where the hell she is.

—Ellen DeGeneres, comedian (1992)

Run Like the Wind

Do you like competition? Does it bring out your best? Or does it drive you off the field and back to your couch? Some women thrive on the challenge that competitive sports bring. Or they compete with themselves to perform at their peak. Others find the whole idea of competition completely irksome. Where do you fall on the scale of competitiveness?

From Atalanta's story that follows, you can see that the idea of women competing with men is not a new one. The idea that a woman might beat a man is also not new. Some interpreters of Atalanta's story suggest that Melanion's golden apples may not have been as irresistible as he thought, and that she may have let him win.

Can you imagine yourself as Atalanta? Have you ever wished that you were a track star like Jackie Joyner Kersee or Florence Griffith Joyner? Maybe you have dreamed of dashing across the finish line of a marathon like Kenyan winners Margaret Okayo or Catherine Ndereba. Imagine that you are the swiftest and most graceful runner. You can easily outpace anyone who dares to challenge you. If you knew you were in excellent physical condition and someone did challenge you to a race you knew you could win, would you run? Would you run your best or would you allow the other person to win? Have you ever let a man beat you in competition just to preserve his ego? Do you ever allow yourself to win? Is competition something that you only engage in with yourself? Or do you avoid any competition altogether? Knowing how you feel about competition can help you to pick a form of exercise that is right for you.

Atalanta, like Artemis, is an ancient Greek Goddess of the hunt and the wilderness. Atalanta was brought up in the forest by bears. Once she was fully grown, she met some human hunters in the woods who took her in. All the people she met marveled at her agility, swiftness, and knowledge of wild places. Atalanta also was very beautiful. She was the only woman to join the famous hunting party that subdued the Calydonian boar, a fierce animal that had been ravaging the countryside. Her participation in that event and her triumph over a well-known male hero in a wrestling match spread Atalanta's fame far and wide and brought about a reunion with her human parents. Her renown also brought her flocks of suitors, to whom she was indifferent. Some say she had pledged herself to Artemis, a maiden Goddess, and wished to remain unwed herself. In fact, some people say that Atalanta is actually an aspect of Artemis herself. (Remaining a virgin in ancient times did not mean abstaining from sex. It indicated a woman who was unmarried and self-sufficient, a whole and complete person "unto herself.") Nonetheless, Atalanta's father urged her to pick a husband. She agreed that she would marry on one condition: Her husband-to-be had to beat her in a footrace, and if he failed, she could kill him.

At first, young men lined up to race Atlanta. Enchanted by her grace and beauty, they thrilled to see her run. Race after race, she beat them, and soon their numbers dwindled. One day, Melanion decided to take the challenge. Because he knew he could not run as fast as Atalanta, he asked Aphrodite, the Goddess of love, for help. She gave him three golden apples that were so shiny and beautiful that no one could resist them.

The race began, and Atalanta easily pulled ahead of Melanion. He pitched a golden apple into her path and she slowed to catch it, but sped up and overtook him. He threw the second apple and gained on her again. Again, she picked it up and then flew past him. She could hear his breath ragged in his throat and knew that he was tiring. Just as they neared the finish, he threw the last apple. Because he was breathing so hard, she felt sure she could slow to scoop up the last apple and still win. She bent down to pick up the golden fruit. Melanion apparently had been exaggerating his fatigue and sprinted forward, crossing the finish line a split second before Atalanta.

Atalanta did marry Melanion, and some say their marriage was a happy one. They did not meet the happiest end, though. Both were eventually turned into lions. Because all myths are about growth and transformation, however, becoming lions is not the worst fate! It represents gaining courage, grace, and physical strength.

If you are highly competitive, running races, playing basketball, or kickboxing may be for you. Or are you attracted to tennis and the grace and power of superstars like Martina Navratilova, Venus and Serena Williams, and Jennifer Capriati? Maybe the great stars of figure skating, women such as Sonja Henie from the 1930s, Peggy Fleming, Dorothy Hamill, Kristi Yamaguchi, and Michelle Kwan are your heroines. For those of you who are competitive, know that the beautiful Goddess Atalanta lives in you. She is timeless. Even though her female form may have been downplayed, de-emphasized, or stigmatized in various periods in history, she has always existed. And she will always exist, just like your competitive spirit.

If you don't like outright athletic competition, there are lots and lots of physical activities at which you can excel, too—jogging, dancing, yoga, and walking, or classes in the newly popular movement therapies, such as Pilates or Neuromuscular Integrative Action (NIA), to name a few. You can feel Atalanta's spirit while hiking or going for a stroll in the woods. Remember, in addition to being a contender, Atalanta is the Goddess of the wilderness. And perhaps your competitive side comes out in other ways than athleticism—in your work, in your garden, in card games, or through your cooking skills. Whatever urges you to excel, heed the call with focus, tenacity, and endurance!

The Dance of Life

Certainly, professional dancers are highly trained competitive athletes. Think of the great ballerinas from the past—Margot Fonteyn, Maya Pliesetskaya, and Gelsey Kirkland. But anyone can enjoy dance, no matter what your age, shape, or size. It seems that humankind has always danced. And the Goddesses dance, too. Dance can be structured or free form. It can be performed as a part of a religious ritual, or it can be a work of art. Dancing is great exercise and great fun, too, and sometimes dancing can save the day.

Uzume comes from the Shinto tradition of Japan. She is known as a Goddess of mirth and dancing, and is also called Heavenly Alarming Female. In addition, she is a fertility Goddess and a shaman. Some descriptions of Uzume say that she is ugly, and some say that she is fat. In one story, Uzume clearly does not care what others think of her appearance, and because she is not hampered by self-consciousness, she is able to save humankind.

Here's what happened: Amaterasu, the sun Goddess and supreme deity in the Shinto pantheon, locked herself in the Rock Cave of Heaven because her brother the storm God had offended her. The earth was plunged into darkness. People on earth prayed for Amaterasu to come out, but she would not listen. Some of the other Gods and Goddesses got together and asked her to come out and let her light shine. She still would not listen. Soon, all 800 deities were gathered outside the cave, and they came up with a plan. They gathered drums, tambourines, and other instruments. Uzume affixed a mirror to a tree outside the entrance to the cave, and she began to dance to the band's accompaniment. She swayed her hips and stamped her feet. The other deities began to clap to the beat. Uzume raised the hem of her skirt and threw herself into the dance, letting the rhythm and movement take over. The assembled divinities whooped and applauded. She pulled up her blouse and wiggled out of one sleeve and then another. The crowd cheered. Uzume continued to twirl, raising her skirt still further, and then, with a flourish, she whipped it off. And Uzume, laughing from the sheer pleasure of her body in movement, continued to dance.

Inside the cave, Amaterasu wondered what was happening outside. Why did it sound like all the other deities were having such a good time? Finally, she stuck her head out and craned her neck to see over the crowd. Shifting from side to side to get a better view, she caught sight of her own reflection in the mirror. She stepped closer to examine the beautiful creature before her. A number of other Gods and Goddesses sprang into action and barricaded the entrance to the cave so that she could not go back inside. And from that day forward, thanks to Uzume and her willingness to dance, the sun has only disappeared at night.

Are you in touch with your inner Uzume? Maybe you would prefer to think of your inner dancing Goddess as the glamorous Ginger Rogers in the amazing dress that she wears at the end of the 1937 film *Shall We*

Dance? Maybe your dancing Goddess looks more like modern dance pioneer Martha Graham—fierce and somewhat angular. Or maybe she is the gamine, young Shirley MacLaine, wearing green stockings the way she did in the film *Irma La Douce* (1963).

Whatever she looks like, Uzume and your dancing Goddess say that you can move and enjoy yourself no matter who you are or what you look like. She also says that moving your body is important, even life-saving. What if Uzume had refused to dance? Perhaps the world would still be in darkness and humankind would have perished. When you move without self-consciousness, without worry about how others perceive you, you will feel alive, and, like the golden light of the sun, that vitality will spread from you to others. Think of Uzume's spirit when you are struggling with grief and loss or are feeling depleted. These feelings can diminish your light. And if you feel bad enough, you may find yourself hiding from life and not letting your sun shine at all. At such times, allow your curiosity to lead you outside. See if you can find Uzume and her sister Goddesses dancing somewhere. Go and join them.

You can keep feelings of self-consciousness at bay by finding a focus for your mind. One way to do that is to concentrate on the breath moving in and out of your body. While your mind is busy watching your breath, you will feel freer to move the way you want to move and, with that fluid freedom, you will look good, too.

66 Doubt yourself and you doubt everything you see. Judge yourself and you see judges everywhere. But if you listen to the sound of your own voice, you can rise above doubt and judgment. And you can see forever.

—Nancy Kerrigan, figure skater (2001) 99

Have you always wanted to take a dance class but felt that you were too stiff, too heavy, too out of shape, or too old? Or maybe you have felt like you have two left feet. But there are many forms of dance, including dancing alone in your living room. (See the second exercise at the end of this chapter.) Know that if you want to dance, you can. Katherine once heard a story about a woman who had worked as an accountant for 40 years, but had always wanted to be a ballerina. After she retired at age 65, she signed up for her first ballet class. She was scared because she didn't know if she would be able to move at all. She had gotten quite heavy and had never had much of an exercise routine. She didn't even know whether she would really like ballet class or whether her old dream was just idle fantasy. But she did like her class. She worked hard, learned, and developed her muscles and her flexibility. And today she teaches classes and serves as an inspiration to her students both young and old. So, if you have been telling yourself that it is too late, know that it is not. If you want to, all you have to do is take the first step. You may want to sign up for a ballet class with your daughter or a salsa aerobics class with your friend. Or try a class in African dance. It's great fun and a good workout, too. If you're feeling shy, why not try a class in African drumming? One way or another, you'll get into a rhythm.

If ballet isn't your thing, you may want to check out a class in the Middle Eastern tradition, known as belly dancing. Many women find this form of dance a lot less intimidating than ballet. One of the big pluses of belly dancing is that you are expected to have a curvy, womanly body. And that body is cherished. If you do look into a belly-dance class, you will learn to move your hips in sinuous and sexy ways and, in the early stages, you won't have to worry about a lot of fancy footwork. There are even belly-dance videos. One is called *The Goddess Workout with Dolphina—Bellydance for Fitness, Body, Mind, & Spirit.* Or look for Dolphina's series of *Goddess Workout* CDs. You may also like Gabrielle Roth's form of freestyle dancing that concentrates on rhythm and movement as pathways to the divine. Roth teaches a popular (and fun!) workshop all around the country called "Sweat Your Prayers."

So, Goddess, do you want the sun to shine? Do you want to dance?

Magic Moves

What's your ambition like? Is it a driving force that leads you to organize and plan? Or is it more like a steady hum in the background? Maybe your ambition hops around from one goal to another. Or maybe your ambition and your goals are fuzzy and unclear. What did you dream of as a child? Many young girls dream of the world of ballet, and, as you probably know, that's not all sugar and spice.

Do you know the movie *The Red Shoes*? It has been extremely popular ever since its release in 1948. Moira Shearer's wonderful dancing in the movie certainly helped make it the classic it is today. And some of the film's popularity certainly must stem from Vicky's ambition to be a great dancer. Many girls and women have shared that dream. Vicky's story also speaks to your ambition, and her dilemma—to live for love or career—may reflect some of the hard choices that you've made in your own life. Can you relate to Vicky's strong drive for success? Have you ever felt torn between your family and your career goals? Unfortunately for Vicky, she lived in a time when women really did have to choose one or the other. In 1948, women were not given the opportunity to engage in the complex balancing act that many women perform today.

The movie *The Red Shoes* (1948) tells the story of Victoria Page, an aspiring ballet dancer, who is played by the real-life ballet dancer Moira Shearer. The film contains a 15-minute dance sequence that presents a ballet, which is also called *The Red Shoes*. Vicky dances her first major solo role in the ballet within the movie.

In the ballet, Vicky plays a young woman who buys a pair of red shoes. The shoes, it turns out, are magical. When she puts them on, they want to dance, and they bring her a high degree of grace and agility. At first, her dance is joyful. What ecstasy to be able to move with such beauty! But the shoes do not want to stop, and she dances on, becoming more and more frantic. She dances and dances through the night. She becomes exhausted, but still the shoes make her spin and leap. Eventually, she dies. The ballet ends when the red shoes are removed from her feet and returned to the shop where she bought them.

In the movie, Vicky achieves her first major triumph in the role of the young woman who buys the red shoes. Her star is rising, and she is happy. She is attaining her lifelong dream of becoming a great dancer. Unfortunately, she is soon forced to choose between her lover and her career. She knows that she cannot live without them both, and she makes a tragic final decision.

In the ballet of the Red Shoes, the dance that brings Vicky her hard-sought fame, the magical shoes help the young woman to dance beautifully. At first they are like her special good-luck charm. They put her in The Zone, that seemingly magical state where her body moves beautifully and without strain. Many dancers and athletes have a lucky pair of socks or a lucky shirt that they feel helps them to reach the mental clarity and physical ease of The Zone. Once in The Zone they can perform at their best. Have you ever had a piece of lucky sports clothing? Or a lucky charm that helped you to perform your best? Think of a time when you were fully engaged in some activity that seemed to take over your entire being. Your movements flowed without effort, and you performed as well as you ever could have imagined. You were overjoyed and felt euphoric. Take a few minutes to remember the details of that experience, and retain that feeling in every part of your being. Know that this is Goddess energy flowing through you.

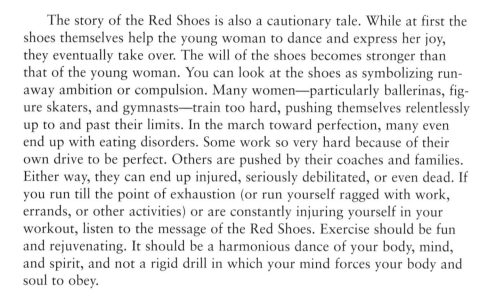

> **"** You listen to your body—it will tell you exactly what you need to do.
>
> —Martina Navratilova, tennis star (2001) **"**

The story of the Red Shoes is also a cautionary tale. While at first the shoes themselves help the young woman to dance and express her joy, they eventually take over. The will of the shoes becomes stronger than that of the young woman. You can look at the shoes as symbolizing runaway ambition or compulsion. Many women—particularly ballerinas, figure skaters, and gymnasts—train too hard, pushing themselves relentlessly up to and past their limits. In the march toward perfection, many even end up with eating disorders. Some work so very hard because of their own drive to be perfect. Others are pushed by their coaches and families. Either way, they can end up injured, seriously debilitated, or even dead. If you run till the point of exhaustion (or run yourself ragged with work, errands, or other activities) or are constantly injuring yourself in your workout, listen to the message of the Red Shoes. Exercise should be fun and rejuvenating. It should be a harmonious dance of your body, mind, and spirit, and not a rigid drill in which your mind forces your body and soul to obey.

Working Body, Mind, and Spirit

Does it seem like everyone you know is suddenly practicing yoga? Yoga has gained a huge North American following in the last 10 years. One of the reasons yoga has become so popular is that it integrates the body, mind, and spirit. The movement and poses, or asanas, that Westerners generally think of as yoga are actually just one of the eight limbs of the tree of yoga. The other limbs in this system of Indian philosophy include the adherence to socially responsible values and ethics, meditation, and union with the divine. In fact, the word yoga is Sanskrit for "union." Practicing yoga asanas is a healing and nourishing way to move. And it's also wonderfully pleasurable!

In the Hindu tradition, Kundalini is the sleeping energy that lies at the base of the spine. She is seen as a coiled snake made of fire. She is also a mother Goddess and is found in all things. Once awoken, Kundalini energy can rise up the spine, activating the chakras, or energy centers of the body. When Kundalini energy passes through the highest chakra at the crown of the head, she unites with Shiva, the God of change, destruction, yoga, and dance, and the practitioner achieves *samadhi*, a union with the divine and a state of oneness.

Kundalini is powerful energy, so powerful that you should not try to raise her on your own. Kundalini can safely be worked with under the guidance of a qualified Kundalini yoga instructor. With proper instruction, dedication, and many years of study, you can learn the techniques to awaken Kundalini and send her on her journey through your body's chakras.

Even if you cannot work with Kundalini right now, isn't it nice to know that her energy is considered female? In the Hindu tradition, the active energy forces are typically seen as female. Each of the three major Hindu Gods—Brahma, the creator; Vishnu, the preserver; and Shiva, the destroyer—have female consorts, who give them energy. These Goddesses are known as Shakti, which means "power." Shakti, the fundamental force of the universe, is a lot like the universe's form of Kundalini. The Shakti also have individual names and energies. Brahma's energizing Goddess is Saraswati, the Goddess of the arts. Vishnu's energizing Goddess is Lakshmi, the Goddess of prosperity. Shiva's energizing Goddess is Parvati or Kali, the Goddesses of birth and death. Shiva and Kali have long been associated with both dance and yoga. Both deities are frequently depicted dancing. In addition, Shiva is known as "The Great Yogi," and the ultimate goal of yoga—union with the divine—is seen as the awakening of the chakras so that the female energy in the body can meet with Shiva at the crown of the head.

But what are chakras, exactly? The word *chakra* means "wheel" in Sanskrit, the ancient language of India. You can think of the chakras as wheels of spinning energy. There are a number of different chakra systems, and it seems that everyone calls them by different names and explains their locations in the body in slightly different terms. What people do seem to agree upon is that your body contains seven primary chakras. They line up along your spine, starting at your tailbone, where the Kundalini lies sleeping.

> 66 Many people do not realize that yoga is simply about learning to pay attention. And since it is through this practice of paying attention, as all spiritual traditions tell us, that life is lived most fully, more and more people are becoming able to see the relevance of such a practice in their own lives, and its compatibility with their own religious beliefs.
>
> —Beryl Bender Birch, yoga instructor and author (1995) 99

Each chakra regulates a different kind of energy in your body. Starting at the base with the most basic needs, the first chakra, or root chakra, is concerned with issues of survival, your physical needs for food, shelter, and sleep. The second chakra rules sexuality, sensuality, and emotions. The third chakra is the seat of your will. This is where you find the energy to make decisions, act independently, shoulder responsibilities, and devise all types of plans. The fourth chakra is all about your abilities to give and receive love. It embodies the energy of the heart. The fifth chakra, located at the base of the throat, regulates your energies of communication and influences your abilities to listen, speak, and find your own voice. The sixth chakra, the third eye, is where the energies of the imagination, visualization, and psychic vision lie. The seventh, or crown, chakra is your door to spiritual wisdom and enlightenment.

Each chakra also has a color associated with it and a sound or mantra. You can help balance your chakras by imagining a ball of color swirling at the place of each of your chakras. Start with your first chakra at the base of your spine and work your way up. To balance your first chakra, imagine a ball of swirling red inside your body at the base of your spine. The color is vibrant and glowing and it moves slowly. You could also chant the mantra for the first chakra, which is *lam*. To chant, all you have to do is repeat the sound over and over again. You can do this in your mind, your normal speaking voice, or you can sing. You may want to pay special attention to the balance of your first chakra if you tend to feel aggressive or nervous, or if you are often passive or depressed. Continue up your spine to the second chakra, imagine a glowing, swirling ball of orange, and chant the mantra *vam*. Continue up the spine till you reach the top of your head. For the seventh chakra, you can sing a prolonged *om* as many times as you desire.

	Location	Color	Energy	Sound
1st	Base of the spine	Red	Survival	*lam*
2nd	Between the genitals and navel	Orange	Sexuality, emotions	*vam*
3rd	Solar plexus	Yellow	The will	*ram*
4th	Heart	Green	Love	*yam*
5th	Throat	Blue	Communication	*ham*
6th	Third eye, center between the eyebrows	Indigo-violet	Vision	*om*
7th	Top of the head	White	Spiritual awakening, enlightenment	*ommmm*

Another way to balance your chakras is by practicing hatha yoga. Each yoga pose has an effect on a different chakra. For example, a pose such as fish (*matsyasana*), which stretches your upper chest, can help to open and balance your heart chakra. You can try a supported version of fish pose by placing a thick book on the floor. Lie down so that the book is under your shoulder blades and your head and arms are on the floor. Breathe, and feel the opening of your heart center. In the pose, you should feel a gentle stretch across your chest. It should feel good. If it doesn't, come out of it. Always listen to your body.

There are many other yoga poses that you can try at home, and there are many books that explain the various poses in detail. Check out the selection of books at your local bookstore or yoga center. If you're interested, check the video section, too. Find out about the yoga studios and health clubs in your area that provide yoga instruction. You may want to talk to several instructors to learn about the many different schools of yoga. Then try a class. But first, now that you are a budding yogini, enjoy the following Goddess exercise!

Exercise #1: Strike a Pose

Have you ever tried yoga? Why not try a yoga pose right now? Goddess pose (*suptha badhakonasana*) can be quite relaxing. It can also help to free up tension in your hips and lower back and help to balance your lower chakras.

Lie down on your back. Bend your knees and move your feet toward your body while keeping them on the floor. Let your knees separate and drop open outward toward the floor. Press the soles of your feet together. Your legs will form a diamond shape with your knees as the two acute angles. Don't try to push your knees down to the floor; just allow them to drop and relax.

You will feel a stretch, probably in your inner thighs and groin. Close your eyes and concentrate on your breathing. When you inhale, imagine that you are breathing into the place where your hips are opening. When you exhale, allow yourself to relax more deeply into the stretch. Does it feel good? If your hips are very tight and this position seems too intense, try placing a pillow under each thigh. If you feel this position too intensely in your lower back, place a pillow under your feet. Or try moving your feet a little farther away from your body.

Once you have gotten settled in the pose, place your hands on your lower abdomen and breathe into your belly. Feel your hands rise and fall with each breath. Count 20 slow and steady breaths.

When you're ready to get up, bring your knees back together. You can use your hands to help move your legs up and into place. Gently roll over on your right side and use your hands to push yourself up into a seated position.

Now you're ready to create your own Goddess pose. Take a look at some of the illustrations in this book, reread some of the Goddess stories, and create a physical position that represents the Goddess of your choice. The position you make up doesn't have to physically resemble the Goddess you have picked. It can be about the Goddess's strength, courage, compassion, or sense of fun. Or your pose can be one that makes you feel like a Goddess.

How are your feet placed in your Goddess pose? Are your knees straight or bent? Do your hips face forward or are they turned to one side? Doing your pose, do you pull your abdomen in or keep it relaxed? Where are your shoulders? Are your arms opened, closed, straight, or bent? Do your hands express the qualities of your Goddess? Move around until your pose feels right to you. Once you have it, stay in the pose and count 10 slow breaths.

Now, draw a picture of yourself in your Goddess pose as a Goddess. Feel free to add long flowing robes, a crown, magical symbols, anything that will help you look and feel like the Goddess you are.

When you're done with your drawing, place it on your altar so that you can look at it. Begin doing your Goddess pose every morning when you get up as a way of greeting the day and recognizing the divine energy flowing through you. Hold the pose for 10 breaths, or longer if you like, meditating on merging with your own Goddess energy.

 Instant Goddess

Every time you move, you strengthen your immune system by massaging your lymphs. Try it right now. Place your hands over your heart in prayerful posture. Now, fling them out and open your heart as your outstretched arms pull back and away from your body. Lift your arms over your head and stretch up. Breathe deeply in and out. Feels good!

Exercise #2: Go with the Flow

Do you like to dance? You don't have to know any fancy steps or smooth moves. All you have to do is move your body. If you feel self-conscious, try this exercise alone. You can even dim the lights. If you feel comfortable, invite your friends or children to join you. Little dance breaks during the day are a fun way to blow off steam and relax.

Get out your favorite CD or tape. Put on your favorite song. Stand in the middle of the room and close your eyes. Sing along, if you like. Let your hips sway to the music. Imagine that you are Isadora Duncan, the great pioneer of modern dance. Duncan's first ideas about dance came from watching waves crash on the seashore. Be one of Isadora's waves. Don't think about what you're doing too much; just follow your body. You may want to leap and crash. Or you may ebb and flow. Let all of your body parts be involved—elbows, shoulders, hands, knees, ankles, feet, neck, and head. Feel the elemental power of your own movement.

Are there other forces of nature that you would like to be? Try dancing as the wind, a thunderstorm, the sun rising over the ocean. Or you could be a bird, a squirrel, a deer, or any animal that calls to you.

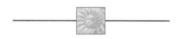

These exercises were designed to be fun and to help you on your journey along the Goddess path. Know that you are like Atalanta with her great competitive drive and Uzume with her boldness and pride in her body. You can learn from the Red Shoes that your ambition is perfectly okay and that it doesn't have to push you to impossible, unsustainable heights. And you contain Kundalini within you, the feminine force whose activation leads to enlightenment. Whatever your physical condition, you can let go of self-consciousness and guilt. You are Goddess. So, act like a Goddess and do your dance.

Do you feel more aware of your body and all of its many sacred parts? Did you work up a healthy sweat reading this chapter? Drink a little water, cool down, and get ready for fun. We hope the Goddesses in the next chapter will work another set of your muscles—your laughter muscles. The next chapter is all about play—the enigma of Mona Lisa's famous smile; the giggles of Kikimora, a Slavic Goddess of the household; Iambe, the ancient Greek Goddess who may have been the mother of the lewd joke; and Bastet, the ancient Egyptian Goddess associated with pleasure, music, and dancing. Yes, more dancing!

Chapter 7

Play: Enjoying Life

Do you enjoy life? Are you happy with your normal everyday existence? Do you take time out from all the many things that you must do for fun? Do you ever play? Play is not just for children, and play can take many different forms—from solitary games of cards to amateur theatrics and make-believe, from a romp on the beach to a museum visit to a ride on a roller coaster or a drive through the countryside.

Have you thought about what fun means to you? If you watch television, you have probably seen many advertisements over the course of your life that promote playing with a certain toy, driving a particular brand of car, shopping at a specific store, or visiting a well-known amusement park as fun. Some individuals would consider these activities to be fun. For others, the toy may seem boring, driving the car tiresome, shopping may be a horror, and the idea of an amusement park may be an exercise in torture. Do you know what you *really* enjoy?

Pleasure in Paint

Looking at beautiful things can be quite pleasurable. There is more than one kind of beauty, of course. Do you like natural beauty? Is the beauty of nature part of your everyday life? And how about art? You don't have to be an art historian or a connoisseur to derive pleasure from works of art. If you're like most people, you probably know more about art than you think you do.

 Mona, Mona, Mona! Leonardo da Vinci's image of the Mona Lisa has been called the world's most famous painting. In 1503, Leonardo started work on this masterpiece, which is painted on a wooden panel, and he painted and repainted it for more than four years. Many people believe that the model for the portrait was a Florentine woman named Lisa del Giocondo, and hence, the painting is known as *La Gioconda* in Italian and *La Joconde* in French. Although Leonardo usually kept detailed records of his models' sittings, no such records exist for the Mona Lisa.

When Leonardo died in France in 1519, he had the *Mona Lisa* with him. After his death, the painting passed into the collection of the French king, who put it on display in his favorite chateau. In 1800, Napoleon Bonaparte, who was soon to become the Emperor of the French, had the *Mona Lisa* hung in his bedroom in the Tuileries in central Paris. In 1804, she was added to the displays of the Louvre Museum, where she quickly became a favorite with the public. She was so well loved, in fact, that she was stolen in 1911. After her disappearance, flocks of people came to the Louvre to look at the empty spot on the wall where she had hung. The public just could not believe that she was really gone. Soon Paris was swept with a Mona craze. Songs about her were sung in cafés, celebrities had themselves photographed as Mona, and *Mona Lisa* postcards sold like hotcakes.

After two years, the *Mona Lisa* resurfaced in Florence, her city of origin, when the man who had stolen her brought her to an antiques dealer. Mona Lisa's abductor, an Italian citizen, had wanted to restore this art treasure to her native land. He was arrested, and before returning to France, the painting went on tour through the major cities of Italy. More than 60,000 people went to see her. In 1963, Mona went traveling again. This time, she visited the National Gallery in Washington, D.C. and the Metropolitan Museum of Art in New York City. A throng of more than a million and a half Mona lovers lined up to see her "in the flesh." Eleven years later, Mona visited Tokyo and Moscow, where another two million art lovers got a glimpse of her famous smile. Today, the painting itself, which measures only about 21 by 30 inches, hangs in the Louvre Museum in Paris.

Why is Mona smiling? People have asked this question for centuries. Some say that she has a secret. Perhaps she possesses special vision, knowledge, and experience. Some say that she smiles because she knows she is pregnant. Or that her smile represents her sexual longing. She has been described as a representation of the returning pagan world; as St. Anne, mother of Mary; and as Leda, the swan from Greek mythology, who was mother to Helen of Troy, the most beautiful woman in the world. Mona Lisa has been called "perpetual life." On the other hand, one critic has suggested that Mona's smile is evil. Sigmund Freud suggested that the facial expression Leonardo reproduced was the smile of his own birth mother from whom he had been separated when very young. Leonardo's biographer, Giorgi Vasari, writing just 31 years after the painter's death, believed that the smile was the result of Leonardo's efforts to keep his model entertained. According to Vasari, Leonardo employed musicians and jesters to keep his model "full of merriment." Consider that Mona Lisa's smile represents a profound secret—her knowledge that she was made up of much more than the outward appearance that Leonardo painted. She knew that she contained Goddess energy, a force that at once brought her a sense of power and a serene inner peace.

Others have seen Mona's identity as a key to her smile. Lillian F. Schwartz, co-author of *The Computer Artist's Handbook* (W. W. Norton & Company, 1992), used computer-scanning techniques to compare Leonardo's image of himself from a 1518 self-portrait to the *Mona Lisa,* and found that the structure of the face in both paintings is the same. Schwartz concluded that the model for the *Mona Lisa* was Leonardo himself. Could Mona's smile be an expression of Leonardo's amusement at all the thought people over the centuries would give to Mona's real identity?

Why do you think Mona is smiling?

- She's imagining the delicious lunch she will get to eat when she and Leonardo take a break.
- She's just met a new special someone about whom she is dreaming.
- She's planning her ideal vacation.
- She's trying to remember a line of poetry that she used to have memorized.
- She's reliving the amazing, earth-shaking sex she had last night.

Does the list of Mona's possible reasons make you smile? Does looking at Mona make you smile? Do you enjoy the mystery surrounding her? What *does* make you smile? Listen to Nat King Cole's 1950 hit song, "Mona Lisa," for inspiration—how are *you* a lovely work of art? Do you enjoy looking at art? For many women, art is a source of great enjoyment. When was the last time you went to a museum or an art exhibit? What kind of art represents your own enigmatic inner passion and Goddess fire? Plan to go look at some paintings or other artwork soon.

> **❝** Religion and art spring from the same root and are close kin.
>
> —Willa Cather, writer (1949) **❞**

Many people find museums overwhelming. There is so much to see! You can make museum-going more enjoyable by planning short visits. Pick out a few works of art that you want to see. (You can preview the collection of some museums on the Internet.) Go and look at the few works that you have preselected, and then leave *before* your feet begin to hurt. Or plan to look at the artwork in just one or two of the museum's rooms. Allow yourself as much time as you would like in front of a painting or sculpture that pleases you. Sit down, if you can. Try to identify what it is about the work that makes you like it. Is it the colors? Does the overall emotion appeal to you? Or do you like the people, animals, things, or place depicted?

Sometimes a little knowledge can help make your experience of art more enjoyable. And you should have as much enjoyment in your life as possible! If it sounds fun for you, read a biography of an artist who interests you. Knowing about the artist's life can shed a whole new light on that person's work, and on their creative process (which is a part of having fun as well!). Or check out some general books on art history and art appreciation. You might look for books by Sister Wendy Beckett, an art historian and nun. (Do you think she would mind if we called her a Goddess? We think she is one!) Or look for videos from her entertaining television series.

Enjoying the creative products of others—such as television shows, movies, theater, music, dance, or artwork—can be fun, stimulating, and fulfilling. Making your own art or just dabbling around with art supplies, playing a musical instrument, performing a monologue from a play, and writing, can also be enjoyable activities. We'll talk more about creativity in Chapter 10. But before you get there, try something goofy. Take out a large sheet of paper and a box of crayons. (If you don't have crayons in your house, buy some. Get the big box of 64. Everyone should have crayons! If you've got kids, then, indeed, you've got crayons. But this isn't an exercise to do with the kids. This is for *you*—be sure that you put everything away when you're done!) Put on some music, lie on the floor if that is comfortable for you. Now, without trying to draw anything in particular, scribble. Just let your hand move to the music.

Are we having fun yet?

Dance with the Dogs?

Music and dancing are also a source of pleasure for many women. Are these art forms that you enjoy? There are many different kinds of music—classical, jazz, rock, country, blues, Latin, easy-listening, and New Age, to name a few. Have you experienced them all? How many of them do you enjoy? And what about dance? Of course, dance comes in many different varieties as well. Do you dance? Do you watch others—your friends, professional performers, or perhaps your pets—when they dance?

Also known as Bast, Bastet is the Ancient Egyptian Goddess of the sun, pleasure, music, and dancing. Worshipped as early as 3200 B.C.E., she is associated with cats and is often depicted as a woman with a cat's head. She carries a special kind of rattle, called a sistrum. Sometimes her body is also depicted as a cat's. And sometimes she has the head of a lion. Often she is shown with kittens crawling over her feet. According to some accounts, when she has a lion's head, she rules over healing and the fertility of the earth and is associated with the sun. When she has a cat's head, she is the Goddess of the moon and the pleasure derived from music and dancing. She has variously been described as the wife, sister, and/or daughter of Ra, the sun God, and the wife of Bes, the God of music, dancing, laughter, marriage, fighting, and protector of women. She has often been confused with Mut, a mother Goddess and the Queen of Heaven, and with Sekhmet, the fiery warrior Goddess of the setting sun who is often seen to represent the destructive side of the sun's power. Bastet was worshipped along with Ra and Sekhmet as Sekhem-bast-ra, a triple deity.

It seems appropriate that a Goddess associated with pleasure would be depicted as a cat. Have you ever watched a cat stretched out, taking a bath in the sun? Cats, and dogs, too, truly know how to derive pleasure from simple, everyday activities. They enjoy their own movements, and they enjoy what is around them—sleeping on your sweater, scratching your couch, gazing out the window, or sticking a nose out the car window when out for a drive. If you have a pet, do you take time to play together? The sheer joy of your dog running to catch a ball or the dance of your cat pouncing on a piece of string is a pleasure to behold. Playing with your pet can be fun for both of you. Enjoy the animal dance and help release your inner Bastet.

Dogs act exactly the way we would act if we had no shame.

—Cynthia Heimel, humorist (1993)

Do you watch a lot of television? Do you ever watch dance programs, concerts, or operas on TV? Consider expanding your enjoyment options. Try watching a new type of program and see if you like it. When was the last time you saw a live performance? Why not go see a dance performance, an opera, or a concert? Certainly, watching television is easy. You don't have to make plans to watch TV, nor do you have to hire a babysitter. But make a commitment to your inner Bastet. Plan to go out to a cultural event soon, even if it's just a movie. If you can, though, go see something live. Dress up for the experience. Part of the joy of live music, dance, or theater is being part of the audience—looking at everyone and being looked at.

You may want to read up on dance, opera, or music to increase your enjoyment of those art forms. The biographies of opera divas are particularly passionate and entertaining. Look for books by or about stars such as Galina Vishnevskaya, formerly Goddess of Russia's prestigious Bolshoi Opera, and co-founder with her husband, world-renowned cellist Mstislav Rostropovich, of the Vishnevskaya-Rostropovich Foundation, a nonprofit organization dedicated to improving children's healthcare in Russia. Learn about Maria Callas, the phenomenal Greek soprano and Goddess, who was romanced by shipping-magnate Aristotle Onassis before he married Jackie Kennedy. Or read the inspiring story of Marian Anderson, another Goddess and the first black singer to perform at the Metropolitan Opera. Or find a book or video about a dancer, choreographer, composer, or musician who interests you.

 We look at the dance to impart the sensation of living in an affirmation of life, to energize the spectator into keener awareness of the vigor, the mystery, the humor, the variety, and the wonder of life. This is the function of the American dance.

—Martha Graham, dancer and choreographer (1935)

And, of course, you can express your own Bastet qualities by singing, making music, and dancing yourself. Did you try the dance exercise in

Chapter 6? Why not do it now? Be as silly or dramatic as you like, and see how much fun you can have. If dancing is not your thing, try playing some music yourself. Consider playing the drums or the guitar. Guitar playing and taking guitar lessons have become an increasingly popular means of musical expression among girls and young women. Guitar manufacturers are even making smaller guitars to meet the needs of women.

Household Fun

You get up in the morning and dash to school or work. You drop your children off, if you have them. You work hard. You zoom to the store for groceries. You rush to complete other errands. Then you pick up the kids and drive them to play dates or soccer or ballet or to the mall. Finally, you arrive home. Time to walk the dog and start dinner! And you realize you didn't have time to pick up your dry cleaning, you haven't called your sister back, and you forgot to buy kitty litter—again! You have barely stepped in the door to your home and already you feel exhausted. Does your life sound like this, at least some of the time? If so, do you ask yourself, "Where is the fun here?"

Although many present-day Russians see her as a bad-tempered swamp demon, the Kikimora has also been described as a household Goddess, who lives either in the house's basement or in the stove. Some people say she is married to the Domovoi, the male house God, and that she may go by the name Domania or Domovikha, all of which come from the Russian word *dom*, which means "house." According to those who see her in a positive light, if treated with respect, Kikimora may help out around the house, but only so long as the place is kept clean. If she suspects laziness in housekeeping, she will mischievously hide small items, break things, and tickle children at night to keep them awake. Some sources suggest that she can be put into a better humor by washing pots, pans, and utensils with a tea made from ferns.

Ack, housework! It's probably not on the top of your list of fun things to do. But there are ways you can actually make it more enjoyable. Have you ever turned putting things away into a game? Many parents find this an effective way to get their children to put away their toys. And it works with adults, too! If you do have children of your own, you can play the pick-up game with them. You can also play it with your roommates, partner, or just yourself. Here are the rules of this simple game:

1. The youngest player gets to go first. Depending on this player's age and abilities, have him or her say either the name of a color or a letter of the alphabet.

2. The next player must pick up and put away an object that is the same color as the selected one or one with a name that starts with the selected letter.

Certainly, having company while you do housework can help to make it more fun. You can also use your imagination. Pretend to be Kikimora and "hide" some objects by putting them away in their proper place. Or think back to make-believe games that you played as a child. Did you ever play house? So why not play house now? Or make up your own fantasy game to help you get some chores done. You could pretend to be Cinderella. Sing "In My Own Little Corner" from the 1964 film musical of *Cinderella* to yourself while you clean. (Remember Lesley Ann Warren? What a Goddess!) Or be Snow White, imagine that the seven dwarves are helping you, and whistle while you work. Any kind of music can help you get the most tedious chores done more quickly and with more fun— vacuuming to opera is one of our personal favorites (look back at the list of Opera Goddesses in Chapter 1 for inspiration). If you're worried about making too much noise—between the music and your howling vacuum— use a portable tape or CD player with headphones.

66 My second favorite household chore is ironing. My first being hitting my head on the top bunk until I faint.

—Erma Bombeck, humorist (1970)

If you have a task that you have been avoiding, try breaking it down into small parts. For example, instead of telling yourself that you have to clean the whole house, tackle just one room. Or plan to work on just one corner. Or go to work on one half of your very messy table. Another trick that may help you is to tell yourself you only have to work for a short amount of time. Set a timer for 10 minutes. When the clock is ticking, you will be amazed at how much you can get done. After your 10 minutes are up, take a break and congratulate yourself for having started. Once you have begun, it will be easier to go back for your next short work session.

You also can lighten the burden of your household tasks by using yogic awareness. Instead of focusing on the results of your actions—having everything put away in its place, clean dishes, or folded laundry—bring your attention to the present moment in which you are working. Take your attention to your breathing, your movements, and the physical sensations that your tasks bring you. Are any of your movements pleasurable? Allow all of your actions to become contemplative. Think of every movement that you perform in cleaning your house as a devotional offering of love and compassion. Know that your housecleaning actions performed with this spirit of mindfulness are, at the very least, the equal of the actions performed by the sage, the rocket scientist, or the surgeon. With a yogic focus, responsibilities and love become one, and your tasks transform into a source of happiness.

The Lewd, the Crude, the Poetic

Dirty jokes and poetry? Do these two things go together? To the modern mind, maybe they don't. Do you enjoy jokes? Do you enjoy off-color or adult jokes? It probably depends on the joke, right? According to classics scholars, Demeter, mother of Persephone, Goddess of the harvest and of the life-giving corn, enjoyed a good joke, including bawdy ones. And she liked poetry, too. Is poetry something that you enjoy?

The ancient Greeks may have been right about the healing power of humor. According to doctors at Stanford Medical School, laughing 100 times is roughly the equivalent of spending 10 minutes working out on a rowing machine or 15 minutes pedaling a stationary bicycle. In addition to providing a cardiovascular workout, laughter boosts the immune system and releases tension and anxiety. So, a laugh attack a day just might help keep illness away. Have you had your daily dose of laughter?

What kind of jokes, if any, do you enjoy? Because humor tends to release tension from areas of conflict in our lives, you may find jokes about men funny. Oftentimes, jokes about men center on the times when men behave badly. Here's an example:

A woman comes home from her annual physical exam and says to her husband, "My doctor reports that I have the breasts of a 30-year-old."

Her husband replies, "And what did he say about your 50-year-old ass?"

"Well," she answers, "you didn't come up."

Did you find that joke funny? Did you actually laugh? Or did you just crack a smile? Do you think Demeter would have laughed at that one? Maybe you prefer lawyer jokes or really silly knock-knock jokes. Maybe your humor is more situational, the kind that you cannot repeat, you just had to be there. Do you know a joke that makes you laugh out loud? If so, write that joke out in your Goddess journal. Then spread the laughter. Share your joke with a friend.

> 66 There comes a time when suddenly you realize that laughter is something you remember and that *you* were the one laughing.
>
> —Marlene Dietrich, actress (1962)

Iambe, in addition to being Demeter's first priestess and a crack joke-teller, was also a bit of a poet. She is credited with inventing her own poetic form. Remember the phrase "iambic pentameter" from when you studied Shakespeare in high school? An iamb, if you recall, consists of a short syllable followed by a long syllable. So, an iamb sounds like this: *di da*. These two syllables as a group are called a metrical foot. Iambic pentameter describes a poem written in lines made up of five metrical feet. In other words, it goes like this: *di da di da di da di da di da*. Or to use an example from Shakespeare: "Now is the winter of our discontent." (Which may have been how Demeter felt before Iambe cheered her by spinning out her wit.)

In some ancient Greek plays, which were written in verse, an iambic rhythm was used to indicate humor, telling someone off, or sexual exuberance. Some scholars believe that writers picked this particular rhythm for the funny, bawdy, or sexy passages in their work because the iambic rhythm was also used in the wilder parts of rituals, such as when women told lewd jokes and mocked others during the celebration of Demeter held at Eleusis, a town 10 miles east of Athens.

Iambe, an ancient Greek Goddess associated with happiness and poetry, was the daughter of Pan, the goat God, and Echo, the mountain nymph. Iambe had a particularly friendly and cheerful nature. In a poem of praise to Demeter that dates from the Homeric era, Iambe is described as "one who knows what is dear and what is not." She understood what was important in life, and high on her list was fun.

When Demeter, in mourning for her daughter Persephone who was stuck down in the underworld, came to the house where Iambe worked as a maid, Iambe cheered her up. Some say that Iambe recited poetry. Some say that Iambe told Demeter jokes. Some say that Iambe told Demeter *dirty* jokes, and that the great Goddess of the harvest smiled. Some sources attribute this joke-telling to a character known as Baubo, who was said to have been Demeter's nurse and was depicted as a headless creature with breasts for eyes and genitals in the shape of a bearded mouth. (A few women in Goddess studies have suggested that Baubo even lifted Demeter's skirts and pleased her sexually to improve the Goddess's mood.) At any rate, because she felt somewhat better, Demeter finally agreed to break her fast, and partook of a drink called *kykeon*, a mixture of barley-water and an herb called pennyroyal. Demeter then began to move from her stuck place of grief into the action that eventually brought Persephone back into the world of light.

Demeter was so pleased with Iambe and her jokes that Iambe became Demeter's first priestess. The story of Demeter's loss and Iambe's wit was reenacted by ancient Greek women every year in the performance of the Eleusinian mysteries, the annual religious rites celebrating Demeter and the fertility of the earth. They even drank *kykeon* and made lewd jokes to elicit laughter, which was thought to promote fertility.

Exercise #1: Laughing Matters

In 1999, award-winning filmmaker Mira Nair came out with a documentary called *The Laughing Club of India*. In this film, which has aired on HBO, Nair traces the development of the more than 450 laughing clubs that have sprung up in India since 1995, when Dr. Madan Kataria, a Mumbai-based physician, started his first group chuckling in hopes of improving health and well-being. Something in his technique of laughter exercises, which include sticking out your tongue and making monkey faces, must be working. The laughing club phenomenon has spread to Australia, Europe, the Far East, and the United States.

So, why not convene your own laughter group? Plan a half-hour where all you have to do is laugh. Invite a bunch of friends, gather your children, and be silly. Tell jokes or funny stories. Have everyone stick out his or her tongue. Make animal noises. Hop up and down on one foot and snort. If those techniques don't tickle your funny bone, try this exercise:

1. Get everyone to lie down on the floor so that you all form a circle. Each person should place his or her head on the stomach of the person to his or her right.

2. Once everyone is in position, get one person in the circle to say, "ha, ha, ha." When this person speaks, his or her stomach will inflate and contract causing the head resting there to bounce. This is usually enough to provoke a laugh that spreads around the circle. If not, have someone else in the circle say, "ho, ho, ho." Pretty soon gales of giggles will ensue!

If you absolutely cannot get a small group of people together to do this exercise, go see a funny movie. Or invite a friend over and rent a video that you know will make you laugh. Try to laugh with other people, if at all possible, because laughter fuels itself and results in more laughter. And we could all use a good laugh!

Instant Goddess

For more fun today, call or e-mail four friends and ask them to help bring some silliness into your life. You may be surprised what each person comes up with! Your friends can help you remember good times and hold on to hope for future fun. Try it; you'll connect in a loving way with people who care about you and know how to help smile.

Exercise #2: Stand Up for Laughter

Have you ever gone to a club to hear a stand-up comedian perform? Hearing stand-up can be fun. And doing stand-up can be even more fun. Gail and Katherine can vouch for this with their own experience—both have performed as stand-up comedians.

In case you're not familiar with the genre, many stand-up comedians poke fun at people or situations in their life that cause anger, fear, worry, or frustration in them. As a stand-up comedian, you don't repeat jokes, but you share your observations. Here's a bit from Katherine's stand-up routine:

The recovery movement's really affected me. I used to smoke too much, drink too much, indulge in recreational drugs. Now I practice yoga; my mind is really clear, and I can see that I used to have a *life*.

At a conference appearance, Gail once dressed up like the great porcine Goddess Miss Piggy and, instead of "Amazing Grace," sang "Amazing Moi!"

You'll find that your routine will grow funnier and funnier as you express your own unique vision and take on life. Try this exercise:

1. Get out your Goddess journal. At the top of a page write, "Don't you hate it when …." Now, keep going and describe a situation that you hate. Feel free to write about your boss, your partner, a difficult friend, an impossible co-worker, the IRS, or anything else that bugs you. Be as outrageous or as cranky as you like. When you have finished describing the situation, write four more "Don't you hate it when"s.

2. Now write, "It makes me really mad when …" and keep going. Write descriptions of four more situations that make you mad.

3. Referring to all of your "I hate it whens" and "it really make me mad whens," make a list of your responses to these aggravating situations. Let your imagination go and imagine what crazy thing you might do. Make your fantasy responses the kind of outlandish, bizarre behavior you might see from a cartoon character or an animal.

4. You now have the basis for a number of different bits in your stand up routine—all transforming anger or frustrating situations and emotions into sources of humor and laughter. What a difference a little perspective can make! Stand in front of a full-length mirror and read what you have written out loud. Edit the parts that sound awkward or confusing. Condense the parts that seem too long.

5. Read your routine to a trusted friend. Be proud of the parts in your routine that make your friend laugh. If your friend is silent for long stretches, edit your material some more. The lines that elicit laughs are your punch lines. In the previous example from Katherine's stand-up routine, the words "I used to have a *life*" make up the punch line. You want to try to ensure that each of your bits has a punch line.

6. When you feel ready and if you're comfortable doing so, get some friends together and try out your stand-up routine. Or go to a bar or club with an open mike and perform your routine for a larger audience. Don't worry about being nervous. Everyone is nervous when

they get up in front of an audience. Recognize the feeling of anxiety for what it is—a feeling that will soon pass, and know that some of what you are feeling is excitement and the movement of your potent creative energy. Whatever you do, enjoy the thrill and have fun!

Have someone snap a picture of you when you're in front of an audience performing your routine. Once you're home, copy out your favorite bit from your routine. Place the photo and your piece of beautifully transcribed wit on your Goddess altar to remind yourself of your amazing, Goddess-like powers of humor.

These exercises, the fun and enjoyment that you have read about, and perhaps experienced yourself while reading this chapter, can help to guide you toward a greater sense of enjoyment in your life. Knowing what you like to do for fun is an important part of life on the Goddess path, and experiencing fun is a crucial Goddess quality. Remember that Iambe made Demeter laugh, and that started the process of awakening the earth from the slumber and barrenness of winter. Know that you embody the mysterious smile of the Mona Lisa. You contain the playfulness and love of music and dance of Bastet. You can be mischievous and harness your Kikimora energy to transform your household tasks. And you can be like Iambe and revel in poetry and sometimes sharp or even lewd feminine humor. Are you smiling?

Now you are ready to move on to Chapter 8, where you will delve into the world of sensation and meet the Venus of Willendorf, an icon of prehistoric womanhood and the feminine powers of fertility; the Roman Goddess Venus and her Greek counterpart Aphrodite, the Goddesses of love and beauty; Ix Chel, the Mayan creator Goddess and Great Mother; and the Yoni Lotus, the Hindu idea, as represented in the ancient Kama Sutra, of the sacred nature of a women's sex.

Chapter 8

Sex: Sensually Spiritual

How do you feel about sex and the images of sex and sexuality that surround you? How do you feel about your own body? And what about the pleasures your senses can afford you? Your answers to these questions may be complicated or simple, and they may shift depending on your mood. You may believe that enjoying sex and physical pleasure run counter to a spiritual life. Many people equate spirituality with celibacy or asceticism. Refraining from sex and physical pleasures is seen as spiritual, but enjoying these experiences is not.

But think about this: In many stories, the Goddesses themselves enjoy sex; some, such as Aphrodite, express a liberal love of sexual pleasure. And, of course, if it were not for a sex act between our biological parents, most of us would not have had the opportunity to manifest ourselves here on earth. In many cultures sexual union—and specifically joyous sexual union—is seen as a spiritual duty and a path to the divine. Try thinking of sensuality as one of the divine gifts that you get for having and maintaining your physical body. In this way, you can begin to see your sexual behavior as sacred.

Power from the Earth

Women have been represented in art since the time before recorded history. Much has been written about the impact that images of women from advertising and the media have on our self-esteem. Have you ever looked at images of women from the period before recorded history? Many women (and some men, too) have become fascinated with archeology because of what it can tell us about women—the way they were perceived in the past, the functions they may have fulfilled in ancient societies, the part that women played in history, and the roles that they play today.

In 1908, a team of archeologists working in a cave in Willendorf, a town near Vienna, Austria, found a small lime-stone statue of a woman with a big belly, huge breasts, tiny thin arms, and stubby legs. The statue measures only 4³/₈ inches (11.1 cm) high, and dates from 24,000 to 22,000 B.C.E. Many other statuettes of similar female forms dating from the Paleolithic era have been found all over Europe—from France to the Balkans to Siberia. Starting in the 1860s, archeologists began to call figures such as the one recovered at Willendorf "Venus," after the Greek Goddess of beauty and love. The term was used with irony. The little obese statuettes did not fit the male archeologists' ideal of feminine beauty.

The Venus of Willendorf became well known because of her being skill-fully carved. Compared to other Paleolithic statues, she is a masterpiece. She also has become a symbol of Goddess worship. Although archeologists tend to agree that Willendorf's carving is superior, they find less common ground when discussing the ancient statue's meaning. Some see her as evidence that a Great Mother Goddess was worshipped all over Paleolithic Europe. Others see her as a fertility charm that may have been carried by a pregnant woman to ensure a healthy delivery. It has even been suggested that she may have been a child's plaything. Archeologists, art historians, feminists, and Goddess studies scholars have all written about the Venus of Willdendorf and pro-posed various theories about her significance. Despite all the discussion about her, we still don't know for sure why one of our Paleolithic ancestors carved her. Neither do we know how the artist or the artist's community felt about the little statue. Today, the mysterious Willendorf remains a powerful icon, and reproductions of her likeness have found homes on the altars of many women.

Have you seen images of the Venus of Willendorf before? You may have studied her in an art history class. You may have seen reproduc-tions of her statue in New Age shops. How do you feel about her? Does her image seem powerful to you? For many women, the Venus of Willendorf has come to represent ancient feminine power. She is the Great Mother, containing the mysterious ability to create life out of herself. She is the one who existed before all time. She is the creator of the world.

Other women see her as the embodiment of a powerful, earthy sexuality. She is female sexuality, unimpeded by society. She is big and bold and immodest, especially if you compare her to ancient Greek statues such as the ones depicting the Greek Venus, rising from the waves. The Greek Venus often reaches with her hands to try to cover her breasts and pelvic area. The Venus of Willendorf displays none of that self-consciousness. She is what she is. If she wished she were thinner, you would never know it from the way that she carries herself. Do you admire her natural poise and forthrightness? Can you imitate her and just be yourself, bold and beautiful?

Some women consider the Venus of Willendorf to be the personification of the fertility of the earth itself. Some scholars have suggested, based on the size of Willendorf's belly, that she is pregnant. Others think that she represents the potential for pregnancy. One art historian, citing the careful carving of the dimples on her knees, has written that she must be a representation of a real-life large woman.

> 66 In traditions that go back to the dawn of civilization, the female vulva was revered as the magical portal of life, possessed of the power of both physical regeneration and spiritual illumination and transformation.
>
> —Riane Eisler, anthropologist (1995) 99

If you feel powerfully attracted by the Venus of Willendorf, you may want to spend more time with her. Having her around can help remind you of your own Goddess qualities of nurturing, strength, and connection to the earth. Reproductions of Willendorf, especially if they are made on the same scale that she is, feel really nice when held in one hand. If Willendorf repels you, you also may want to find an image or reproduction of her for further study. What is it about her that makes you uncomfortable? Can you imagine being her? Is something about that scary to you? Of course, we are not suggesting that you should look like Willendorf, but can you imagine having her raw power? In such ancient times, when the Venus was carved and humankind struggled to advance and survive, certainly a woman's ability to bring forth life from her body must have been profound. And so it is, today.

Mirror, Mirror, on the Wall

In fairy tales, movies, and on television, the pretty girl usually gets the mate of her choice. And generally, it's the pretty "young" girl. (Consider older actors such as Robert Redford starring opposite younger stars such as Demi Moore and Michelle Pfeiffer ....) But is this "success" of fairytale beauty true in real life? Do you imagine that if you were more beautiful (however you perceive "beautiful" to be), you would feel more fulfilled in your love life, both sexually and emotionally? How can the stories of the Goddesses—who were, well, Goddesses—have anything to say about your feelings that you may lack beauty? Well, even Goddesses sometimes worry about their looks and their lovability.

If you've ever heard the expression "the face that launched a thousand ships," the face in question was the one belonging to the beautiful Helen. Doesn't it seem terrible that her looks seem to have gotten her into a situation of armed combat? Doesn't it seem tragic that Aphrodite, Hera, and Athena worried so much about their attractiveness and that their worries eventually led to war? Don't you wish you could have given them a good talking to? What would you have told them? Perhaps you would have said something like this: *Aphrodite, you are gorgeous! So what if Hera has bigger breasts than you do? So what if Athena is taller? Why compare yourself to others? You are you! You are unique, and you have your own special beauty.*

Next time you start feeling insecure about your looks, try repeating this little speech to yourself. It really is true. You are beautiful in your own unique way. You have probably seen pictures of Venus and Aphrodite. What do you think of these images? Do you find them attractive? Do their slender shapes inspire you, or do they leave you feeling that your body and your beauty do not measure up? Aphrodite and Venus are just one ideal, in the same way that models in fashion magazines are just one very limited idea of female attractiveness. As Susie Bright, the prolific writer, "Sexpert," and Goddess, says, "sexual attraction is possible in every package." Know that you are beautiful enough to get the kind of love and sex that you want. It doesn't matter what you look like. You don't have to have a perfectly flat stomach, long legs, and shiny hair. It doesn't matter that you think you have fat ankles or jiggly upper arms. It doesn't matter how old you are or how many children you have had (or not had). You deserve to get what you want. Of course, real beauty, as every Goddess knows, is not merely physical. Real beauty comes from within, from the self-confidence and self-acceptance that grows with your own understanding of your true Goddess nature.

Aphrodite, the ancient Greek Goddess of sexual love and beauty, was one of 12 deities who lived on Mount Olympus. Originally, she was probably an even more ancient Goddess from the islands of the Eastern Mediterranean. In that form, she was seen as a Mother Goddess and Queen of Heaven. The Greeks saw her as the daughter of Zeus and Dione, a daughter of Gaia, the earth mother, and Uranus, the sky. She was also said to have risen from the foam of the sea. The name Aphrodite comes from the Greek word *aphros,* which means "foam." She is often depicted as a beautiful young woman rising naked from the waters of the sea or poised inside a large seashell. Aphrodite was married to the rather unattractive Hephaestus, the God of fire and the forge. She had many affairs, with Gods and mortals alike, and bore as many as 18 children, including Cupid, the God of love whose gold-tipped arrows pierce the heart and ignite desire. In her Roman version, she is known as Venus, and she was thought to be the mother of the Roman people. Venus's temple in ancient Rome was the largest of all the city's places of worship. In addition to being a love Goddess, Aphrodite/Venus enjoyed laughing and did so often.

Despite the fact that she was a Goddess, Aphrodite's beauty was not always a source of pleasure for her. Even she sometimes suffered from insecurity and jealousy. Once all the Gods and Goddesses were gathered at a wedding. All but one, that is. Eris, the Goddess of discord, had not been invited. When she found out about this snub, she tossed a golden apple into the crowd of guests. On the apple were written the words "For the fairest." Aphrodite; Athena, the Goddess of wisdom; and Hera, the Goddess of marriage and protector of women, all wanted the apple. The other Gods and Goddesses did not want to get involved in this fight because they knew that the two Goddesses not chosen as the most beautiful would bear grudges. So, they asked Paris, a shepherd, to decide which Goddess should keep the apple.

Each Goddess tried to persuade Paris to pick her. Hera promised him power and great wealth. Athena said she would give him glory and heroism in war. Aphrodite promised that she would find him the most beautiful woman in the world to wed. Paris gave the apple to Aphrodite. From that day forward, the other two Goddesses considered him an enemy. Aphrodite kept her promise and took Paris to meet Helen. Unfortunately, Helen was already married to Menelaus, the king of Sparta, one of the Greek city-states. After much effort and help from Aphrodite, Paris convinced Helen to run away with him. He took her to Troy where his father was king. Menelaus asked his friends to help him retrieve his wife. A thousand Greek ships set sail for Troy and lay siege to the city, and that was the start of the Trojan War.

Sex appeal is 50 percent what you've got and 50 percent what people think you've got.

—Sophia Loren, actress (1973)

How much of what you want sexually are you getting? Do you have orgasms? Do you have orgasms as often as you would like to? Do you have enough closeness and physical intimacy in your life? Enough hugs and kisses and pampering? Do you feel loved? If not, don't act like an insecure and jealous Aphrodite, but take matters into your own hands. You can learn a lot about your sexual response on your own. Okay, masturbation has gotten a bad rap in this country, but what better way to learn about yourself? Through self-exploration, you can learn what pleases you without the pressure that your partner can sometimes bring. You can learn if what sounds like an interesting idea is ultimately going to light your fire or leave you cold. For many women, masturbation is the most effective way to learn to have an orgasm. Or, if reaching climax is not difficult for you, you can learn to prolong and intensify your pleasure. Betty Dodson and Joani Blank are two sex educators (and Goddesses!) who have helped thousands of women to learn about their own sexuality. If this topic interests you, look for their books and videos, or check out Betty's website at www.bettydodson.com.

 Sex pleasure in woman ... is a kind of magic spell; it demands complete abandon; if words or movements oppose the magic of caresses, the spell is broken.

—Simone De Beauvoir, writer (1953)

And of course, there is much more to your sensuous life than the actual sex act—either alone or with another. Do you allow yourself other sensuous pleasures? There are many simple delights that you can enjoy every day. Really nice underwear, a silk shirt, a velvet jacket—all of these things may appeal to your senses and help you to feel sexy and beautiful. Bubble baths—alone or with a partner—can be great clean fun. And don't forget your sense of smell. Some perfume, scented oil, potpourri, or scented candles can help turn your home, or your bedroom, into a temple of delight.

The Path to Ecstatic Union

Do you have a partner? Do you have a good relationship with your partner? Do you communicate well most of the time? Is your sex life fulfilling? Sometimes do you wish there was more to it? Do you yearn for greater closeness and more pleasure? Do you find that the feeling of magic in your closeness that you used to share has faded away? Or do you just feel like exploring and trying something new?

Yoni is a Sanskrit word that means "womb" or "abode." Yoni is also seen as a Hindu Mother Goddess. In the Kama Sutra, a fourth-century Hindu text on sexuality, *yoni* is the word used to describe female genitalia. In Hindu art, the yoni, the seat of fertility and creativity, is often represented as a lotus flower in full bloom. The lotus and the yoni are both symbols of life, death, and rebirth. In the Kama Sutra, the yoni is honored as the gateway of birth through which a being passes from a solely spiritual existence and into the physical existence of a flesh and blood human. The yoni is also seen as a special place because of the pleasure that it can bring a woman. In Tantric practices, an ancient Hindu system of philosophy and psychology that seeks to unite the apparent opposites in life, the yoni is also revered. The energy of Shakti, the one universal power and energizing force, lives in the yoni. Sexual play awakens Shakti and causes her energy to grow and intensify.

Does the word *yoni* sound funny to you? And how do you feel about *your* yoni? One way to improve your sex life is to examine how you relate to your own sexual parts. Do you think of your yoni as a creepy and dirty thing? Is your yoni a place of wonder and pleasure? Or is she one big mystery? Maybe you don't think about your yoni at all. Have you ever really looked at your yoni? (Remember that scene with Kathy Bates in *Fried Green Tomatoes?*) Have you ever touched your yoni ... other than to insert a tampon, that is? Maybe you have experienced childbirth, but have you ever *seen* a yoni transform or expand in the act of childbirth? In your role as caregiver, maybe you carefully diaper a girl infant's delicate yoni or assist your 90-year-old grandmother with bathing and dressing. All yonis are sacred, and beautiful!

How would you describe your relationship with your yoni? Is your yoni …

a. Your best friend?

b. A source of amazing pleasure and fun?

c. A fun place to visit every once in a while?

d. A dark secret?

e. Yoni? Oh, you mean down there?

If you haven't already, there are many ways to begin to get acquainted with your yoni. One easy thing you can do is look at her. Pose nude in front of a mirror one night after your bath or shower. Feel connected to the sacred sexual energy stored in your body, your heart, and your soul. When you gaze at your yoni, do so with love for her and for all parts of your Goddess body. Many writers have produced excellent books on women's relationships with their bodies and genitalia. Working with these books can be educational and liberating, and actually quite fun.

> **"** If sex and creativity are often seen by dictators as subversive activities, it's because they lead to the knowledge that you own your own body (and with it your own voice), and that's the most revolutionary insight of all.
>
> —Erica Jong, writer (1972) **"**

Eve Ensler, the author of the hugely successful play "The Vagina Monologues" (and a Goddess!), has written that she began working on her play because she was "worried about vaginas," including her own. So, she interviewed hundreds of women about their vaginas and how they feel about them. From those interviews, she developed character monologues that are touching, sad, funny, fascinating, and ultimately liberating. If you have the chance, go see the play, or read the book. For many women, learning about the experiences of the myriad women in Ensler's piece has served as a stepping stone to greater self-love and self-acceptance.

In addition to Ensler, many other women have made art centering around or containing images of female genitalia—Georgia O'Keefe springs to mind. Judy Chicago's installation "The Dinner Party" is one famous example of a woman using female genitalia as a motif. In the mid- to late 1970s, Chicago created a large, triangular table with 13 place settings on each side. Each place setting commemorates a Goddess, a woman from history, or an important female figure. The plate at each place is hand-painted with images of female genitalia. Each plate has its own style, depending on the women represented and the historic period in which she lived. Chicago has described her work as a "symbolic history of women in Western civilization."

> ❝ Sex itself must always, it seems to me, come to us as a sacrament and be so used or it is meaningless. The flesh is suffused by the spirit, and it is forgetting this in the act of love-making that creates cynicism and despair.
>
> —May Sarton, poet (1980) ❞

The Kama Sutra also honors a woman's genitals with a great deal of attention. This ancient Hindu text not only details 64 elements of sexual loving and the importance of a woman's pleasure, but it also provides guidelines for how to live properly within a marriage. The Kama Sutra can help you to add an element of ritual to your lovemaking, if that is what you want. Many women feel that an element of ritual—from candles, mood music, and seductive scents to special lighting, sensuous sheets, or exotic locations—make lovemaking more special, intense, spiritual, and celebratory.

The Origins of Life

Are you a mother? Or do you want to become one? Perhaps you are pregnant right now. If you are pregnant, chances are that you got that way as a result of sex. Many women find that the sex they have while trying to get pregnant is the best they have ever had. Relieved of worry about birth control, when trying to get pregnant they feel they can really let themselves go. Other women find that trying to get pregnant becomes a source of anxiety itself and that their lovemaking takes on an air of rote duty.

During pregnancy many women feel more connected to the life-giving properties of the earth. Some women report that they feel especially sexy and sexual when pregnant. And many women also feel tired, cranky, and bloated. Whether you are a mother or not, whether you desire to be one, you certainly recognize that motherhood is an awesome and amazing creative power.

Ix Chel is the Mayan Goddess of childbirth, sex, sorcery, healing, and weaving. She is also associated with destructive floods, the moon, and night. She is known as "Lady Rainbow" or "Old Goddess with Tiger Claws." She is often depicted with the claws of an eagle or a tiger, a crown of feathers or a serpent headdress, and carrying a water jug. Sometimes she wears a cape or a skirt made of bones. She was worshipped by weavers and by women to ensure a healthy pregnancy and delivery. Her shrine on the island of Cozumel, Mexico, was probably still in use at the time the Spanish first arrived on the Yucatan Peninsula in 1518.

Ix Chel is a great creator. She creates new life. She makes magic, and she is the patroness of weavers, one of the most important artisans in Mayan culture. Do you allow yourself to feel your own creative force and passion? You may express your creative power through mothering your children. Or you may let it out with your pets, through gardening, your career, hobbies, teaching, or volunteer work. Whether you are biologically fertile or not, you still contain the magic of Ix Chel inside you. Even if you have not believed it until now, you are, like Ix Chel, a magnificently creative being.

Do you ever feel that all your knowledge—your basic understanding of human biology, chemistry, and physics—has taken some of the magic out of your life? Don't you still feel that magic when you look at an infant with its perfect, tiny little toes and fingers? Do you feel the magic when you look at a beautiful work of art or a sublime natural landscape? When you feel and acknowledge that sense of magic, you are also connecting to the Ix Chel aspect of your own inner Goddess.

Like many mothers, Ix Chel can also be stern and fierce. She will protect her children and fight to the death if necessary. She holds the power over life and death in her own magical claws. Have you ever felt that kind of power inside of you?

Exercise #1: This One Is Just Right

In the classic children's tale *Goldilocks and the Three Bears*, Goldilocks found the right chair, bowl of porridge, and bed through trial and error. Prior to sitting in the chair, tasting the porridge, and lying in the bed, she probably had not given much thought to what she actually wanted from those things, but she did recognize her own discomfort when they did not suit her. Is that how you live your life? Sometimes getting what you want may seem as if it is up to chance or fate. Sometimes it may seem difficult or even completely out of your reach. But, as you've probably heard, imagining what you want is the first step toward getting it.

You're going to imagine your ideal partner, and you're going to throw in all the traits and little details—physical, mental, emotional, spiritual, and sexual—that feel important to you. (Of course, you know that no one person is perfect, and no one can make you happy unless you are happy with yourself.) If you don't have a partner, this exercise can help you to find someone. If you do have a partner, coming up with your list of ideal traits can help you to appreciate what you do have and can act as a road map to help you work toward what you want.

Get out your Goddess journal and a pen. Without thinking about it too much, answer the following questions. Write down the first thing that comes into your head. If you stare at the page and nothing comes to you, try closing your eyes and repeating the question to yourself. Then write down whatever you think of. If that still does not bring you an answer, skip the question, and write down what you do know. You can always come back and add to your answers later.

1. How does your ideal partner look physically? Is he or she tall or short or somewhere in between? What color eyes does your ideal partner have? What color hair? Is your ideal partner thin, muscular, or on the soft side? Where does your ideal partner live? Does he or she live with you, in your neighborhood, in your town, or in a different state or country? Are there any other physical traits that your ideal partner should have? List them now.

2. Is your ideal partner super smart or of average intelligence? Is your ideal partner smarter than you, the same as you, or not as smart as you? How much education has your ideal partner had? Does he or she speak a language other than English? Many women find that they are more comfortable with a partner who has an educational background similar to their own. You may find that someone with the same level of education as you shares more of your interests and aspirations in life. Is there some kind of specialized knowledge that you would like your ideal partner to have?

3. Is your ideal partner very emotional? Do people, places, or things easily affect him or her? Does your ideal partner express emotion easily? Or is your ideal partner more reserved and placid in nature?

Would your ideal partner cry openly at a sad movie, hide his or her feelings, or remain pretty much unaffected? Is your ideal partner affectionate physically and verbally? Would you like your ideal partner to be affectionate out in public or would you rather that such attentions were reserved for private time between the two of you? How close do you want to feel to your partner? Do you want your relationship with your partner to be your highest priority, or are other things in your life—such as your work, children, or aging parents—more important?

4. How commitment-oriented is your ideal partner? Do you want to be monogamous with your partner or would you both be able to see other people? Would you want your relationship with your ideal partner to lead to a longtime commitment, such as marriage or living together, or would you prefer to see each other only on weekends?

5. Is your ideal partner a spiritual person? How important is spirituality to your ideal partner? What kind of spirituality does your ideal partner practice? Is your ideal partner's spiritual practice similar to your own or different? Does the lifestyle that goes along with your ideal partner's spiritual practice suit you? You may imagine that your ideal partner teaches yoga and meditates regularly. But will he or she be able to accommodate your love of hot dogs and late nights out on the town?

6. How passionate is your ideal partner? How often does he or she like to make love? Is your ideal partner someone who plans sexual encounters or is he or she spontaneous? Are there sexual techniques or habits that you would like your partner to practice?

7. If you enjoy drawing, draw a picture of your ideal partner. You may want to place your picture on your altar to remind you of what you already have and to inspire you to reach for what you deserve.

If you don't have a partner and you want one, read over your list every night before you go to bed. Close your eyes and imagine your ideal partner. Imagine what it would feel like to be with that person. Imagine how you would feel giving and receiving pleasure in that person's physical presence. When you wake up in the morning, take a moment to imagine your partner and those loving feelings again. If you do these things, be prepared. You just may meet a special someone soon! Feeling the love of your imagined partner can help you love yourself, because it is your own love that you are experiencing, after all. When you feel secure in your own love and don't feel desperate to find love from outside sources, you are more likely to draw people toward you. Self-love is the core or the essence of being able to love someone else. From the spiritual perspective (and maybe ours), until you can love the Goddess within, you will find it a challenge to manifest and link to another Divine (human) being.

If you already have a partner, go ahead and imagine giving and receiving pleasure with your ideal mate. Think about how your real-life partner does meet the criteria on your list. How your actual partner relates to the description of your ideal partner may be obvious. Perhaps one of the traits you have listed for your ideal partner is being tall, and your own real-life partner is tall. On the other hand, some of the traits you desire may exist in your partner but not be readily apparent. Perhaps physical affection is a trait that you have listed, and maybe you don't feel that your partner is affectionate enough. If so, try asking your partner for what you want.

Sometimes without realizing it, we expect our partners to be mind readers. Perhaps your partner has been interpreting your grunts of pleasure as grunts of indifference when he or she touches you. If, for example, you feel your partner doesn't display enough physical affection toward you outside of bed, talk to him or her about your feelings. When you do this, avoid making "you" statements. Don't say, "You never hug or kiss me when I need it. You only touch me when you want to have sex." Such a statement will sound like an accusation to your partner, will probably lead to an argument, and will not help you to get more of what you want. Instead, try saying something like this: "I love being with you, and I love it when you touch me. I'd like for us to kiss, hug, and hold hands when we go out or when we are just hanging around the house."

 Instant Goddess

Some anthropologists say that painting lipstick on your lips is really a way to evoke the yoni force and attract a mate. Whether or not you agree, who couldn't use a new lipstick? Try a different shade, then pucker up, smile, grimace, bite, growl, sing, and express the many moods of your passionate, sexual self!

Look over your list again. Are there any traits that you have named as desirable for your ideal partner, which are actually qualities you would like to develop in yourself? We may think that we want to be with someone who has an exciting job, a passionate commitment to political activism, or a serious yoga practice, when in reality we would really like to be engaged in such activities ourselves. As one of Katherine's friends used to say about the lead singer of the band Roxy Music, "Do I want to be *with* Bryan Ferry or do I want to *be* Bryan Ferry?"

Exercise #2: Shakti Power

Here's a sex exercise you can do with a partner. If you do not have a partner, imagine that you are doing this exercise with your ideal partner. Whether your partner is real or imaginary, focus on how it feels to give and receive love in your partner's physical presence.

One of the unions, or positions, described in ancient Tantric teachings is called "Shakti Expressing her Energy with Shiva." Because Tantra is a spiritual path, this union is more than just another sexual position. In Tantra, sexuality becomes a vehicle for self awareness. Sexual loving is not only an act of pleasure, but it becomes a means of transformation and enlightenment.

Before you try this union with your partner, you may want to meditate together or spend some quiet time just listening to each other breathe in order to prepare your mind for a sharing of energy and to bring you both into a shared heart space. Once you feel that kind of connection, you can begin love play.

When both partners feel fully aroused, you can move into the union of "Shakti Expressing her Energy with Shiva." In this union, the woman is the more active partner. If you are a woman whose partner is a woman, you get to decide who will play the Shakti role and who will be Shiva. Have Shiva lie on his (or her) back, legs outstretched. As Shakti, you sit or crouch over Shiva and take his lingam (penis) into your yoni. Feel the union of your bodies, minds, and spirits. Feel the wisdom and energy of Shakti and give that power to your partner.

When practicing a Tantric union, relax all your muscles and your mind as your sexual excitement rises. One way to help you do this is to keep breathing slowly and evenly.

At the point of orgasm, allow your mind to be still and empty. Relax, keep breathing deeply and slowly, and look into your partner's eyes.

Let the orgasm take you by keeping your muscles relaxed. Continue to breathe deeply and slowly.

Was it good for you? Did you feel the power of your Shakti energy?

There are many books and videotapes available on the Kama Sutra and Tantric sex. If the subject interests you, you may want to start with *The Complete Idiot's Guide to the Kama Sutra* (Alpha Books, 2000), or check out www.tantra.com online.

These exercises and the material you have read about in this chapter will help you to know yourself and your desires better. Do you feel sexy? Is it hot in here? It looks as if your Shakti energy has been heating things up! Can you feel the powerful sensuous quality of life on the Goddess path? You are earthy and strong like the Venus of Willendorf. You are beautiful, lovable, and deserving of the sex that you want, just as Venus and Aphrodite are. Like the beautiful Yoni Lotus, you are a portal to the divine. And like Ix Chel, you hold the power of motherhood and creation inside you no matter what your age.

Now you're ready to move on. In the next chapter, we'll look at some more feminine forms of power: Kali, the Hindu Goddess of destruction and death; Oya from Africa, the Goddess of sudden change and stormy weather; Amaterasu, the Japanese sun Goddess and Supreme Deity; and Baba Yaga, the powerful witch from Russian and Slavic folktales who lives in a house in the forest that stands on chicken feet.

Chapter 9

Strength: Centering Power

What is personal strength? Where does it come from? You know that you can make your muscles stronger by working out at the gym or taking dance or aerobics classes. But what about your mental, emotional, and spiritual strength?

Let the Goddesses in this chapter be your new gym, a place where you can look at yourself and recharge with powerful Goddess energy. Goddess energy, as you probably know by now, takes many forms and can be used in many ways. Most important, Goddess energy can be used to improve your life and make you feel great.

Fierce Energy

You know that you are not all sugar and spice and nice, nice, nice. But do you pretend that you are sweetness and light all the time? Do you ever get angry? How do you deal with anger? Do you harbor your anger? Do you replay moments in your head in which you felt that you were right and someone else was wrong? Do you lash out at others, or do you turn your anger on yourself? Perhaps you stuff your anger down inside you with food, drugs, alcohol, or overwork. Are you conscious of what you do with your anger?

Kali, the Hindu Goddess of destruction, is also a symbol of the eternal nature of time. She is usually considered to be an aspect of the Goddess Durga. She is known by many different names, including the Black Mother and Kali Ma. In addition to being a destroyer of demons, she is a powerful creative force. She can also represent freedom and independence. Shiva, the God of destruction, dance, and yoga, is her husband and she is his Shakti, or active energizing force. The city of Calcutta takes its name from the Kalighat, Kali's temple. Kali is said to have invented the Sanskrit alphabet. She is often depicted as either blue or black in color, and she has a protruding tongue. Kali has four arms. In one hand, she holds a sword and in the second a severed head. Her two other hands form *mudras* (signs or gestures), one of which removes fear, and the other indicates her willingness to help you if she is asked. Kali is often depicted wearing a necklace of skulls and a girdle of severed hands. Sometimes she is shown standing on her husband, Shiva.

In one version of Kali's story, the deities asked the Goddess Durga, a many-armed warrior who is also associated with death and destruction, to fight against the demons who had taken over the celestial kingdom. Armed by her fellow deities and accompanied by her tiger, Durga marched out for battle. When she saw the evil countenances of the demons Canda and Munda, she furrowed her brow in fury, and Kali sprang from her forehead. Although she had just been born, Kali jumped into the fracas. Wielding her sword, she sliced off the demons' heads and presented them to Durga.

In another version of Kali's tale, Durga led the other deities into battle against the demon Raktabija. The fighting was especially fierce because every time a drop of Raktabija's blood spilled, a hundred new demons, exact replicas of Raktabija, materialized and sprang into action. Durga had just dispatched a group of these Raktabija clones, when another hundred of them appeared. Furious at what appeared to be a never-ending stream of evil, she furrowed her brow and Kali burst forth. Kali polished off the new pack of demons, and then grabbed Raktabija carefully. She did not want to even scratch him lest a drop of his blood fall to the ground and create a new demon battalion. Kali raised Raktabija to her lips, bit him, and sucked every last drop of blood from his veins, and the evil demons were vanquished. Some say that Kali chopped off Raktabija's head and that the severed head she carries with her is his. Others say that the head she carries belongs to Shiva.

Kali is often perceived to be an angry Goddess. Some people even see her as bloodthirsty. Her devotees, on the other hand, point out that she is the slayer of duality. Harboring anger at another person creates duality by causing you to feel separate from that person. Kali attacks and roots out the misperception that anyone or anything is separate from divine consciousness. Kali did drink all of Raktabija's blood, but that blood is seen as the human mind's infinite ability to generate negative thoughts. Kali sticks out her tongue to catch those thoughts and relieve you of them. Are there any thought demons in your life that you could use Kali energy to slay? Are your negative thoughts about yourself interfering with your life and ability to relate to and enjoy others? Is your anger keeping you separate from the people around you? Kali will lick up all the nasty drops of your negativity and leave only divine love.

> This, it seemed, was one of those angry natures that feeds on grievance; nothing would madden her more than to know that what she complained of had been put right.
>
> —Mary Stewart, writer (1965)

You may think of anger as a negative emotion. As Pema Chödrön, an American Buddhist nun who lives in Nova Scotia, has pointed out, in Buddhism, emotions are said to contain wisdom. All emotions contain wisdom, not just the happy ones. What can you learn from your anger? If you can detach yourself from the story of whomever or whatever is making you angry, you can experience anger as just another form of energy. Chödrön writes this: "When emotional distress arises uninvited, we let the story line go and abide with the energy. This is a felt experience, not a verbal commentary on what is happening. We can feel the energy in our bodies. If we can stay with it, neither acting out nor repressing it, it wakes us up."

Where in your body do you feel your anger? Is it in your stomach, your chest, running along your limbs, or is it somewhere else? Do you feel your anger at all? What does your anger look like? You might try writing about your feelings in your Goddess journal. Or draw a picture of your feelings. What color is your anger? Does it resemble Kali at all? What part of Kali's image attracts you? What would you like to do with your four arms? What would you like to do with your sword? Would doing these things rid you of fear? Do your feelings have a taste? A smell? If your angry energy could accomplish three things, what would they be? Try not to censor yourself, and allow yourself to write or draw whatever you desire. Just remember that actual physical violence, toward yourself or others, is simply not an option. Hold the image of yourself as a powerful many-armed warrior in your mind.

Next time something makes you angry, watch yourself. Remind yourself that you have choices: You can let your anger grow and fester, you can try to smash anger down inside of you, or you can choose another way. Just as an experiment, try this: Note where the angry energy is in your body. See what happens if you let the feeling be there without clutching at it. Make sure that you keep breathing. Holding your breath is one way to hold on to an emotion. Some people grab their anger and use it to mask other emotions or to keep themselves from feeling vulnerable or uncertain. Equally, try not to push your anger away or lash out to make the feeling go away. Continue to breathe. Focus your attention on your third eye, the place on the forehead from which Kali emerged during the most difficult of times. Let Kali clear away your reasons for anger and then dissolve, leaving simply space. Observe for a few moments and notice if anything inside you has changed. Do you sense another feeling? What do you become aware of?

Are there times when you have reacted very strongly to an only somewhat irritating event? Say that your boss has been critical of your work, and what she said has left you furious. Have you ever felt mystified by the power of your own response? Have you ever felt that your anger was too strong a reaction? In such a situation, your boss's comments may be stirring up old feelings for you. Perhaps your mother was critical of you when you were a child, or maybe one of your teachers was overly demanding with homework assignments. If your anger at a situation or event in your present life seems super strong, think a moment and see if the feeling or situation is reminiscent of something from your past. If so, take some time to honor the pain from that past event that you've been carrying. Much of our reactivity as adults is due to unresolved grief from childhood. So be gentle with yourself as you recognize and exorcise the inner demons, or false beliefs, that were planted in the past. Remember that old encumbrances must die to allow a rebirth and a release of newness and potential.

> 66 It's when we are given choice that we sit with the gods and design ourselves.
>
> —Dorothy Gilman, writer (1992) 99

Certainly, anger can be a useful emotion. It can protect you when someone has crossed your boundaries. It can spur you into action. Has someone ever made you mad by either saying or implying that you were not capable of carrying out an action or a project that interested you? How did you react? Did you get mad? Did you allow the fuel of your anger to help you to complete your project the way Erin Brockovich, the real-life single mother and environmental activist who was played by Julia Roberts in the popular film, did? Or did you abandon your project, stuff your anger down, and let it eat at you?

You always have the choice to act. And your action can be a small one. Maybe you'll allow your anger to help you update your resumé or make a phone call you've been putting off. Or your anger can motivate you to clean out that scary, disorganized front-hall closet. Imagine Kali's arms organizing things quickly and her long tongue lapping up all the junk and dust inside. Let Kali help you to destroy your self-limiting demons, whether they are physical or mental, and walk proudly with her on the Goddess path.

The Winds of Change

Like the wind or the weather, emotions are ephemeral. They change all the time. Allowing your anger to help you clean out a closet or engage in some necessary business could lead to a small change in your life. Allowing your anger to transform into a powerful passion for service could change your life in a big way. How do you feel about change? Do you resist it? Does it scare you? Or do you seek change, challenges, and new experiences in your life?

Present-day practitioners of Orisha worship (see the following side-bar), such as Philip Neimark, a writer and adept, have pointed out that Oya and the other Orisha are elemental energies. Neimark feels that the anthropomorphized stories of the Orisha, like the ones presented in the following sidebar, have led to confusion about the nature of the Orisha. Oya is not a person; she is not a mythological character. She is the essence of sudden change. Of course, her association in these stories with death and thunderstorms is an attempt to explain the nature of her sudden change. Try to see her as a swirl of potent energy rather than a person.

It may not always feel true, but, like Oya, you have the ability to instigate change in your life. You have probably already made some changes to your life just in the course of reading this book. You may think that change has to be huge, sweeping, and dramatic. You tell off your boss, quit your job, throw out all your work clothes, and buy a small bed-and-breakfast place in the country. You dump your partner, sell your possessions, and jump on the next plane bound for Paris or Tahiti.

Oya is one of the *Orisha*, or natural forces, from the religion of the Yoruba people of Nigeria, West Africa. Today she is associated with rainstorms, wind, the river Niger, and the Amazon. She is the energy of sudden change. She is swirling energy, a spiral, and the wind. When the peoples of West Africa were brought to the New World as slaves, some of them preserved their religious traditions. Eventually, these traditions mixed with Christianity and over time, the idea of Oya changed. Some people equate Oya directly with deities of the New World. Accordingly, in Puerto Rico, she is thought to be Olla. In Central America, her Catholic counterpart is Our Lady of Candelaria, Saint Theresa, or Saint Catherine. In South America, she may go by the names Saint Teresita, Oya-bale, Oya de esteira, or Yansa. On the other hand, many modern-day practitioners of Orisha worship stress the differences between the New World African religions and the original African tradition.

There are many stories about Oya, who in her personified form is seen as a tall woman who wears nine skirts that swirl around her when she dances. In one story, her husband Chango came running home pursued by an angry mob and asked Oya for help. Oya decided that the best thing for them to do was to switch places and fool Chango's enemies. So, she dressed Chango in her outfit of nine skirts, and she donned Chango's clothing. Chango was just about to step out the door when he turned back, went into his room, and closed the door. Oya peered through the keyhole and saw Chango drink from a mysterious-looking bottle. Oya knew right away that this must be Chango's secret formula that enabled him to create lightning. As soon as Chango had left the house, striding like Oya herself and deceiving his pursuers, Oya grabbed the bottle and took a swig. She snorted, and fire sprang from her nostrils. She stepped out of the house and at that moment, Chango turned and began to attack his enemies. He zapped them with lightning, and when they turned to run from him, they faced Oya and her newly acquired fire-breathing powers. The two Orisha quickly subdued Chango's enemies, and, although Chango was a bit annoyed that Oya had stolen his lightning-producing powers, from that day forward they have both used this awesome power and fought together, side by side.

In another story, Oya is the one who gets tricked. A long, long time ago, Oya ruled over the ocean and Yemaya presided over the cemetery. Yemaya was tired of the cemetery. So she took Oya on a walk not far from her deathly home. She pointed out the beautiful trees, the swaying grass, the chirping birds. All Oya could see was the beauty of the plants and the peaceful setting. Yemaya had made sure that no graves would be visible from their path. Yemaya gestured to her domain and asked Oya if she would like to trade responsibilities. Oya jumped at the chance, and as soon as she had agreed, Yemaya took off for the sea. Oya approached her new home and was furious to discover that it was full of graves. Ever since that day, she has been guardian of the cemetery.

Sometimes change is dramatic, but it doesn't have to be. Are you using the drama of your ideas about change to scare you from taking a small step that could make you happier? You don't have to totally upset your life to begin to follow your dreams. Your dreams are part of your Goddess path. When working toward your dreams, you can start small. Begin by naming one thing that you would like to do. Break your goal down into the smallest parts that you can. Do you actually want to quit your job and open a bed-and-breakfast? If so, your first step, before you even contemplate talking to your boss, may be to check out books on the subject from your local library. Learn as much as you can about the subject. Your new knowledge will help you decide if this dream is something that you really want to pursue, and it will help you in planning your next steps along your Goddess path.

Change is the only constant. Hanging on is the only sin.

—Denise McCluggage, racecar driver (1977)

A Path to Wholeness

Change can come into your life in many forms. Sometimes you initiate change in your life by choice. Sometimes change foists itself upon you as in the case of accidents, illness, or death. Some changes in your life are reversible. (You can always let your hair grow out and try a different color next month!) Other changes can never be undone. And some changes bring about unexpected results.

Baba Yaga, the great witch from Russian folktales, is seen by some to be a Goddess of the dead. She is also the guardian of the Water of Life and Death. She is said to sprinkle corpses with her magic waters so that they can be reborn. She is triune, embodying Maiden, Mother, and Crone. She has been described as a Slavic version of the Three Fates. She represents fertility and new life, maps out the course of your life, and determines the hour of your death. In some stories, she rules over the rising and setting of the sun. According to some, she is quite dangerous, but she also can help the virtuous. She lives deep in the woods, in a house that is supported by chicken feet. In some accounts, the house has four pairs of chicken feet, one pair at each corner. The center of the house is supported by a shaft on which it can turn. Others have described the house as walking around on one pair of chicken legs. The house is surrounded by a fence made from human bones.

In one Baba Yaga story, she is both fearsome and benevolent. Vasilissa the Fair, an eight-year-old girl, had been sent into the forest by her stepmother to fetch a light for the family's stove. Vasilissa's father was away, and very late one night her stepmother had let the stove go out on purpose so that she could send Vasilissa to see the old witch. The stepmother was fairly certain that her lovely stepdaughter would not return from her errand.

Vasilissa set off with her doll under her arm. She carried the doll, which had been a present from her dead mother, everywhere. Her mother had told her that if ever she needed help, all she had to do was feed the doll, and the doll would do her bidding. Vasilissa trod through the dark forest. She walked and walked, and then the thundering of hoof-beats filled her ears. From behind her, a horse galloped up, and she leapt from the path; the white horse with its rider, a man clothed entirely in white, galloped by her, and at that moment, dawn lit up the sky. Vasilissa, wondering why the horseman rode to Baba Yaga's house and at such speed, continued on her journey. Soon she heard a horse behind her again. She turned to look and just had time to dash out of the way when a red horse with a rider entirely outfitted in red galloped passed, and the sun cleared the horizon and sent its rays down into the thick forest. Vasilissa wondered at the horseman's tremendous haste and stepped back to her path. She walked and walked. Finally, she arrived at a clearing in the woods. In the middle of the clearing, surrounded by a high fence, stood Baba Yaga's house. The top of each fence post bore a human skull. Shivering with fear, Vasilissa hesitated, and another horseman thundered up. This one rode a black horse and was dressed entirely in black. He galloped through the gate of Baba Yaga's house, and night fell. Much to Vasilissa's horror, the skulls on the fence posts lit up. And, to make matters worse, Baba Yaga appeared at that moment, riding in her mortar and waving her pestle, which she used like an oar to propel herself forward.

When Baba Yaga heard why the girl had come, she invited her in and agreed to give the girl a light in exchange for some work. Baba Yaga warned Vasilissa that if she failed in her assigned tasks, she would be eaten. Each time Baba Yaga gave Vasilissa a seemingly impossible chore, such as removing all poppy seeds from a mound of dirt or separating all the stray seeds from a pile of wheat, Vasilissa secretly set her doll to work. At the end of three days, Vasilissa had performed all her tasks to perfection, and Baba Yaga said that she could go. Before Vasilissa left, she asked the witch about the horsemen. Baba Yaga explained that the white rider was Bright Day, the red was Fair Sun, and the black one was Dark Night. All three were her servants. Her curiosity satisfied, Vasilissa accepted a skull glowing with fire from Baba Yaga's fence and headed home.

When she finally arrived home, Vasilissa was about to throw the skull away. Surely her stepmother and stepsisters had gotten a light in all the time she had been gone. But her doll told her to keep the skull. Vasilissa's step-family was distraught. The whole time she had been away, they had been unable to light any fire. So, they greeted her warmly and welcomed her and the light she had brought from Baba Yaga's. As soon as Vasilissa entered the house, flames leapt from the eyes of the skull and burned Vasilissa's stepmother and stepsisters till nothing was left but a pile of ash.

Later that evening, Vasilissa's father returned home, and he rejoiced to hear that his daughter had survived the ordeal her stepmother had put her through. He was also glad to be rid of his wicked wife and her two daughters.

Some folklore scholars have pointed out that the story of Baba Yaga and Vasilissa contains all three of Baba Yaga's aspects—fertility Goddess and protector of life, the one who maps human fate, and death herself. Vasilissa's stepmother can be seen as Baba Yaga's death aspect. Baba Yaga herself, in this story, fills the role of the mapper of fate, and the doll is the protector of life. Of course, there are many ways to interpret such a complex story.

Because Vasilissa is the heroine of this story, you may also want to look at what happens from her point of view. When the story has hardly begun, Vasilissa already has a hard time of life. She loses her mother when she is very young. But she carries her mother's gift, in the form of the doll, with her wherever she goes. The doll has magical, even miraculous, skills.

In return for Vasilissa's care and kindness, the doll uses her powers to help and protect Vasilissa, much the way Vasilissa's mother would have had she remained alive.

Vasilissa also has to contend with a stepmother who wishes Vasilissa were dead. Despite the help that she receives from the doll, Vasilissa has no choice but to obey her stepmother's wishes and face her own possible death. So, she sets off on the dangerous journey to Baba Yaga's. While walking her path, she encounters the great power of nature in the forms of Bright Day, Fair Sun, and Dark Night. And then she meets the fearsome Baba Yaga, who turns out not to be quite as scary as her reputation.

Much in the way that Dorothy does in *The Wizard of Oz*, Vasilissa learns about all the parts of her psyche on her journey. Although at first Baba Yaga seems to play the same archetypal role as the Wicked Witch of the West, in actuality she turns out to be the Wizard. In Jungian terms, Baba Yaga and the Wizard both represent the Trickster archetype. Vasilissa is able to complete Baba Yaga's tasks because she listens to her Divine Child in the form of her doll. Vasilissa then takes what she has learned and integrated into herself and confronts the real evil, which is the archetype of darkness and death, in the form of her stepmother. (No offense to all you stepmothers out there! In fairy tales, the stepmother represents the projection of evil and the unconscious hatred for a mother who is felt to be abandoning.) Because Vasilissa has learned and grown on her journey, she has the strength to vanquish her stepmother and her fear, and is able to lead a whole and happy life ever after.

In your own life you have probably faced Baba Yaga in the form of fear. And maybe you have come face to face with death—either your own or someone else's. An understanding of your own mortality can change you. And grief can change you. When faced with loss, do you allow yourself to grieve? Or have you decided, after the initial shock has worn off, that you should be done with feeling bad and force yourself to move on? Grief is a complex state involving many shifting emotions. Many writers and psychologists have described the grief process as a spiral that moves you through stages of denial, anger, bargaining and obsession, depression, and finally acceptance of the loss. When you experience a loss, you may move through the spiral several times, and the emotions may not follow the exact same order each time. As co-author Gail has pointed out in her book *Taking Advantage of Adversity* (Little Brown UK, 2002), "Acceptance is the point where we finally overcome our fear and transform our grief into awareness and self-expression." Gail stresses that loss, grief, and growth are natural cycles, just as the changing of Earth's seasons are.

You have probably encountered many forms of loss in your life—from the very small, such as misplacing your favorite umbrella or losing a special sock in the wash, to larger losses, such as the crushing of a fantasy, losing your address book (and the handful of people whose addresses you know you'll never be able to retrieve), leaving your old neighborhood for a new one, or more serious losses such as the death of a pet or the chronic illness or death of a family member or loved one. Each of your losses deserves to be mourned at its own level of intensity. By allowing yourself to move through the stages of grief, you learn about yourself and you become more aware in your own life. In expressing your feelings associated with grief and recognizing that depression is an aspect of unresolved grief, you continue your growth process and become stronger, more whole, more creative, and better able to live and appreciate your life. In short, you become more in tune with the Goddess that you truly are.

> **❝** I have always fought for ideas—until I learned that it isn't ideas but grief, struggle, and flashes of vision which enlighten.
>
> —Margaret Anderson, editor (1969) **❞**

Let There Be Light

Do you enjoy all of your gifts? Do you acknowledge and recognize your own energies, strengths, and natural talents? How comfortable are you with your own power?

Do you act like an upset Amaterasu (see the following sidebar)? Sometimes do you hide your light? Many women choose to pretend that they are not as powerful, smart, or beautiful as they really are. As Marianne Williamson has written in her book *A Return to Love: Reflections on a Course in Miracles,* "Our deepest fear is not that we are inadequate. Our deepest fear is that we are powerful beyond measure. It is our light, not our darkness, that most frightens us." Do you let your light shine? Perhaps you only let your light shine around selected friends or associates. Maybe you only share your light with your children or your pets.

Know that you were born to be the best that you can be. You are not responsible for someone else's success or failure. Neither are you responsible for the jealousy that someone else may feel toward you.

Choosing to be your best self, allowing your Goddess to shine, only makes the world a brighter place for everyone. So, don't cower in a cave out of fear. Get out there and be a shining example of your own special Goddess power!

Amaterasu is the Shinto Goddess of the sun. Her name means "she who shines in the heavens." She is worshipped throughout Japan as the supreme deity of her pantheon. She is also said to be the divine ancestor of Japan's royal family. She invented the art of weaving and the cultivation of rice, one of Japan's most important crops, and she is the grandmother of the God of rice. She also taught people to grow wheat and silkworms. Her temple on the island of Honshu, Japan's largest island, is dismantled every 20 years and then rebuilt anew to exactly the same specifications. Roosters, because they greet the rising sun each morning, are considered sacred to Amaterasu. She is honored each year on July 17 with the celebration of the Great Festival of the Sun Goddess, and she is celebrated on December 21, the day of the winter solstice, when the dark night begins to grow shorter and the hours of daylight start to grow longer.

The most famous story about Amaterasu is the one in which she gets upset and hides in her cave, leaving the world in darkness. You probably remember this story from Chapter 6. Despite the pleas of all the other deities, Amaterasu refuses to come out. Finally, Uzume, the Goddess of mirth and dancing, tempts Amaterasu from her cave, and the world is reborn in her light.

> 66 The women of my mother's generation had, in the main, only one decision to make about their lives: who they would marry. From that, so much else followed: where they would live, in what sort of conditions, whether they would be happy or sad or, so often, a bit of both. There were roles and there were rules.
>
> —Anna Quindlen, journalist and novelist (1988) 99

Exercise #1: Harness Your Solar Power

Do you lack energy? Do you have difficulty making decisions? Are you incapable of saying no? Do you start projects, but lack the drive to follow through and finish them? Do you shrink from responsibility?

If you answered yes to any of these questions (and even if you didn't!), you may want to work on balancing your third chakra, which is known as the *Manipura* chakra in Sanskrit. As we first mentioned in Chapter 6, chakras are energy centers in the body that lie inside along your spine. Each of the seven chakras regulates a different energy in the body. Your third chakra, which is located at your solar plexus, governs your will.

Did you know how the solar plexus got its name? The solar plexus is actually a network of nerves that is located inside your body behind the stomach. These nerves branch out from a central point like the rays of the sun. Although the third chakra is usually associated with the planet Mars, you can think of your solar plexus chakra as the home of Amaterasu, the Goddess of the sun.

To balance your third chakra, sit up on the floor or in a chair, or lie down. You want your spine to be straight. If you like, lie in Goddess pose. (See Exercise #1 in Chapter 6.) Place your hands over your solar plexus and continue to breathe. Imagine Amaterasu's swirling yellow energy inside you. With each exhalation, allow any clouds of worry or distracting thoughts to leave your body. With each inhalation, see Amaterasu's light inside you grow brighter and clearer. Feel her calm and centered power. Then repeat the following affirmation to yourself:

I make balanced decisions that aid me on my spiritual path.

Say this affirmation over and over. You can say this to yourself at any time during the day. Or write the sentence out a few times on a piece of paper. For right now, try to say it at least 20 times. When you are done, write about your experience in your Goddess journal. Or draw a picture of Amaterasu's light shining from inside you. Place the picture on your altar to remind yourself of your own Goddess power.

 Instant Goddess

Here's another yoga pose that can help you tap instant centering and instant power: prayer pose. Stand up straight with your feet together, bend your elbows so they stick out to the side, and push your palms together in front of your heart center. Breathe and feel your Goddess power!

Exercise #2: All You Need Is Love

Sometimes you're angry and you know the source all too well; your anger accompanies you as if it were an old friend—or nemesis—ever-present, walking with you everywhere. You nurse your anger like nursing a grudge, tending it with care and holding it tightly to you. After all, this anger or resentment, over the years, has become a more steadfast, faithful companion than some of the closest people in your life. You begin to suspect that you can *never* let go of your anger, as it has become so much a part of your daily experience of life that you would not know who to be, or *how to be* without it.

Sometimes you are angry and you don't know why, only that you *are*. The anger surges up inside you, accompanied by a fierce feeling of consuming, blinding validation. You have a *right* to this anger. You can see nothing, and no one else, not even yourself.

It's never too late to examine your anger and to make a mental map of how this emotion affects you. When you feel ready and you find a solitary moment, sit quietly for at least half an hour and contemplate your hurt. What does your feeling of anger accomplish in your life that is truly positive? Are you ready to transform your anger into the drive to heal your relationships, to heal your own life? Or do you feel that your anger has made this too difficult, too impossible—all that is left to you is the anger to hold. And when you attempt to express the anger, to channel it outward, by lashing out at others, at yourself, or by hitting a pillow, all you do is increase the angry energy, or violence. Expressing the anger does not help it to dissipate, or better, to heal. Are you ready to believe that there is another way? Are you ready to face the sorrow behind the anger, to feel the pain of loss, and to risk being vulnerable enough to restore love in your life?

After your 30 minutes of meditation about your anger, compose a love letter. This letter can be to a person with whom you have a strained relationship, to a place where you hold your anger, or even to yourself. As you hold the pen to begin writing, visualize your anger as a flower you set adrift on the water and watch it float away. Now, without the protection of your anger, you have reached a new place to start on a path of love. Without your anger in the way, what would you say, and how do you feel? Write it down, and the emotions of healing and love that emerge after the pain and anger are gone may surprise you. If you feel that you can, share your letter, and ask for a letter in return. The old saying is true, "Hate will destroy you, but love will restore you." Listen to your heart, connect at the point of love—not anger—and believe!

With your balanced third chakra, you will feel better able to make decisions and exert your will. After contemplating your anger map, do you understand yourself and your feelings better? Do you feel the power—your own Goddess power? Do you feel your own Goddess power? Like Kali, you are a slayer of demons. You possess the strength, compassion, and fearlessness to harness your anger and use the energy without letting it use you. Like Oya, you are an agent of change. You can make the changes that you want in your life, whether they are big, small, or somewhere in between. From Baba Yaga, you have learned that death and the grieving your losses are natural parts of a healthy life. And you shine with the radiant power of Amaterasu.

Did those exercises leave you feeling creative? Well then, get ready to move on. Creativity is the subject of the next chapter. Prepare to meet Tarot's Empress, the archetype of the fertile Earth Mother; Sappho, the famous poet from ancient Greece who has been called the tenth Muse; Sheherazade from the Arabian Nights, who told stories to save her own life; and Sarasvati, the Hindu Goddess of the arts.

Chapter 10

Creativity: Fertile Imagination

Do you admire creative people? And what about those who have lots of imagination? Do you have a favorite artist, musician, singer, or writer? Does what these individuals do with paint, music, or words seem like a magical secret? Does creativity seem like a mystery to you? Or is creativity something that you practice in your own life?

Do you have a good working relationship with your imagination? There are many kinds of creativity and many different kinds of lives that express creativity. Is yours one of them? Accessing and expressing your creativity is one way you can get in touch with and release your inner Goddess. Goddesses are creative, and they love to see creativity expressed in all its myriad forms.

Nurturing Growth

Who are the Earth Mothers in your life? What do you most admire about these women? What qualities do you share with them, or pull away from? Motherhood was once one of the few spheres of creativity open to women. And motherhood is still a profound, and possibly the most elemental, of creative acts. The creativity of motherhood rests not only in the biological act of bringing forth new life, but in the day-to-day tending of the lives entrusted to you. These lives may be the lives of your children, or perhaps the lives of plants and animals. And don't forget yourself! The way that you mother and take care of your *self* also demands imagination and is a creative act.

The Empress is the third major Arcana card in the Tarot deck. She is the Earth Mother, and she represents fertility, growth, generosity, and healing. She is often depicted seated on a well-cushioned chair, with a scepter in one hand and a 12-pointed crown on her head. Her shield, which is heart shaped and bears the astrological symbol for Venus, the planet of love, rests at her feet. Her association with Venus links her to the two astrological signs ruled by Venus—Libra and Taurus, both of which have strong ties to the home. The Empress often is surrounded by luxuriant nature—golden wheat and leafy trees, and, in some Tarot decks, a stream flows behind her. In a Tarot reading, the Empress card indicates future happiness, fertility, prosperity, or abundance.

Psychiatrist Carl Jung described the Tarot's Empress as the Anima, or the feminine side of the self. Everyone, men included, has an Anima. Some Tarot readers see the Empress as the mother of all things. She is also a symbol of beauty, grace, and the flow of creativity. Like all the Tarot cards, you can look at the Empress as a key that will unlock your relationship to the qualities and situations the card expresses. Studying Tarot's Empress, you can learn about your own Earth Mother qualities. You can also clarify your feelings about the people in your life who manifest these qualities. Looking at an image of the Empress, what do you feel? Do you embody her generous fertility?

Are you in touch with your inner Empress? You express your Empress in many creative ways. What? You say you're not creative? *Everyone* is creative. Creativity is not a special quality that only professional artists, writers, or musicians possess. Every time you solve a problem at home or at work, fix your car or a leaky faucet, plant your herb garden and then cook a fabulous meal from your homegrown efforts, you are using your creativity. When you play with your children or pets, you are also being creative. When you tenderly care for an aging parent or grandparent, you are being creative. The clothes that you select, the items you have chosen to decorate your home, the people who inhabit your life—these are all examples of your Empress in the act of joyous creation.

In her book *Taking Advantage of Adversity*, Gail defines creativity as "the art of growing self-expression." So, even if you don't do any of the things we've just mentioned, observe yourself and learn about your "signature self-expression." Ask a trusted friend or anyone who loves you to verify that you really do have a creative side. One woman, who positively believed she lacked creativity, was told by her friend that she possessed a natural gift for storytelling, always describing events in a humorous and delightful way. Signature self-expression is simply your own way of being creative. Honor and nurture this part of your Goddess self.

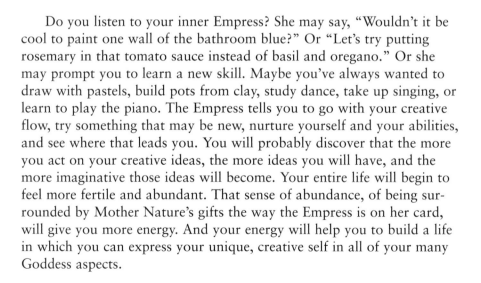

> **"** Every moment of your life is infinitely creative and the universe is endlessly bountiful. Just put forth a clear-enough request, and everything your heart desires must come to you.
>
> —Shakti Gawain, teacher and author (1978) **"**

Do you listen to your inner Empress? She may say, "Wouldn't it be cool to paint one wall of the bathroom blue?" Or "Let's try putting rosemary in that tomato sauce instead of basil and oregano." Or she may prompt you to learn a new skill. Maybe you've always wanted to draw with pastels, build pots from clay, study dance, take up singing, or learn to play the piano. The Empress tells you to go with your creative flow, try something that may be new, nurture yourself and your abilities, and see where that leads you. You will probably discover that the more you act on your creative ideas, the more ideas you will have, and the more imaginative those ideas will become. Your entire life will begin to feel more fertile and abundant. That sense of abundance, of being surrounded by Mother Nature's gifts the way the Empress is on her card, will give you more energy. And your energy will help you to build a life in which you can express your unique, creative self in all of your many Goddess aspects.

Let It Flow

Do you enjoy the arts? Do you create art? And what about crafts? If you don't have any artistic habits or hobbies now, you probably did when you were a child. What did you like to do best? Did you draw, paint, or make things out of clay? Maybe you used to knit, crochet, or form models from papier-mâché. Did you tap dance or play a musical instrument? Or maybe you are, or were, a writer of poems and stories or a devoted journal keeper. Take the time to let yourself practice these activities today. Yes, now!

Sarasvati is the Hindu Goddess of the arts. She also rules over knowledge, learning, and science. Some see her as being particularly associated with the performing arts, such as dance, music, and the recitation of poetry. She is known as the Goddess of speech and eloquence, and is said to have invented spoken language, the ancient language Sanskrit, or the script in which Sanskrit is written. Words are said to flow from her mouth in a beautiful cascade. She is the patron of poets and writers, and is honored in libraries with offerings of flowers, fruit, and incense. In some areas, she is considered especially sacred to people who sing or play musical instruments. She shares her name with the river Sarasvati, which flows through northwest India, and she is said to originally have been the Goddess of that river. She either got her name from the river, or the river was named after her. Because of her association with water, she is known as The Flowing One.

Sarasvati is the consort and Shakti of Brahma, the God of creation. She is pictured riding on a swan or seated on a lotus. She always has a pale complexion and is dressed in white, cream, or light yellow. She often has a crescent moon on her forehead, and she has four arms. She plays a stringed instrument called a vina. Buddhists and Jains, another religious group of India, also worship Sarasvati because she is the source of knowledge. Hindus, particularly in the north and east of India, worship her alongside Durga, or Devi, whom some consider to be her mother, and her sister Goddess Lakshmi, who is associated with prosperity and wealth. Sarasvati's festival, Sarasvati Puja, is held on the cusp between winter and spring, the moment when nature is budding and about to create itself anew for the coming season.

Have your experiences of practicing the creative arts been joyful? Or do you mostly remember the frustrations? Perhaps you suffered through piano lessons and never quite learned to read music. Or maybe you tried a ballet class only to discover your inner klutz. Everyone, even the amazingly graceful and talented, has experienced frustration when learning a new artistic skill. We have a tendency in North American culture to view artists as natural geniuses. People say that artists are born that way, as if all their skills and knowledge were born with them.

It may very well be true that you were born with a natural affinity for music. Or perhaps you have an inborn ability with language. But even geniuses need to learn the skills of their craft, and must work to master those skills. For example, singer and songwriter (and Goddess!) Tracy Chapman had to learn to play the guitar before she was really able to create music. The same is true for Joni Mitchell, Rosanne Cash, Gillian Welch, and Mary Chapin Carpenter. You can learn to express yourself through the art of your choice, too. Your first efforts might not sound pleasing or look like much. Your first drawings or paintings may seem more like muddy blobs than works of art, but give yourself the room to be a beginner. Because Sarasvati is also the Goddess of learning, her image speaks to the beginner's state of learning. Sarasvati often sits on a lotus. The lovely lotus represents the truth of creativity. Just as the lotus grows up out of the muck at the bottom of a pond, beauty is born of mud. When you are learning a new artistic skill, give yourself some time to grow out of the mud and become a beautiful lotus. You will become more creative by doing so, and you will have more fun in life. And isn't more fun one of the things that you want in your life?

Psychologist Mihaly Csikszentmihalyi began studying fun in the 1960s. He wanted to know what makes experiences enjoyable. After doing many interviews with all kinds of people, he identified a state that he called flow. Flow is the feeling that you are being carried away, that everything is moving smoothly and seemingly without effort. When you are in a flow state, you are highly focused on the activity you are per-forming. You no longer worry whether you are performing well or badly. Your sense of time may be altered, and the work you are doing comes to feel like play. In making art or engaging in physical activity, it is the balance between the challenges of what you're trying to achieve and the execution of the skills that you have that leads you to the plea-surable and fulfilling state known as flow. Without the challenge there is no flow. That's why watching television can be entertaining, but it's unlikely to be one of your peak fun experiences. To experience flow and have real fun, you need to use your skills to face a challenge. Athletes as well as practitioners of the arts also experience the flow state and some-times call it The Zone. Have you ever experienced flow? What were you doing when you felt yourself in the flow state? Can you promise yourself that you will engage in more of your flow-producing activity?

Sarasvati, the Flowing One, challenges herself and uses her skills of eloquence and beautiful speech. Words of beauty flow from her mouth. She also plays an instrument. It seems like no accident that Sarasvati, in addition to being the Goddess of the arts, is also the Goddess of knowledge. You need some knowledge in the form of skills to practice your art and achieve the Goddess-like state of flow.

Sarasvati with her name, The Flowing One, reminds us that painting or dancing or playing the piano or writing should be pleasurable activities that can lead you into a flow state. You may feel there's no point to playing the piano if you're never going to be a professional musician. Why paint if you'll never sell your paintings? Why study ballet if you'll never be invited to dance with the American Ballet Theater? You do it because it's fun! The Flowing One tells you to enjoy the process. The Flowing One says you don't have to worry about the results—whether you engage in your art in private or in public, whether you choose to express your Inner Goddess through music, dance, painting, knitting, the verbal arts, through the joy of process in doing your job (whatever you define your job to be), or in any other activity of life in which you nurture your creative spirit. Some people express their creativity by facilitating the self-expression of others. Acting coaches, actor's agents and managers, writing teachers—mentors of every type express their creativity behind the scenes and thus enable the creative spirit of others. The Flowing One shows you that it is part of your Goddess nature to be artistic. All of life is creation. So, set yourself an artistic challenge and go with *your* flow.

Express Yourself

Do you enjoy poetry? Do you ever read poetry? Or do you like to listen to someone else reading poetry out loud? Perhaps you write poetry of your own. Or maybe you wrote as a child or teenager. One of the wonderful things about writing poetry is that you don't need any special equipment. A pen and a piece of paper, and you are good to go. And you can write almost anywhere!

> ❝ The process of writing, any form of creativity, is a power intensifying life.
>
> —Rita May Brown, writer (1988) ❞

When was the last time you read a poem? Does reading poetry seem difficult to you? Does it remind you too much of boring classes in school? Today there are many women writing many different types of poetry. If you have not read any poetry recently, then you may want to check out the books of some contemporary female poets. Deborah Garrison's collection, *A Working Girl Can't Win* (Modern Library, 2000), is both accessible and witty, and it might give you ideas for poems that you could write. Marie Howe's book *What the Living Do* (W.W. Norton, 1999) transforms personal loss into redemption, revelation, and, ultimately, celebration. In *Mr. Bluebird* (Painted Leaf Press, 2001), which gets its name from a type of rose, Gerry Gomez Pearlberg writes about Brooklyn, nature, birds, and the women she loves with both wit and delight. Another entertaining poet, although she is not contemporary, is Ho Xuan Huong, an eighteenth-century Vietnamese concubine. Her book *Spring Essence* (Copper Canyon Press, 2001), translated by John Balaban, is funny, suggestive, poignant, and sexy. If you want to learn more about poetry in general, or if you find reading it difficult, check out Molly Peacock's *How to Read a Poem … And Start a Poetry Circle* (Riverhead Books, 2000). Peacock, who is herself a well-published poet, provides detailed explanations of 13 of her favorite poems with infectious enthusiasm and a joyous passion for language.

Sappho and her passionate poetry have served as inspiration and role model for many poets and for many women. Catullus, a first-century B.C.E. Roman poet, named a cycle of poems after her about a romance that he had with a married woman. The American poet Amy Lowell (1874–1925), who won a Pulitzer Prize for poetry in 1926, cited Sappho as one of her important influences. And the imagist poet Hilda Doolittle (1886–1961), who wrote under the name H.D., explored the divinity of the Goddesses, and has been credited with developing a woman's mythology, also found inspiration in Sappho's poetic work.

Some women are drawn to Sappho because she has come to represent lesbian love. Even the word *lesbian* comes from Sappho's home Lesbos. Interestingly enough, the Greek verb *lesbiazein*, which literally means "to play the Lesbian," is said to refer to enthusiasm for all sorts of sexual experience. When Sappho lived on Lesbos, many young women came to study with her, and based on her poetry, she may have fallen in love with a number of them. She celebrated these loves in her passionate and sensual verse. But you don't have to love women in the erotic sense to learn from Sappho. Sappho expressed her passion and her love through her art. She did not concern herself with what others might think about her feelings. She allowed herself free rein to express herself. The society in which Sappho lived, one where women were cherished, valued, and educated with great care, can also be an inspiration that you can learn from today.

Sappho was a poet in ancient Greece, and she lived on the Isle of Lesbos, which is in the Aegean Sea off the coast of Turkey. Sappho was born between 630 and 612 B.C.E. into an aristocratic family. She married a wealthy merchant and had one daughter. Sappho is considered one of the great poets. As evidence of her high status in ancient times, the philosopher Plato called her the "tenth Muse" and on Lesbos, coins were minted bearing her image.

Sappho wrote lyric poetry and was known as a lyrist because her poems were written to be read while accompanied by the music of the lyre. She made certain changes to the standard meter in which lyric poetry was written. The metric form that she used came to be known as sapphic meter. Another of Sappho's poetic innovations was in the content of her poetry. Most ancient poets wrote about the Gods and Goddesses. Sappho wrote about personal experience, and she did so using the first person. In other words, she used "I" in her poems of personal longing and love. Often the love she wrote about was for another woman. Very little of Sappho's poetry has survived into the present day. In fact, only one of Sappho's poems still exists in its entirety. The rest of her poems are only available in fragments. You can read her work in a translation by Mary Barnard. Look for *Sappho: A New Translation* (University of California Press, 1999).

In what ways do you express your passion and love creatively? This is not to say that your artistic expression has to be about sex or love, per se. Write, dance, or draw sex if that sounds like an interesting artistic challenge for you. Sappho's lesson is to make art about the things that matter to you most, the things that excite you, and the things that you love. You may want to write about trees. Or you may be inspired to draw birds or flowers. Your love and excited anticipation may lead you to learn to knit a difficult pattern in honor of a new baby in your circle of friends. You can share your feelings and your secrets in your art. Let Sappho be your guide and your inspiration. Let her give you permission to not worry about what other people will think. Listen to your own creative voice, your own Goddess-given passion. Learn what it tells you to learn, express what your passion wants to express, and be true to releasing your Goddess within.

66 I can always be distracted by love, but eventually I get horny for my creativity.

—Gilda Radner, comedian (1989) **99**

Tell Your Tale

You probably tell stories naturally in the everyday course of your life. "I went to the store," you tell a friend, "and I ran into my neighbor who …" We are all natural storytellers. Do you prefer true stories or made-up ones? Do you ever add details or exaggerate just a little to make a story about your life more interesting? Do you ever make up stories entirely? Perhaps you tell your children fantasy stories about adventures with pirates or fairies. Would you rather tell a tale or listen to one?

Do you know the stories of the Arabian Nights? Besides Sheherazade's story, the other most famous tales in this collection include "Ali Baba and the Forty Thieves," "Sinbad the Sailor," and "Aladdin." You may want to look for N.J. Dawood's translation *Tales from the Thousand and One Nights* (Penguin Classics, 1973). Many of the stories in the collection involve the human conflict between passion and power. Ultimately, the stories affirm the value of women and the feminine. Several critics who have studied the tales suggest that the collection acts in an almost therapeutic way to correct the king's negative attitudes toward the feminine principle, or Anima. Some scholars believe that the tales may have originated with women shut up in a harem who imagined a world in which they could play free and have active roles in society.

Sheherazade is a character from the world-renowned collection of stories known as the "Arabian Nights" or "Thousand and One Nights," and she may have been a real woman. The stories of the collection, which were originally recorded in Arabic around the year 1000 C.E., are held together by the story of Sheherazade, the teller of the tales. Sheherazade tells her stories to keep her husband, King Shahryar, from killing her. The king had been previously married, and because his wife had been unfaithful, he had her put to death. To fend off his despair, he then married a succession of virgins whom he had killed after their wedding night, thus murdering each new relationship and ensuring that his brides would remain faithful to him.

To save the women of her country, Sheherazade volunteers to marry the blood-thirsty king. On her first night in the king's palace, she tells a story. The king is awed and asks her to tell another one. Sheherazade tells him that her next story is even better than the first one, but that she cannot tell it because dawn is already starting to break on the horizon. Because he wants to hear her next story, the king orders Sheherazade's execution postponed.

The next night, Sheherazade entertains the king with another story. And again, he asks to hear more, and Sheherazade sighs that her next story is even better, but that the sun is already up, and she must stop. Once again, the king postpones Sheherazade's execution. This goes on for a thousand and one nights. By the end of that time, the king has fallen in love with Sheherazade and no longer wishes to have her killed. Through her eloquence, skill, and bravery she has saved not only her own life, but also the life of the king and the lives of thousands of her fellow countrywomen.

Do you write stories? Do you dream of writing them? Or perhaps you are attracted to storytelling in its oral form. Writing or telling stories can be fun. It also, as Sheherazade's story indicates, can be a crucial and even life-saving activity. When you write or tell stories, you communicate, sharing an important part of your Goddess self. Sharing yourself in that way is a generous act. Through your words, you can reach out to other people and help them feel less alone in the world. Of course, sharing your words can also help you to feel more connected to others. And writing your words down can help you feel more connected to yourself and your Goddess aspects. Committing your words to paper or to your listening audience is a commitment to yourself. Writing and storytelling are one way of letting yourself know that your experience of the world and your thoughts and feelings matter. And they *do* matter.

Most writers read a lot. When you begin to write, even if you have never met another writer, you join the community of other writers by reading, wrestling with, and loving the written word. As Anne Lamott has described in her book *Bird by Bird: Some Instructions on Writing and Life* (Anchor Books, 1995), you may find yourself writing a story or a book or a poem back to another writer whose work you admire. Maybe you will want to write a story for Sheherazade or for Sappho. Perhaps you will find inspiration in the stories of some of the other Goddesses or you will write about the unique combination of Goddesses that is you.

> 66 He had a different face; he had a different thumbprint. He was a different person. His story is valid, but that doesn't mean that mine's not. I really, really … came to terms with that—that you don't have to copy other people or even ever try. You just bring yourself to your fullest, whatever that is.
>
> —Carolyn Chute, novelist (2001) 99

Exercise #1: Unlock Hidden Treasure

You get to go on a field trip! In fact, it's going to be a treasure hunt of sorts. You are going to go looking for the keys to your creativity. You can use tarot cards, of course, as keys to unlock your relationship to the archetypes. You have looked at the Empress as a metaphorical key to your Earth Mother aspects. The keys you are going to hunt for now are not metaphorical keys, but actual keys and preferably old ones.

Ideally, you want to find the old-fashioned kind of key that has a metal loop on one end, a cylindrical shaft, and a bit on the other end—the part that actually turns the lock open. These types of keys often fit interior locks within a house, such as the lock on a bathroom door. You can also look for small keys, like the type used for desk drawers or jewelry boxes. You may have to comb your local antiques stores, flea markets, and thrift shops to find just what you are looking for. If you come up empty handed, you could try a shop that sells reproductions of antique locks and keys, but these keys, which are often made of brass, can be rather expensive ($5 to $12 each!), and old keys seem to hold more mystery and excitement.

Once you have found a key or two, use them to call up the various facets of your creativity. Maybe the shape or size of one particular key brings to mind your math skills. You may decide that another key opens up the power of your drawing talents, and a third may unleash your writing aptitude or your problem-solving skills. Keep adding to your key collection.

You can make labels for each key if you like. Your label could bear the name of one of your creative talents, for example, music, dance, organization, or poetry. Or you could name your keys after the Goddesses that you associate with each activity. You could have an Empress key, a Sarasvati key, a Sappho key, or a Sheherazade key. You can make your keys shine with a little metal polish, or you can leave the patina of the years on them. You can even paint your keys with a little fingernail polish. Keep your key collection on your altar, and use them whenever you need them to open the door to your creative Goddess source. You may get out your math key (or your problem-solving key) when you are about to sit down and balance your checkbook. Use your writing key to help you get started on that poem you have been thinking about. Or get out your planning or organization key when you are coming up with ideas for a child's birthday party.

If you are ever stumped for a gift to give a friend, why not try a creativity key? It is easy to make, and you don't have to worry that the key will not fit! If your friend is an aspiring poet, give her a poetic inspiration key. If your friend is remodeling her house, you could give her the key to a beautiful and peaceful home. Once you decide which kind of key you are going to give, make a pretty label that identifies the key's purpose, wrap it in a piece of velvet, and put it in a gift box. You can even decorate the box with images of creative Goddess power in action.

Instant Goddess

Danish writer and adventurer Isak Dinesen, played by Meryl Streep in the classic 1985 movie *Out of Africa*, wrote this line: "Would the full moon throw a shadow over the gravel of the drive that was like me?" Think of a question that describes—embodies within itself—your relationship to the universe, and write it down in your Goddess journal.

Exercise #2: Song of the Self

Get out your Goddess journal, a pen, and a sheet of scratch paper. Imagine that you are one of the Goddesses of creativity from this chapter. Go through your journal and, using the scratch paper, write down words or phrases that you particularly like. Think about the sounds of the words as well as their meanings. Say them out loud so you can appreciate their music. Look up their meanings in the dictionary and see whether the words have secondary meanings that are intriguing or unexpected.

Once you have a list of words and phrases, read it over as the Goddess. While still imagining yourself as a Goddess of creativity, use the words and phrases from your list to paint a verbal picture of who you are. What is it about yourself that you cherish? Feel free to add the words that you need, even if they are not on your list. Let the sounds of the words guide you, but don't feel that you have to make rhymes. Allow the words to flow out of you. If you like, include information about your past, your present, and your future. What did you love about yourself as a child? What do you hold dear now? And what qualities or achievements of your own do you imagine you will cherish in the future?

If you like, you can write the first section of your poem in the voice of one of your creativity Goddesses. Then write the next section in the voice of another of your inner Goddesses. See what the two Goddesses, and the two parts of you, have to say to each other.

When you feel that your poem is done, type it up. Use a fancy computer font if you like. Or write your poem out on nice paper in your best handwriting, or use calligraphy if that is something you enjoy. Put your self-portrait poem on your Goddess altar, and let it inspire you to greater and greater Goddess-like creative acts.

Do you feel like writing or drawing or singing? Has this chapter helped you to find some of the keys to your creativity? For more inspiration, be sure to take a look at the list of suggested reading in Appendix B. What is your inner Empress saying now? Remember that the Empress represents the fertility and abundance in your life. Do you acknowledge her importance on a regular basis? Do you feel more likely to listen to what she has to say? Are you excited by the idea that you could learn a new artistic skill? Know that Sarasvati will guide you in your endeavors, and Sappho will help you to express your passion and focus on what is really important to you. Sheherazade tells you that your ideas and imaginings are not only important, but that they are filled with the power to sustain life.

Now it's time to move on to the next chapter where, through the art of meditation, you will learn to access the Greek Muses, the Goddesses who have provided heavenly inspiration for artists and writers for centuries. You will read about St. Teresa of Avila, the Carmelite nun who wrote about her meditation experiences and her visions of the divine. And you'll meet Shekinah from the ancient Canaanite civilization and Ennoia, an angel from Gnosticism, an early Christian sect of the Near East.

How to Find Your Inner Knowing

Elizabeth Bowen wrote "When you love someone, all your saved-up wishes start coming out." The path to love begins by loving yourself, by releasing your Goddess within! In Part 3, we help you learn how to look inward to gain insights and self-understanding that will radiate outward from you to your loved ones, community, and world at large with the beautiful golden glow of compassion and loving-kindness. It's time to use what you have learned, to love yourself, to know yourself, and to *be* the Goddess you are. To quote another remarkable woman, Helen Keller: "When we do the best that we can, we never know what miracle is wrought in our life, or in the life of another." Use your Goddess power with confidence, strength, and love.

Chapter 11

Meditation: Calm and Aware

What exactly is meditation? Doing nothing, you might answer. And, in a way, you're right. During meditation, you do sit still and appear to be doing nothing. But meditation is not just doing nothing, and neither is it the same as sleeping or spacing out. In meditation you actually are doing something.

When you meditate, you focus your mind, and as you have probably noticed, your mind can be a pretty busy place! Sometimes your mind may feel full of clutter and noise—shopping lists, a few bars of a song you heard on the radio, the nagging feeling that you have forgotten to do something really important. Other times, your mind may seem sluggish—refusing to wake up and get moving—or stubborn—picking over the same conversation again and again and again. The good news is that meditation can help you in all these situations. Meditation teaches you that you are more than your thoughts and feelings. Through meditation, you can learn to let go of the mind's clutter and experience your own inner divinity.

Meditation is like a workout for your mind. When you meditate, you train your mind's muscles. With practice, you will develop better abilities to shed stress, stronger powers of concentration, and an overall feeling of well-being. Scientific studies have proven that meditation lowers the blood pressure and relaxes both mind and body. Electroencephalogram (EEG) tests, which measure the brain's activity, also prove that a person in a meditative state is having a unique experience. EEG printouts show that meditation produces slower brain waves than the ordinary waking state or sleep.

Have you ever tried to meditate? Does it sound too difficult, esoteric, or just plain boring? Like many other activities, meditation sometimes is boring. When you meditate, though, your occasional feelings of boredom are offset by the benefits that you receive. Have you ever started a workout routine that you dreaded only to discover, after it had become part of your schedule, that you began to look forward to it and actually felt a lack if you had to miss exercising? Meditation is like that. And meditation doesn't have to be mysterious or complicated. You don't have to be a Buddhist or a Hindu to meditate. Christians meditate, Jews meditate, Muslims meditate, atheists and agnostics meditate. Everyone and anyone can meditate. All you have to do is find some place quiet, sit down, and breathe. And be patient. In the West, people tend to expect immediate results. You may be inclined to try something, but then give it up a short time later if you feel you haven't achieved results. As meditation teacher, Jon Kabat-Zinn once commented, "Try it for a couple of years and see how you like it."

The Breath of Inspiration

Do you know what inspires you? Do you feel inspired right now? Perhaps reading about creativity in the last chapter got your juices flowing. (We hope it did!) Perhaps you're interested in experiencing the state of flow that we discussed. Have you ever felt that kind of total engagement and inspiration when working on a project or doing sports? In general, though, we could all use a little more inspiration in our lives. Don't you agree?

Inspiration is a special type of excitement combined with focus. Inspiration can also be someone or something that provokes that excitement. The word *inspiration* also means "divine guidance." And it can mean "inhalation," the act of breathing in. So, think of it this way: Every time you breathe in you could be inhaling the inspiration of the Muses. Meditation is one way to help you access your inspiration, and one of the simplest ways to meditate is to focus on your breath. Because it's often difficult for people to settle down into meditation, various meditation traditions have come up with ways to help. In the yogic tradition, the poses of hatha yoga are the preparation for sitting meditation. You can also use yogic breathing exercises to help you to relax and prepare for meditation.

The ancient Greek Muses are the Goddesses of the arts, sciences, and inspiration. Do you remember from Chapter 10 that Sappho had been called the tenth Muse? Well, now you're going to meet her Muse sisters. In different parts of Greece, there were thought to be varying numbers of Muses. The Muses that you generally hear about today are the nine honored in Athens. The daughters of Zeus and Mnemosyne, the Goddess of memory, they are as follows: Calliope, Muse of epic poetry; Clio, Muse of history; Erato, Muse of erotic poetry; Euterpe, Muse of lyric poetry; Melpomene, Muse of tragedy; Polyhymnia, Muse of sacred song and poetry; Terpsichore, Muse of dance; Thalia, Muse of comedy; and Urania, Muse of astronomy. The Muses watch over and give inspiration to artists of all kinds. In ancient times, they were said to raise their exquisite voices in song to celebrate the marriages and funerals of deities and humans alike. Our English word *muse* comes from the Greek word for muse, *mousa*, from which we also get the words *mosaic* (literally, belonging to the Muses), *museum* (place of the Muses), and *music* (art of the Muses). The Muses are the very spirits of inspiration.

66 The most beautiful thing in the world is, precisely, the conjunction of learning and inspiration.

—Wanda Landowska, musician (1964)

Here's a breathing exercise that will help to calm your mind. Sit in a comfortable position with your spine straight. You can sit on the floor or in a chair. Keep your elbows at your sides and hold up your right hand. Bend your index and middle fingers into your palm. Take a comfortable breath in and hold it. Close off your right nostril with your thumb. Exhale through your left nostril to a count of four, and then inhale through your left nostril to a count of four. Release your thumb and close your left nostril with your ring finger and pinkie. Now exhale through your right nostril for a count of four. Then inhale through the right nostril to a count of four. Switch fingers and exhale through your left nostril again; inhale and continue this pattern until you feel centered and calm.

After you've practiced this version of alternate nostril breathing for a while, you can begin to retain the breath for four counts at the end of each inhalation and exhalation. You can also lengthen the exhalation to a count of six or eight. Once you are a real adept, you can begin to lengthen the breath retention up to 6, 8, or even 16 counts. If you find yourself struggling, return to a pattern and rhythm that feels comfortable. The practice should be focused, calm, and comfortable.

Do you feel those Muses hovering around you? Do you feel ready to focus in meditation? If you do want to meditate, you will need about 20 minutes of quiet time alone. Before you start a meditation session, check the following:

- Did you turn the ringer on the phone off (or unplug the phone)? You don't want any interruptions. This goes for your cell phone, too.
- Have you fed the cat? What about the dog? Often it's easier to meditate if you can keep your pets in another room.
- Go to the bathroom, even if you don't feel like you have to. You don't want the urge to go to distract you from your meditation experience.
- Make sure that you are comfortable when you sit down. If you are sitting on the floor, give yourself sufficient padding. If you are sitting in a chair, make sure that your feet touch the ground while your back remains upright.
- Make sure that your clothing is comfortable, too. Don't wear anything that binds or causes you to itch.
- Did you just have a double espresso? If so, this is probably *not* the best time for you to try to sit down and calmly contemplate your breath.

Meditation practice can help you to gain better focus, and better abilities to focus will aid you in achieving the flow state that we talked about in Chapter 10. By practice, we don't mean trying and trying to get meditation "right." When you meditate, there is no right or wrong. The point is just to do it. And that is what practice means—doing it habitually and preferably every day. Because the Muses sometimes bestow good ideas during Gail's meditation sessions, she likes to keep a pen and pad next to her chair.

Explore Your Inner Mansions

Does the idea of some quiet time alone sound great to you? Or do you try to avoid being alone? If you're not used to it, alone time can feel a bit like a vast desert. But it doesn't have to. After all, you have yourself and all of your inner Goddesses for company! When you are alone, you have a great opportunity to look at yourself—both inside and out. You probably look in the mirror every day, right? But when was the last time you really looked into your soul?

What exactly is the difference between prayer and meditation? Some people would say that prayer is outward-looking, sent out toward someone or something outside of the self, while meditation is inward-looking and is focused on the present moment. There are four methods of prayer: colloquial, petitionary, ritualistic, and meditative. In the colloquial form, you talk to your deity (or deities) in your own words, sharing concerns, experiences, or gratitude. In petitionary prayer, you ask for help with a specific problem. You might, for example, ask for a physical healing. Ritualistic prayer is usually the recitation of a sacred text. Meditative prayer is considered to be the simple stilling of the mind. Saint Teresa's description of the mansions (in the following story), or dwelling places, of the soul sounds very interior, and yet her visions were thought to come from a divine source outside of herself. Saint Teresa's visions and her practice of prayer brought the divine into her everyday life. Meditation can be combined with any form of prayer to bring you a feeling of greater connection with your own Divinity, the Goddess, and the many divine blessings all around you.

> ❝ … St. Teresa in a single process seeks to be united with God and lives out this unity in her body; she is not the slave of her nerves and her hormones: One must admire, rather, the intensity of a faith that penetrates to the most intimate regions of her flesh.
>
> —Simone de Beauvoir, philosopher (1953)

Saint Teresa of Avila (1515–1582) was a Carmelite nun and a mystic. Born in Spain, she entered a convent as a young woman and became a passionate reformer, the founder of a religious order, and leading figure in the church. She founded 17 convents in her lifetime, and also wrote books. Her works—a spiritual autobiography and several volumes on prayer and meditation—are considered some of the most remarkable writings about personal faith in existence. She wrote with humor, vigor, common sense, and a good deal of self-abasement. Saint Teresa described the soul as an interior castle that holds the Trinity at its center. Through prayer, the individual moves through the many mansions of the castle toward the center and God. (Mansion is translated from the Spanish *moradas,* which means "dwelling places.")

Saint Teresa advocated silent prayer and, like her predecessor Joan of Arc, the French heroine and saint, often experienced visions when she prayed. In one of her visions, the Saints Mary Magdalene and Augustine of Hippo came to her and showed her what hell looked like. This vision spurred Saint Teresa to live a more devout life. Her most famous vision, which came to her over and over, involved a beautiful young angel with a flaming, golden spear. In her vision, the angel stabbed her several times in the heart, leaving her "inflamed with a great love of God." Saint Teresa's vision was immortalized in a statue by the sculptor Giovanni Lorenzo Bernini (1598–1680), which today stands in the Cornaro Chapel in the Church of Santa Maria della Victoria in Rome. "Ecstasy of St. Teresa" depicts the saint, her armed angel, and Saint Teresa's remarkable, rapturous expression.

Saint Teresa was beatified in 1614. Because of controversy about her—some argued that her visions may not have been divinely inspired—she was not canonized as a saint until 1622. In 1970, she was the first woman to be honored with the title Doctor of the Church. Today, because of the mental stress that some of her visions caused her, she is invoked against headaches. Her feast is held on October 15.

"But wait a second," you say. "Isn't meditation done in silence, while prayers have words?" Well, yes and no. Contemplative prayer can be silent, and you can use words while meditating. In meditation, some people like to use a mantra, a word or phase that is repeated, either silently to the self or out loud. Chanting a mantra can help you to attain a meditative state and is often a good way for Westerners to ease into the inactivity of meditation. When you are chanting, you will feel like you are doing something and that feeling can make it easier to sit still.

In Transcendental Meditation (TM) a guru (which is Sanskrit for "dispeller of darkness") gives everyone his or her own secret mantra. You can pick any word you like for your mantra. You could repeat the word "om," the Sanskrit syllable that represents the vibration of the entire world. Or you could say "amen"; "peace"; "shanti," which is the Sanskrit word for "peace"; "shalom," which is Hebrew for "peace"; "love"; or "light." Pick a word that will help you calm down, focus, relax, and feel good. If a short phrase from the poem you wrote in Chapter 10 feels right, you can even use that as your own personalized mantra. If you want to keep track of how many times you have said a mantra, you can use prayer beads, such as a rosary or a *mala*, a Sanskrit word for prayer beads that literally means garland of flowers. You can turn other types of small hand motions into meditation as well. In many Eastern traditions, the power of a mantra increases in proportion to the number of times you repeat it. While in a meditative state, you can easily loose count of the number of times you have chanted your mantra. Mala beads can help you keep track. In addition, when passed over the fingers, mala beads help to stimulate certain meridians, or energy, points, which can help to reduce stress and deepen your meditative state.

Have you ever folded origami figures from paper? Many people find making origami figures, particularly the origami crane, a satisfying meditative activity. Origami is an ancient art form. Some people claim that origami developed in China around the year 105 C.E. Others believe that this art form was born in Japan in the sixth century. What we do know for sure is that the word *origami* comes from the Japanese words for fold and for paper.

The crane, a symbol of good luck and long life, has been a popular motif in Japanese art for centuries. Since the mid-1950s, it has also been a symbol for peace. In 1955, Sadako Sasaki, a young Japanese girl, developed leukemia from the effects of radiation caused by the bombing of Hiroshima. While in the hospital, she began folding a thousand paper cranes in the hope that the Gods would grant her a long life. After folding 644 cranes, Sadako died at the age of 12, but her story spread across Japan. Today a statue of her, holding a golden crane, stands in the Hiroshima Peace Park and commemorates all the children killed by the atomic bomb.

Why not learn to fold a paper crane and then try crane-folding as a form of meditation? You can find directions for how to make a crane in most origami books. Check your local library or look for Katherine's step-by-step directions in *Paper Magic: The Art of Origami* (Troll

Communications, 1998). Perhaps your children already own a copy. When you are learning to make the crane, have patience with yourself. Remember to keep breathing as you work. If you're having a hard time, take a little break. Roll your shoulders around and shake the tension out of your arms and hands. The first few times you make a crane, try using a large piece of plain paper. After you have become adept, you can use smaller and fancier sheets.

If you can't find origami paper, you can make squares of paper from colorful wrapping paper, other pretty colored paper, or use white paper and decorate your cranes with crayons or paint after you are done folding them. To make a square from a piece of $8^1/_2$" × 11" paper, fold the paper on a diagonal so that the bottom short side meets the long side on the right. Make sure that your fold runs through the bottom-right corner of the paper. You will end up with a double-layer triangle shape, with a single-layer rectangle above it. Using the edge of the top layer as a guide, cut off the rectangle. Unfold your triangle, and you should have a perfect square.

Once you have learned to fold an origami crane, you can use the act of folding cranes as a meditation. If you'd like to fold a thousand cranes, organize some friends and make the cranes as a group meditation for world peace. Know that your action honors all children who have died as a result of war. If you're working on your own, try folding cranes as a meditation for 15 or 20 minutes. Before you start, make sure you have plenty of paper. So that you won't have to break your meditation by wrestling with a package, remove your origami paper from its wrapping and place a stack of it on the table where you are working.

To turn your paper-folding experience into meditation, just focus on your breath while you make each fold. Breathe slowly and regularly. Feel the paper under your fingers. When thoughts come up, just let them go and bring your awareness back to your breath and the physical sensations of the paper folding. If you practice crane-folding every day as a personal meditation, regardless of how many cranes you create, you will find yourself experiencing a deep sense of inner peace. Give your cranes flight by stringing them into mobiles, or give them as gifts.

Clearing Your Mind

Where are my keys? Did I turn off the oven? What did I do with the phone bill? And what are we going to eat for dinner? Do these thoughts sound anything like yours? Of course, you are busy. You have a zillion things on your mind. But how much of your energy is eaten up with worry about the past and anticipation of the future? How much of your time do you spend focused on present events, the now that is right in front of you?

 Ennoia is the Gnostic Goddess of thought and knowledge. The Gnostics were an early mystical Christian sect that developed in the Near East. The word *gnostic* comes from the Greek word *gnosis*, which means "knowledge," and in this case specifically the knowledge derived from intuition and insight. Ennoia is one of the Aeons, angels of great manifested thought, who created all things. Ennoia's sister Aeons include Charity, Sophia (wisdom), Aletheia (truth), and Zoe (means of life). Ennoia has been described as the same as or similar to Sophia. On the other hand, she is also said to be the mother and creator of the malevolent angels of the lower world who pulled her from heaven. On earth, she lives inside women and can fan the flames of their passions to cause them difficulties. The Greek word *ennoia* means the act of thinking, consideration, or meditation; a thought, notion, or conception; mind, understanding, will, or manner of feeling and thinking. Ennoia has been described as possessing knowledge of magic, which she passed on to the Gnostic Christians. For more about these early mystics, look for Elaine Pagels's book *The Gnostic Gospels* (Vintage Books, 1989).

In Ennoia's story, thought creates all things, both good and bad. Thought created the unique and Goddess-like you! And thought can also enflame your passions and cause you strife. Does your mind ever seem too full of thoughts? Do you ever have the same thought circling around and around inside your brain? Perhaps you have met a special someone. You wonder if he or she is going to call you. And you wonder, and you obsess, and you cannot seem to stop your mind from going over every last detail of the conversation that you had. Or maybe you have a problem from work that persists in zooming around your head all evening and into your weekend. Sometimes it can be enough to make you shriek, right?

But shrieking doesn't usually help, at least not for long. One thing that you *can* do in this kind of situation is to meditate or chant. Or you can go about your business, doing whatever it is that you have to do and reminding yourself gently, but repeatedly, to bring your awareness back to your breath. You can also steer your mind to the physical sensations that are happening in your body and observe them in the present moment. One of the great things about learning meditation techniques is that you begin to gain greater control of your mind. You start to feel that your thoughts are just thoughts and, as such, they can be changed.

Learn to recognize that you can choose your thoughts. Try the method known as "changing the channel." Imagine that your mind is a television that is playing an annoying show. See yourself change the channel to another program, one that is soothing and agreeable. Take the time to imagine all the details of the new show you are watching. Take yourself into your show, your own special place, and notice all the elements that bring you pleasure. Clearing your mind of the thoughts that are not helpful to you can fill your life with more peaceful and satisfying Goddess energy.

> 66 Her thoughts were busy enough, and though some reasons against the carrying out of her plan ventured to assert themselves, they had no hope of carrying the day, being in piteous minority, though she considered them one by one.
>
> —Sarah Orne Jewett, novelist (1884) 99

You Had to Be There

You've probably had the experience of recounting a funny event to a friend, only to have her stare at you blankly because she clearly doesn't understand what about your story is funny. "Well, I guess you had to be there," you may say. How do you react in such a situation? Do you feel a bit annoyed because your friend doesn't understand you? Or do you actually feel that somehow your experience could not be put into words?

How do you know what you know? Some of what you know you learned from reading books or going to school. Other knowledge you obtained through experience. Given an infinite amount of time, could you put all your knowledge into words? Many people would say no to that last question. Shekinah says there is some knowledge that cannot be described with words. What do you know of the divine? Do you only know what you can see or hear, or is your knowledge wider and deeper?

Is what you know something that you can feel? In mystical traditions, from Kabbalah to Christianity as practiced by Saint Teresa to Zen Buddhism and yoga, the divine is experienced directly. And guess what? The divine is often experienced through a form of meditation. Some people would even say that, although mystical truth can be contemplated in meditation, it can never be fully understood by the human mind because of its divine nature.

In Judaic thought, Shekinah (or the Shekinah) is the manifestation of divine presence on earth. She is also referred to as Divine Grace, Holy Spirit, or the Tree of Life. Unlike God, who, in the Jewish tradition, is a limitless Being and thus cannot be described, Shekinah is tangible; she can be seen and heard. She is the aspect of God that dwells among people. She represents pure compassion, and has been described as a beautiful being of light. A few scholars argue that the Shekinah is a concept and is neither male nor female. Others point out that the language of the Talmud clearly indicates that Shekinah is female. During biblical times, when the Israelites built the desert Tabernacle, Shekinah came to live within it. The Shekinah is said to dwell wherever 10 people are assembled. Like God's servant, the sun, she shines all over the world. She is the Divine Light inside the human heart. Shekinah is seen to comfort the sick and to aid repentant sinners. She can also, when necessary, bring death, an end to suffering.

In one story, because Moses was so pure, the Angel of Death could not come for him. So, Shekinah kissed Moses to release his soul and carried his body on a long journey to his secret burial place. In the Kabbalah, a mystical Judaic text, Shekinah and the feminine aspects of God are further elaborated. There is even a system of meditation based on the Tree of Life that will help you feel more connected to her. Because Shekinah's name is transliterated from Hebrew, there are a number of different English spellings, including Shekhina, Shechina, Shechinah, and Shekina.

How do you deal with things that you don't understand? Do you hunt down answers and explanations until you "get" it, whatever it is? Do you pound your head in frustration? Or do you figure that you pretty much know what you need to know and if you need to learn something new, you will when the right time comes? When you think about sitting down in meditation, does it feel as if you would be facing a big mystery? It's difficult to put the experience of meditation into words, partially because everyone's experience is different and partially because the experience can transcend words. So, why not try a little transcendence? Look into your own mystery, breathe, see the Divine Light inside your heart, and discover your Goddess within. Talk to her, ask her to talk to you, and be still so you can listen for her loving response.

 The unknown is the largest need of the intellect.

—Emily Dickinson, poet (1894)

Exercise #1: Mala Meditation

Why not try making your own set of mala meditation beads? A mala has 108, 54, or 27 beads plus one larger bead known as the guru bead, from which hangs a tassel of string. The numbers 108, 54, and 27 are considered auspicious because they are all multiples of 9 and thus break down, from a numerological point of view, to 9, which is the number of completion. You can use plastic pony beads, wooden beads, glass, semi-precious stones, or any material that resonates for you (craft stores sell a wide selection of beads). Your mala becomes a precious representation of your commitment to your meditation practice, and to an experience of your inner Goddess. Keep it on your Goddess altar, or carry it with you!

You will need the following:

- 108, 54, or 27 beads
- One guru bead, slightly larger than the other beads
- String or silk cord
- A paper clip or toothpick
- Clear glue or fingernail polish

Make sure that the beads you select for your mala are large enough for you to handle comfortably. When you use them in meditation, you will count each one between a thumb and finger. Avoid beads that are too tiny, such as seed beads, which will probably give you hand cramps.

Tie one end of your string around the paper clip or toothpick, which will act as a bead holder to keep your beads from getting away. String all your beads onto the other end. When you have strung them all, add the guru bead.

Carefully untie the cord from your bead holder. Slide that end of the string through the guru bead, too, so that both ends of the string point in the same direction. About ¼ inch from the guru bead, take both loose ends of the string together and tie them in an overhand knot.

Check to make sure there is enough room on your string for the beads to move slightly. A little play in the string will make counting your beads easier. If the beads feel too tight, adjust your knot so that there is more room for the beads to move. When it feels right to you, secure your knot and add a drop of glue or nail polish to make sure it holds. Now your customized mala is ready for use!

Before you start to chant, hold the guru bead between your fingers and take a few centering breaths. When you're ready, start chanting. After each repetition, count off another bead with your thumb. After a while, your chant will start to push all the worries and debris out of your head. You may start to feel a delicious peace and sense of space inside your body. That calmness is inside you. Be present with it and melt into it. That feeling of stillness and well-being is part of your Goddess-self. You can come here and experience it any time you choose. Meditation is the key.

 Instant Goddess

Writer Joyce Carol Oates says, "In love there are two things—bodies and words." Close your eyes, take a deep breath in, hug yourself, and breathe out. Love! Om! The universe! Spirit! Goddess! You!

Exercise #2: Walk for Peace

Okay, sitting still to meditate is a challenge. The good news for you restless types is that you can practice walking meditation. There are many different kinds of walking meditation. You can walk indoors—around your altar, around a room, or up and down a corridor. You can walk outdoors in a park, garden, along a city street, through a meadow, or down a forest trail. Some people even walk in specially designed labyrinths. A meditative labyrinth, like the medieval one on the floor of Chartres Cathedral in France (shown in the following illustration), has one circuitous path that leads to the center. Your route to the labyrinth's center is like a miniature version of the journey Saint Teresa described. You move through the mansions, or dwelling places, of your spiritual castle toward your own inner Goddess.

When you walk as meditation, you will want to walk with awareness. Some do this by walking slowly—taking one step per each inhale/exhale combination. That's pretty slow! Get up right now and try walking around your chair, taking one step with each full cycle of your breath.

How was it for you? Perhaps a little too slow? Try taking two steps for each inhalation and two for each exhalation or try four steps with each part of your breathing cycle.

If you can, take a walk outside at that pace, or even a little faster. Feel your feet touch the ground. Notice the colors of all the things that you pass by. Listen to the sounds of nature or the city or the combination of both. Smell the air. What do you notice? Feel the breeze on your skin. Is it cool or warm? Dry or moist? Try to walk and be mindful of every sensation for 20 minutes.

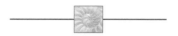

Does your mind feel as if it's had a workout? Do you feel refreshed? Or are you tired? Did you have fun doing the exercises in this chapter? Do you feel as if you have moved further along your Goddess path? Know that you have. You have learned about the inspiration of the Muses and how to access that power. You have met Saint Teresa, the great Christian mystic, and toured your own soul. Through Ennoia, the Goddess of thought and knowledge, you have learned that you can master your thoughts, and in reading about Shekinah, the divine light that dwells in your heart, you have discovered the joys and mysteries of mysticism.

In the next chapter, you will have the opportunity to further celebrate your mind. You will take a look at what you know in the form of your inner wisdom. In the process, you will hear the story of Athena, the Greek Goddess of wisdom, and Arachne, the weaver. You will meet the women from Shakespeare's plays and learn about their identities. You'll also come face to face with the High Priestess from the Tarot deck, the archetypal key to your intuition and psychic abilities, and Morgan Le Fay, the enchantress from the British Isles.

Chapter 12

Knowing: Your Inner Wisdom

As you are certainly aware, there are many kinds of knowledge and many different ways to learn. Do you excel at book learning? Or do you learn best from experience? Perhaps you prefer a combination of the two.

Do you feel that all of your accumulated knowledge has added up to wisdom? How would you define wisdom? Perhaps you see wisdom as belonging to someone else. Maybe you see wisdom as the provenance of the elderly, and you feel you're too young to yet possess it. Or is wisdom something that only the Goddesses control? Consider that you, too, hold wisdom, and that your wisdom is as unique and personal as your own budding inner Goddess.

Web of Ambition

You know, you are one smart cookie. Otherwise you would not be reading this book! Are you comfortable with your intelligence? Do you feel that you should be smarter? And how do you feel about your skills and education? Are you always working to improve? Do you rest on your laurels, or do you like to show off your knowledge and skills just a little?

Arachne, whom some describe as an ancient Greek Goddess associated with weaving, and whom others consider a mere mortal, was known throughout the land as a remarkably skillful weaver. She was so good at her craft and moved at her loom with such grace and speed that people came from miles around to watch her work. Such was Arachne's talent that even the nymphs of the forest stopped by to watch her work. Arachne enjoyed the attention that her weaving brought her, and she was rightfully proud of her work. One day, a member of Arachne's audience proclaimed that Arachne must have derived her skills from none other than the great Athena, who, in addition to being a warrior Goddess and the patron of the city of Athens, embodied wisdom and the arts, particularly the art of weaving. All the attention must have gone to Arachne's head because she sniffed and muttered that she could outweave anyone, even Athena.

Athena heard about Arachne's arrogance and, disguised as an old woman, went to watch her at work. Stooping as if with infirmity, Athena warned Arachne to be careful lest she offend the Goddess. The warning only egged Arachne on; she declared that she would test her skills against Athena's own. At that, Athena dropped her disguise. The rest of Arachne's audience, the nymphs included, drew back in fear. Arachne blanched, but stood her ground, and the contest was on.

Athena went to work on a wall hanging depicting her victory over Poseidon, God of the sea, for the city of Athens. Her weaving, of course, was exquisite. Arachne chose Athena's father, Zeus, as her subject. More specifically, she chose to portray Zeus's misdeeds—he was a terrible womanizer—with mortals. The beauty with which she rendered the scenes caused the onlookers to catch their breaths. Some say that Athena worked just slightly faster than Arachne and finished her work first. Others claim that the two competitors completed their work at the same time.

Looking over Arachne's shoulder, Athena, the great Goddess of wisdom, was infuriated by her rival's choice of subject matter. She snatched Arachne's shuttle from her hand, rent the weaving into many pieces, and struck Arachne on the brow. The blow from the Goddess's hand caused an overwhelming shame and guilt to well up inside Arachne. She fashioned a noose braided from her strongest threads, and hung herself. When Athena saw what had become of her rival, she was moved to pity. She sprinkled Arachne's body with a brew made from aconite, and almost immediately, Arachne's body began to stir with life. Her fingers grew longer and turned into legs; her head shrank and morphed until she was transformed into a spider. And from that day forward, Arachne, whose name in Greek means "spider," and her descendents have continued to weave the most delicate and beautiful of webs.

Just as you can with characters in many stories, you can look at Athena and Arachne as two aspects of one being. Arachne, with her arrogance and defiance, is the shadow side of Athena, who usually embodies the calm strength of wisdom. When Athena engages in competition with her shadow, she stoops to her level, and violence ensues. The story of Athena and Arachne can serve as a reminder that you want to achieve a balance between pride and humility, and that on your spiritual journey there is always more to learn.

Would you have challenged Athena? What if you knew that your weaving abilities were the absolute best in the entire world? You read about athletic competition in the story of Atalanta in Chapter 6. But how do you feel about competition involving your skills and knowledge? Are you a killer Scrabble player? Do you slay the competition around the card table? Or do you deal with competition by refusing to play the game? Maybe you are competitive about your craft skills or artistic abilities. Or are you more one for history, scientific fact, and general knowledge? Do you show off what you know or do you keep it to yourself? Do you ever act as if you know less and are less intelligent than you actually are? Even today, many women feel pressure, in certain circumstances, to hide their intelligence, education, and knowledge from others. In an editorial on career women, marriage, and fertility, Maureen Dowd cited women students at Harvard Business School, who told the columnist that they are often reluctant to tell men they are dating that they are graduate students at Harvard. Many men, it seems, are not drawn to smart, educated women! Of course, a man with a Harvard Business School degree is seen as a "great catch." His level of knowledge and education acts as a magnet to draw mates to him. For women, though, this high level of education is seen to drive men away.

This oddly negative impact of education on women's lives can be measured much more quantitatively as well. In her Pulitzer Prize–winning book *Woman: An Intimate Geography* (Anchor, 1999), Natalie Angier cites a study by Virginia Valian, a professor of psychology at Hunter College, in which Valian found that in the United States, although a man with a Bachelor's degree earns $28,000 more per year than a man without such a degree, a woman with a B.A. earns just $9,000 more per year than a woman without. In addition, a man with a degree from a high-prestige college earns $11,500 more per year than a man with a degree from a less-respected school, and a woman with a degree from a top-flight school earns $2,400 *less* than a woman with a degree from a less prestigious school. Is it any wonder that some women feel compelled to hide what they know!

> **❝** Knowledge is happiness, because to have knowledge—broad, deep knowledge—is to know true ends from false, and lofty things from low. To know the thoughts and deeds that have marked man's progress is to feel the great heart-throbs of humanity through the centuries; and if one does not feel in these pulsations a heavenward striving, one must indeed be deaf to the harmonies of life.
>
> —Helen Keller, author, lecturer (1903) **❞**

Do you hide your knowledge and intelligence from men? Have you ever done so? How does doing that make you feel? Do you feel that it's safe to show your real intelligence to other women? Do you compete with other women in this arena? Of course, there's nothing wrong with showing off your smarts a bit. You have a right to feel proud of all your abilities. Take a tip from Arachne, though, avoid challenging Athena and seek balance in your self-expression. Vicious rivalry between adults is no more attractive than the squabbles that break out between siblings. When you really know yourself, you can express your identity through your integrity rather than through squelching other people. Most great athletes say that they compete only with themselves. They work to increase their strength, stamina, and skill to better their own records. When they step out to compete, they know that the results will speak for them.

Is All the World a Stage?

Arachne knew that she was a great, and maybe even the greatest, weaver. But Athena knew her intrinsic power could overcome any threat to her greatness. Do you know who you *really* are, or just who you pretend to be? Part of your inner knowing is having an understanding of your own identity. Identity can be complicated. You play many roles in life, and sometimes they may seem to conflict with one another. There may be times in your life when it will seem impossible to be both a good employee and a good mother, a good daughter and a good life-partner, a good friend and a good sibling. The conflict of roles can sometimes lead you to question. These questions and their answers can partially define who you are. Are you someone who puts family first, or is career more important to you? Or are they both equally important? Questions such as these often form the basis of theatrical dramas. Sometimes studying a character in a play (or a book) can help you to shed some light on your own conflicting roles.

"But soft, what light through yonder
window breaks? It is the east, and Juliet
is the sun."

So says Romeo of his Juliet, although they have only
just met. *Romeo and Juliet* is probably the most famous
love story in Western culture, and Juliet is the archetypal
young woman in love. She is also a girl just coming into
her own identity as a woman. You have heard the story
of Romeo and Juliet, but do you really know it?

Tragically, Juliet's family, the Capulets, have been involved in a feud with
Romeo's family, the Montagues, for years. Because the young men of the families keep getting into fights on the street, the Prince of Verona has declared
that anyone caught fighting will be exiled from the city. Paris, a relative of the
Prince, asks Juliet's father if he can marry her even though they do not know
each other. Juliet's father says that she is too young to marry, but if Paris will
wait two years, they can perhaps work something out. He invites Paris to a
party he is hosting, in the hopes that Juliet will fall for him. Juliet, who is 13,
the age that many women of her era wed, has not thought about marriage,
but promises to consider Paris as a possible partner.

At the party, which Romeo and his cousin Benvolio crash, Romeo and
Juliet meet for the first time. Without even knowing each other's names, they
fall instantly in love, and they kiss. Unfortunately, Juliet's cousin has recognized that Romeo is a Montague and thus an enemy. When Juliet learns that
Romeo is a Montague, she is distraught. Leaving the party, Romeo sneaks
back toward the house to catch a glimpse of Juliet in her bedroom. She
appears at her window, and Romeo compares her beautiful radiance to the
sun. It is here that Juliet says, "O Romeo, Romeo! Wherefore art thou
Romeo?" She goes on, "O, be some other name! What's in a name?" She
wishes that Romeo was not a Montague and suggests that she will trade herself if he will give up his name and his identity as an enemy of her family. She
knows that she cannot remain a member of the Capulet family and love a
Montague. Although they have just met that evening, they agree to be wed.

The next day, Juliet meets Romeo at the friar's house and they are secretly
married. When Romeo kills Juliet's cousin, who had challenged him to a duel
he did not want to fight, the Prince exiles Romeo from Verona. The friar
makes arrangements for Romeo to see Juliet and consummate their marriage
the night before he is sent into exile. They spend the night together and part
tenderly, not knowing when they will meet again. As soon as Romeo leaves
Juliet's room, Juliet's mother arrives to announce that everything is set for
Juliet to marry Paris. Juliet hurries to the friar's house, and he comes up with
a plan. Juliet will drink a potion and appear to be dead. Because her family

thinks that she is dead, she will be free of her Capulet identity and will be able to run away with Romeo. According to plan, Juliet drinks the potion. Her family believes that she is dead and goes into mourning. The only hitch is that the friar has not told Romeo about the plan, so he also thinks that Juliet is dead. Romeo decides to kill himself and drinks poison at her tomb. Juliet wakes up from the potion, sees the dead Romeo beside her, plunges his dagger into her own chest, and dies.

Poor Juliet! If it were not for Juliet's identity as a Capulet and Romeo's status as a Montague, their story, in all likelihood, would not have ended in tragedy. Did you see the 1998 movie *Shakespeare in Love*, which contains Gwyneth Paltrow's Academy Award winning performance? Remember how her character, Viola De Lesseps, has to pretend to be a boy so that she can act in *Romeo and Juliet?* Disguised as a boy, Viola rehearses the part of Romeo in the play. Playing opposite to her as Juliet is a boy dressed as a girl. All this cross-dressing, of course, leads to confusion much the way it does in Shakespeare's comedies. The theme of mistaken identity is a staple of the comedies. In cross-dressing and acting the role of a man, some of the women in Shakespeare learn about their true identities as women.

66 I am because my little dog knows me.

—Gertrude Stein, writer (1936) 99

In fact, many of Shakespeare's women, both in the comedies and in tragedies, such as *Romeo and Juliet*, have identity questions, and in the course of their respective plays, they learn about themselves and the audience learns, too. For example, when Lady Macbeth finds out that the king, whom she plans to murder, is coming to spend the night at her castle, she descries her own identity as a woman and as a person with feelings. "Come, you spirits/That tend on mortal thoughts, unsex me here/And fill me, from the crown to the toe, top-full/Of direst cruelty!" Her question is, Can I play this murderous game of politics? She does commit the murder, but then she goes mad. So, ultimately, although she performs the murderous act, the answer to her question is no. She is not capable of playing the vicious and deadly political game of her era.

Shakespeare's heroines! What a collection of awesome Goddesses—from the pure, young love of Juliet cut short in full flower to the frightening ambition of Lady Macbeth, from Cleopatra's mature flirtatiousness and shrewd queenship to Desdemona's bawdy tongue and fatal innocence, from Titania's enchanted love of a beast to Viola's frustrated, but ultimately satisfied, love for Orsino. Here's a quick rundown of some of Shakespeare's women and their questions of identity.

Heroine	Play	I.D. Question
Lady Macbeth	*Macbeth*	Am I someone who can play the murderous game of politics or not?
Cleopatra	*Antony and Cleopatra*	Am I a woman in love, a skilled manipulator, or both?
Rosalind	*As You Like It*	Am I an emotional, feeling being or is love just a game for me?
Titania	*A Midsummer Night's Dream*	Am I powerful, proud, and in control, or am I loving and passionate? Can I be both powerful and loving?
Cordelia	*King Lear*	Do I become hardened and evil as my sisters have or do I remain loving and true despite being sent into exile by my father?
Desdemona	*Othello*	Can I be sexually aggressive and self-assertive and retain my good reputation?
Ophelia	*Hamlet*	Can I choose between a daughter's duty, a sister's loyalty, and a lover's affection?
Gertrude	*Hamlet*	Can I choose between the memory of a husband's love and his faded power, his brother's caress and the crown it comes with, and a son's anguished devotion?
Viola		Am I lovable the way I am for the real me or must I hide behind my wit and a disguise?

If you were a Shakespeare Goddess, what would your identity question be? Do you face love forbidden by your family, as Juliet did? Are your ambitions butting up against your sense of what is right and good the way these two forces clashed for Lady Macbeth? Do you, like Cordelia, feel that you have to choose between being a good daughter and being honest and truthful? Or are you more like Cleopatra, whose character was based on the real-life historical Queen of Egypt (reigned 51–49 B.C.E. and then again 48–30 B.C.E.) and a love Goddess in her own right? Cleopatra, it is said, wrapped herself in a beautiful tapestry, unrolled at Caesar's feet—power and beauty in one queenly gesture. If you have never seen the 1963 film version of Cleopatra's story, starring screen Goddess Elizabeth Taylor, check it out and see which aspects of your Goddess she releases.

Look Through the Veil

Have you ever had a sudden flash of insight? From out of the blue, you instantly understand something that previously you did not. "Ah-ha," you say, "*now* I get it!" Where do those flashes of understanding come from? Sometimes it seems that something in your brain just suddenly clicks. Other times you may feel that you just mysteriously know who is on the other end when the phone rings. You may think of this kind of knowledge as coming from your gut, or you may call it your sixth sense or intuition. Do you have a strong sense of your own intuition? You probably have flashes of intuition at least some of the time. With a little attention, you can cultivate this quality of knowing in yourself and learn to use it every day.

You probably trust and act on your intuition at least some of the time. For example, on a given day you may just know that you will be better off avoiding the highway and taking your back route home from work. Halfway home, you turn on the radio only to hear that there is a nasty traffic jam on the highway! Or perhaps you've had a strong feeling all day that you're going to run into your friend Joan. You go to the grocery store, and there she is. Events like these can seem like weird coincidences, or they can seem that they were meant to be and are examples of pure synchronicity.

The High Priestess represents the balance between logic and spirit. She is a scientist of the emotions. She tells you to pay attention not just to your rational knowledge, but to your subconscious knowledge, your intuitive awareness, and all things secret and mysterious. She embodies the pull and balance of apparently opposed forces—black versus white, visible versus invisible, secret versus known, sun versus moon, inside versus outside. You can strengthen your powers of intuition by balancing your sixth chakra, the seat of vision and imagination (there's more about the chakras in Chapter 6). The High Priestess is the Wise Woman, and she reminds you that you are, too!

The High Priestess is the second Major Arcana card in the Tarot deck. She represents your intuition, instincts, and hidden talents. She is frequently depicted seated between two pillars—a black one, inscribed with the letter B, and a white one, bearing a J. Behind her, a screen or veil decorated with palm fronds and pomegranates hides the inside of the temple and the unknown. Some have suggested that the area behind the screen represents the subconscious, and others see it as the collective unconscious. In her lap, only half visible, rests the Torah of Divine Law, the representation of truth. She wears a solar cross, a symbol for the power of the sun, on her chest. A crescent moon rests at her feet, and on her head she wears a horned diadem with either a full moon or a globe in the center.

The High Priestess, poised on the threshold of the temple, represents the doorway between the ordinary, mundane world and the unseen world of energy, dreams, and spirit. On the journey of the Tarot, she is the origin of connection to your higher self. She is your psychic self, and she is you—open to and in tune with your own inner Goddess. She is associated with the moon and the development of your sixth sense. She is Glinda, the Good Witch, from *The Wizard of Oz*, and she tells you to trust yourself and your gut reactions. She is Persephone returned from the land of the dead. She is the mystic Oracle at Delphi, a priestess who sat on a three-legged stool over a vaporous spring and foretold the future. She is also associated with the Virgin Mary and with Shekinah. In a Tarot reading, the High Priestess card reminds you that you have the ability to look beneath the surface of the situations in your life and discern the truth of what is really happening.

> 66 One of the many sad results of the Industrial Revolution was that we came to depend more than ever on the intellect, and to ignore the intuition with its symbolic thinking.
>
> —Madeleine L'Engle, writer (1980)

A Good Witch or a Bad Witch

There are many different types of Wise Woman—from the High Priestess to your fourth-grade teacher (she was a Goddess, wasn't she?) to actress Shirley MacLaine and Billie Burke as Glinda the Good Witch of the North. Sometimes, though, women with certain types of specialized knowledge are seen in a less favorable light. During various times in history, wise women have been deemed evil, called sorceresses, and sometimes even been killed because of the knowledge they had.

If you're a fan of tales about King Arthur and the Round Table, then you have probably heard of Morgan Le Fay. A Goddess from England and Wales, she is associated with water, magic, and healing. Some scholars believe that she was originally a sea goddess who, over time, transformed in the popular imagination into a sorceress. Some say that she has been confused with Mórrígán or Morrigu, the three-part Celtic Great Queen and Goddess of war. Others claim that she has been confused with Morgause, the Celtic Goddess of the moon. And still others believe that she originally was the Goddess Modron, who presides over health, healing, and medicinal plants and is married to the God of the underworld.

In Arthurian legend, Morgan Le Fay is the queen of Avalon, an island in the western sea on which she dwells with her eight sisters. She possesses specialized knowledge of medicinal plants and healing. Some consider her knowledge to be magical. She may have learned her skills in a convent, or she may have been taught by Merlin, the wizard. In some versions of her story, Morgan is King Arthur's half-sister and his enemy. Despite the conflicts of their relationship and a number of incidents in which Morgan seems to be trying to get Arthur killed, she takes him, after his last battle, to her home on Avalon where she uses her special skills and heals him. Sometimes Morgan goes by the name Morgana or Fata Morgana, which is also the name given to a mirage, particularly one that appears off the coast of Sicily, which was thought to be caused by her magic.

Morgan Le Fay may have gotten her nasty reputation from medieval monks who did not understand that women with knowledge of healing, which often was considered magical, were not practicing the "dark arts." Many scholars believe that the Catholic Church made a concerted effort to stamp out any vestiges of folk beliefs, including healing traditions, by telling people that their old practices, Goddesses, and fairies were evil. Some scholars even argue that the rise of a class of professional medical practitioners and their desire to increase their patient base helped to fuel witchcraft hysteria and led to the murder of thousands of women healers.

In North America, during the last 25 or 30 years, there has been a huge upsurge of interest in the traditional healing arts. People have been studying herbalism, going for acupuncture treatments, and practicing reiki and other healing modalities that work on the energetic level. Learning about natural medicine and other modes of healing—from Bach Flower Remedies to foot reflexology to ayurveda, the ancient Hindu science of healing—can be both empowering and fun.

Nationwide, common medicinal herbs, such as Echinacea, have gained huge popularity; supplies at health-food stores often sell out, especially during the cold season. Susun S. Weed, a popular author, wise woman, and green witch, has written the *Wise Woman Herbal Series,* five volumes of helpful, practical, and easy-to-use information on herbal medicine for women. Why not gain some more special knowledge and look for one of her titles? Or check out your local health-food store for classes in herbalism or the healing science of your choice. Morgan Le Fay says explore and learn. Possess and study any knowledge that feels right for you. Feel the healing power of the Goddess within you, and use your power, be it magical or mundane, to heal the earth and all of its creatures.

66 Why not walk in the aura of magic that gives to the small things of life their uniqueness and importance? Why not befriend a toad today?

—Germaine Greer, feminist, writer (1991) 99

Exercise #1: Six Senses

Here is an exercise in creative visualization that will help to balance your sixth chakra and open you up to imagination, vision, and all of your six senses. The sixth chakra, which is also known as the Third Eye, is located on your forehead between your eyebrows.

First, pour yourself a glass of water. Dehydration can constrict the sixth chakra and make it hard for you to visualize or use your imagination. Imagine, as you drink the water, that it has been drawn from the

Fountain of Wisdom. It is filling you with the swirling violet light of insight. Close your eyes. See the light centering and focusing at your Third Eye. Are you breathing? Keep breathing! Imagine this orb of violet light spinning and pulsing.

When you have the violet spinning energy of your sixth chakra clear in your mind's eye, imagine that you see someone or something you love inside it. You could imagine your partner, your child, your pet, or a tree. Try to see all the details and feel your connection to the image. Spend as much time looking at the image as you like. Love is timeless. When you feel done, let the image go. Imagine the swirling violet energy of your sixth chakra again, and open your eyes.

Take out your Goddess journal and write about your experience. Do you feel that you gained any new insight from looking at your vision? With regular practice, your sixth chakra will become more open and your ability to visualize will expand with Goddess strength and power.

Instant Goddess

All women need, postulates Virginia Woolf in her book, *A Room of One's Own*, is an independent income and a space to create—and, perhaps, time to grow. What do *you* need to fulfill your ambitions? Read Woolf's book, or another book by a woman who explores women's potential, such as Eleanor Roosevelt's *You Learn by Living*.

Exercise #2: Guidance from the Great Beyond

Psychics, mystics, and visionaries throughout history have used a variety of different tools to help them get in touch with information from the unseen realm—from Tarot cards to crystal balls; from the *I Ching*, an ancient Chinese book that describes a system of 64 different life situations to Ouija boards; from runes, ancient Northern European alphabets, to the flight patterns of birds. Carl Jung, the great pioneer of human psychology who described the archetypes, studied many of these tools and found that they can help you connect with the collective unconscious.

A pendulum is a fun means of exploring guidance from the other side. You can use your pendulum to answer yes or no questions. You can make this simple tool at home.

You will need the following:

- Thread
- Scissors

- A small object to act as a weight (such as a ring or other piece of jewelry, a fishing weight, a crystal, or a piece of hardware)
- A piece of heavy paper or cardboard
- A pen
- A ruler or straight edge

Cut about 10 inches of thread. String the weight onto your length of thread. Secure it with a knot.

Now make an answer sheet for your pendulum. Draw a dot in the center of the paper. This dot will represent your neutral starting point. Draw one line through the dot that is parallel to the bottom edge of the paper. Draw the other line so that it is parallel to the paper's sides.

Decide which of your lines will represent "yes" and which will mean "no." Mark the answers on the sheet. If you want, you can draw in diagonal lines to stand for "maybe" and "wait for your answer."

To use your pendulum, place your answer sheet on a table. Hold your pendulum's thread between the thumb and forefinger of one hand and rest your elbow on the table. Allow the weight of the pendulum to swing freely. (If it hits the surface of the table, pull the thread up a bit.) Let the weight hang directly over the neutral center point on your answer sheet.

Now you're ready to ask your pendulum a question. Start with something easy. "Should I wear my new jacket tomorrow?" you may ask. At first it may seem that your pendulum does not move at all, but after a while you will see it start to sway along your "yes" axis or along the one for "no."

As you become more comfortable with using your pendulum, you can ask more difficult or emotionally charged questions. Remember to phrase what you want to know as a yes-or-no question. And don't ask questions that you don't want to have answered! When you're not using it, keep your pendulum on your altar so that it can soak up Goddess energy.

Does a pendulum really connect you to a higher power or a source of wisdom outside of yourself? Some people would argue that the answers you get from a pendulum merely reflect your subconscious knowledge or desires because, without being aware of it, you must be manipulating the pendulum to give yourself the "right" answers. The answers that you get from your pendulum could very well represent your subconscious, but your subconscious contains inner wisdom. Don't you want access to as much of your own Goddess-like knowledge as you can get? Could some of your knowledge come to you from another plane? Shall we see what your pendulum has to say about that?

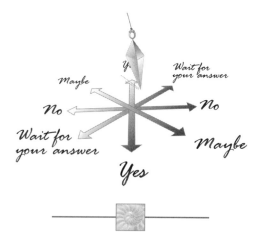

These exercises have helped to link you to your own Goddess wisdom. Can you feel it? You now have the knowledge of Athena and understand the lesson of Arachne and the grace to know how best to use your knowledge. You possess the self-understanding necessary for a Shakespearean heroine and can act your many roles with skill. Like the High Priestess, you balance scientific fact with your intuition, and you can see below the surface of people and events to understand the real truth. And like Morgan Le Fay, you contain healing magic, your own special brand of Goddess wisdom.

With all of your newly felt wisdom, you're ready to move on to the next chapter, where you will be poised to put your wisdom into action. By looking at the Tarot's World card, you will learn about your role on earth. You will meet Gaia, the original Earth Mother and supreme power. In addition, you will enjoy an encounter with Oshun, the Yoruba Goddess who represents the essence of pure joy. And you will feel the compassion of Kwan Yin, the Goddess of mercy in several Asian countries, who chose to remain on earth after reaching enlightenment to help others to attain that blissful state.

Chapter 13

Action: Help Make the World a Better Place

Of course, you want to help make the world a better place. You want life to continue. You want your children, if you have them (or the world's children, if you don't), to be able to grow up on a planet that is free of war, crime, pestilence, and pollution. You may feel that the list of things that you simply must do is so long. How can you ever find the time, between buying food, folding the laundry, and going to work, to create world peace?

It's hard to remember, as you go about your busy day, that all your actions, no matter how small, have consequences, and that you—yes, even you—can have an impact on the entire earth by the choices that you make in your daily life. When you align your actions with the good of the planet, you feel more in touch with the earth and all of her creatures. This feeling of connection helps to release your inner Goddess. In addition, when you act for the good of the earth, you are behaving like a Goddess. And acting like a Goddess will make you feel like a Goddess, too!

Journey's End

Do you remember your high school graduation? How did you feel? Were you proud, excited, or a little scared and sad? You probably experienced a combination of all these feelings. Finishing school, of course, is an end, but it's also a new beginning. At the moment of graduation, you celebrate the knowledge you have attained, but you also step off onto a new path, one in which you get to use all your knowledge, skills, and abilities—the journey of your life.

The World is the last Major Arcana card in the Tarot deck. It represents attainment, integration of life-lessons, and self-actualization. The center of the World card depicts a maiden dancing. She carries with her two wands that represent her connection to all of the lessons she has learned while on her path to her present happy position in life. She dances with joy. She feels her wholeness and understands her place in the universe. She has achieved the highest level of success—self-actualization and spiritual knowing. She is liberated from petty concerns and self-doubt and is ready to apply her knowledge and global awareness in service. She is also ready to begin again on a new path of learning and discovery.

In pop-culture terms, she is like Dorothy in *The Wizard of Oz*, after she has returned to Kansas from her adventures in Oz with a newfound sense of strength, courage, and mental clarity. The dancer in the center of the World card is flanked by representations of four Zodiac signs, one from each season of the year—an angel for the winter sign of Aquarius, an eagle for the fall sign Scorpio, a lion for the summer sign of Leo, and a bull for the spring sign of Taurus. In a Tarot card reading, the World card appears to tell you that you have all the talents and tools that you need. You can move ahead, teach others, travel, or start on a new path of further self-discovery.

The Major Arcana cards of the Tarot represent your journey from the innocence of the Fool through the High Priestess, the Empress, the Star, and culminating in the World. The World card says, "The world is now your oyster!" Can you feel the message of the World card? Do you sense and acknowledge all of your attainments? How do you feel now that you have read this book, done the exercises, and traveled along the path to release and accept your inner Goddess? You may want to get out your Goddess journal and reread some of your early entries so that you can see where you were then and compare that space to where you find yourself now.

Have you ever imagined what it would be like to be Dorothy in *The Wizard of Oz?* In a sense, you *are* Dorothy. At some point in your life, you leave home or life as you know it and set off on your life's adventure. As you travel the yellow brick road of your life, your experiences help to destroy your illusions. Like Dorothy, you probably started your journey thinking of yourself as "small and meek." As you travel, though, you learn that you are strong. When you use the Tarot, you are guided on your journey by the archetypes mapped out by the Major Arcana cards. Ultimately, you learn, as Dorothy did, that you have the resources to reach home, that you contain happiness, strength, and love in your own heart. Have you ever imagined what Dorothy's life would be like after she has returned to Kansas with all of her newfound wisdom? When you reach the end of your own yellow brick road, you will continue to learn and you will begin to teach your truth to others. What are you learning right now? How will you celebrate coming home to your heart and discovering your Goddess within? Will you dance for joy in your ruby slippers?

66 Spiritual energy brings compassion into the real world. With compassion, we see benevolently our own human condition and the condition of our fellow beings. We drop prejudice. We withhold judgment.

—Christina Baldwin, teacher and writer (1990) 99

Mother of Us All

Where did human beings come from? How would you answer this question? If you have children, you may have already been asked. If you have young children, you may want to prepare for the future by thinking about your answer. And what about these: How was the earth formed? And where are we, as a species, going in the future? These are questions that people have asked for thousands of years. Perhaps the story of one of the Goddesses can help to bring some illumination.

While the antics of Gaia and her family sound hellish and dysfunctional, the story does bear a message. You can look at this story as one of transformation. When the masculine aspect threatens to stop the force of life, Gaia, the feminine Earth Mother, cuts off that masculine drive and transmutes it into life-giving love in the form of Aphrodite. Some people see the masculine drive as one that attempts to dominate and control nature. The subjugation of nature can lead to the destruction of many life forms. Some people believe that our present environmental crisis is due to this dominating effect of the masculine drive. You've probably heard all kinds of dire predictions about the end of the world. Since the 1960s, writers, activists, and scientists have been sounding the alarm about the state of the world's environment—the hole in the ozone; global warming; the poisoning of our oceans, rivers, and streams; the dangerous level of pollutants in the air. Despite the earth's amazing abilities to renew herself, our throw-away, fossil fuel–burning society may have pushed her too far.

Gaia, or Gaea, is the ancient Greek Goddess of the earth. She is also the earth itself. After Nox, the Goddess of the night, laid the egg that hatched Love, Gaia and Uranus emerged from the eggshell. Some say that Gaia, like Nox, emerged from primordial chaos and gave birth to Uranus, the sky, so that he might cover her. Then she formed the mountains and the sea and all the physical features of earth's landscape.

Gaia and Uranus became the parents of a group of giants who each possessed 100 hands, the 3 one-eyed giants know as Cyclopes, and the 12 Titans—6 females and 6 males. Uranus was so horrified by the giants that were his children that he had them all locked up. Gaia then had her son Cronus, who was a Titan and the God of time, chop off Uranus's genitals and throw them into the ocean. Gaia then gave birth to the Furies, the Goddesses of vengeance. And Aphrodite, the Goddess of love, came into being from the Union of Uranus's severed parts with the sea.

Among Gaia's Titan children were also Mnemosyne, the Goddess of memory and mother of the Muses. Cronus, together with Rhea, another Titan who was considered to be both Mother Earth and mother of the Gods, became the parents of the Olympic deities Zeus, Hera, Demeter, Hestia, Hades, and Poseidon. Some classical scholars also consider Gaia to be the mother of the Three Fates and many other lesser-known deities. Gaia is a supreme being, a primordial deity, and the creator of life. In art, she is depicted as a mature woman, seated on a throne. She often holds fruits, grains, and vegetables spilling out of a cornucopia, which rests in her arms or on her lap.

Life scientist James Lovelock's Gaia theory postulates that the earth functions as a self-regulating organism—in essence, that the earth is, in a way, alive. He says: "I am, of course, prejudiced in favor of Gaia and have filled my life for the past 25 years with the thought that the earth might in certain ways be alive—not as the ancients saw her, a sentient goddess with purpose and foresight—more like a tree. A tree that exists, never moving except to sway in the wind, yet endlessly conversing with the sunlight and the soil. Using sunlight and water and nutrients to grow and change. But all done so imperceptibly that, to me, the old oak tree on the green is the same as it was when I was a child."

Because of the heavy load of pollutants that are already in the environment, now more than ever, everything that you do, whether you realize it or not, has an impact on others and on the earth herself. Like adult children of aging parents, we, as children of the earth, are now in a position where we have to take care of our mother. Do you love your Earth Mother? Do you do your part to protect her environment?

Do you participate in your community's recycling programs? Most all cities in North America now recycle to some extent, and you probably do, too. But do you buy goods made from recycled materials? In recent years, there has been a huge supply of material coming in to be recycled and, in the case of paper in particular, not enough of a demand for new recycled products. Next time you buy paper, why not look for paper with at least some recycled content? You can find recycled computer paper, drawing paper, and even toilet paper and paper towels. Recycling what you can of your office and household waste is important, but the circle is not complete unless you buy recycled products, too.

> **"** The "control of nature" is a phrase conceived in arrogance, born of the Neanderthal age of biology and philosophy, when it was supposed that nature exists for the convenience of man.
>
> —Rachel Carson, marine biologist and writer (1962) **"**

There are many other ways that you can help protect Gaia and her environment. Instead of driving to work or school alone every day, you could set up a carpool, which would conserve gas and pump less car exhaust into the air. If you just have a few quick errands to do, why not walk or bicycle to the store instead of driving? A short bicycle trip can also serve as a nice break during your busy day, and it's good exercise, too. And don't forget about public transportation. Sometimes taking the bus or train is easier than driving. You don't have to worry about parking or traffic and you can relax, read, or just look out the window while on your trip.

And what about your household water consumption? Have you installed low-flush toilets? If you live in an old house, the tanks on your toilets could hold almost 4 gallons of water. Water-use experts estimate that the average person in a home with old-style toilets flushes away 19.3 gallons of water per day. Those with low-flush toilets flush only 9.3 gallons per day. Multiply those gallons per day by the days in a month or a year, and you're talking about a lot of water! You may want to look into your flushing situation, especially if your household water bills are high.

How high is your electric bill? Have you done all you can to keep it down? Of course, you turn off the lights and the air conditioner when you're not home, but have you checked to make sure that all your appliances are running properly? Check your owner's manuals for proper maintenance procedures and make sure to follow the manufacturers' recommendations.

And what about those portable sources of energy—batteries? Do you dispose of used batteries properly? In some communities, dead batteries are picked up along with recycling or with hazardous wastes. In other areas, you are left to fend for yourself. Used batteries are extremely hazardous and must not be placed with your regular trash. Batteries contain acid and a whole range of poisonous heavy metals. They can also explode when exposed to flame. If your community does not have a regular means of collecting used batteries, find out where you can safely dispose of yours and make a commitment to Gaia to do that.

> All parts of the living body of the earth are linked. All things are interconnected, including the human and natural worlds.
>
> —Starhawk, spiritual teacher and writer (1989)

Another way we all make an impact on the environment is with our food choices. We talked about buying organic produce in Chapter 3, and how organic farming spares the consumer, the farmer, and the environment from hazardous weed-killers, fertilizers, and pesticides. Do you buy food grown locally? Besides being fresher and tastier, local food has not had to travel via truck and a fossil fuel–burning motor to get to you.

Do you eat a lot of meat? In her book *Diet for a Small Planet* (see Appendix B), Frances Moore Lappé makes a convincing case for both the ethical and environmental benefits of vegetarianism. Yes, you need to eat protein to live. But you can get that protein from nonanimal sources, which are less damaging to other beings and ecologically more efficient. As Lappé says, "it takes 16 pounds of grain and soy beans to produce just one pound of beef." So, instead of feeding four people with a pound of hamburger, imagine how many people you could feed on 16 pounds of rice and beans! Even if you feel that you cannot give up meat completely, cutting down on your meat consumption can help Gaia have enough to feed all her children.

O Joy!

Your world is made up of many things—the physical world of objects, other people, and places. And you have ideas, emotions, and a spirit, which you can feel and articulate, but you cannot always see. You have thought about ecology on the physical level, but what about an intellectual, emotional, and spiritual ecology? What would this kind of ecology look like? What would it feel like? Ecology is all about balance. So, in maintaining a spiritual ecology, you would want balance of thought, emotions, and spirit. What are your daily thoughts like? Can you improve them? And what about your emotions and your spirit? Do you have joy in your life? Try moving through one whole day observing your "joy quotient." Notice the nature of your thoughts and which emotions seem to predominate. Are your thoughts positive, neutral, or negative? Do your emotions feel heavy or light and buoyant? Let your inner Goddess help you release all negativity from past patterns. Let her help you to be joyous in thought, feeling, and action.

Oshun! O Joy! For that is what and who she is. But what is joy exactly? As Philip John Neimark, author of *The Way of the Orisa* (see Appendix B), writes, "True joy must come from the exaltation that we feel in recognizing the beauty and symbiotic relationship we have to our loved ones, our community, and the planet we live on." In other words, you are connected to your loved ones and your community. You are also connected to Mother Earth. And it is through the understanding and celebration of those connections that true joy comes. You will not find true joy by watching television, shopping for new clothes, buying a fancy car, or riding a roller coaster. While those experiences may give you pleasure, that joy doesn't last. You cannot buy true joy, but you can cultivate it, and causing it to grow in your life will help to make the world a more joyful place.

Oshun, from the Yoruba tradition of West Africa, is the essence of pure joy. She is the Goddess of love; fresh water, particularly that of the Oshun River; fertility; sensuality; and food. Some consider her to be associated with money, in the sense that prosperity can be an aid to happiness. Sometimes she is known as the Mother of Charity and is a healer, especially of the womb.

When personified, she is seen as a beautiful, seductive young woman. Alternatively, she can be a tall and dignified older woman. She is often accompanied by a peacock or a parrot. In some traditions, she is given honey, cinnamon, or pumpkins as offerings. In one story, Oshun wanted to learn to tell the future by reading divining shells. Only Obatala, the ancient creator deity, knew how to read the shells, and Obatala refused to teach her. One day Oshun was walking along the banks of the river when she happened to see Elegba, the trickster God, run off with Obatala's clothes. She continued her walk and came upon the angry Obatala standing in the waters of the river. Oshun told Obatala that she would help, but on one condition: She wanted to learn to read the shells. Obatala agreed, and Oshun set off for Elegba's house. A short while later she returned with Obatala's clothing. Obatala then taught Oshun the art of divination. As soon as Oshun had mastered her new skill, she taught it to all the other deities.

Do you recognize that we are all truly one? You may say, "Yeah, I know that." And you probably do, but do you *feel* it? Have you *ever* felt it? Perhaps you feel it some of the time. Your sense of connection and joy grows when you spend time with people you love, when you cook and share food with them, when you dance and sing and share your inner light. Of course, you can cultivate your joy on your own. Enjoying your own body, walking in nature, appreciating art or music— these are all experiences that can help your joy grow. Have you felt joy? Or maybe caught a glimpse of it? Joy comes when you make your art or garden or brush a child's hair, when you do the things you love. Joy is the fuel that propels you on your journey along the Goddess path.

That's why Goddesses dance. They dance their joy. It's not that they never feel bad, but Goddesses recognize that emotions are fleeting. One moment you may feel happy, the next disappointed or sad. The joyful

Goddess takes the sadness, the disappointment, or the anger, and celebrates it for what it is. The joyful Goddess says, "Wow, look at this amazing intense feeling! Isn't it wonderful to be alive and be able to feel?" Then the passing emotion is gone and a new one comes, but joy remains. And joy is contagious, so why not pass it on? Spread your joy by being an example. Walk (or dance!) your Goddess path. Encourage others to make their own journeys. Share what you know, and learn what you can from others.

> **66** Surely the strange beauty of the world must somewhere rest on pure joy!
>
> —Louise Bogan, poet (1953) **99**

Love and Kindness

You want to be a loving person. You want to feel that you are kind. Do you behave the way a kind and loving person does? Maybe you do some of the time and maybe not. If not, what gets in your way? Do you carry unresolved grief inside you that needs to be melted away with self-compassion? Can you decide to cultivate your own love and kindness? Have you ever tried to grow compassion? Why not start today?

You may not aspire to become a Bodhisattva, but your practice of some simple spiritual principles can help to make your world a better place. In your daily life, as you hurry from one place to the next, how do you greet the people you encounter? Are you friendly? Do you smile? And how do you feel inside? Are you actually smiling with gritted teeth and thinking that you really don't want to take the time to stop and talk to your neighbor because all she does is complain? And what about the people you don't know? You probably don't say hello, but what do you say in your heart? For example, you are pulling out of the parking lot of the grocery store. How do you respond to the cars that are whizzing by on the street? Do you curse them for being in your way? Or do you feel frightened by them? What is your voice inside saying to them? What would Kwan Yin (the Chinese Buddhist Goddess of mercy) say?

Do you realize that you are actually connected to your complaining neighbor and to the cars that zip past on the street? What if, like Kwan Yin, you greeted them with compassion? What if each and every time you encountered another living being, silently and to yourself, you wished that being well? Instead of thinking "Oh, no! I don't want to hear about how badly she slept last night," you might say to yourself: "May she be free from suffering." Or, "May she feel peace and happiness." Try doing this as an experiment for one entire day. See how it feels. See if looking through the lens of compassion alters your perceptions. In her book *Lovingkindness: The Revolutionary Art of Happiness* (see Appendix B), Sharon Salzberg explains how to cultivate your sense of compassion and how doing so can benefit you and the entire world.

Kwan Yin, the Chinese Buddhist Goddess of mercy, is also a fertility goddess, a protector of women, and a bringer of rain. She is the spirit of compassion. She is known as the Queen of Heaven, the Mother of Compassion, the Divine Voice of the Soul, the Melodious Voice, and "the one who hears the cries of the world." She is a Bodhisattva, a spiritually advanced individual who has achieved enlightenment and qualified for nirvana, but has chosen to remain in the world to assist those who have not yet reached that state. Just as Kwan Yin was offered the opportunity to step out of this world and all its suffering, she stepped back in, vowing to remain until she has assisted every being out of the world of suffering and into the bliss of enlightenment. As a Bodhisattva, Kwan Yin's essence is pure knowledge, and in the future, she may become a Buddha.

According to scholars, Kwan Yin has taken 33 or more forms. In Japan, she is known as Kannon, Kwannon, or Kwannung. In Korea, she is Kwanseieun. In China, she is also known as Kwan-she-yin and as Miao Shan, who was said to be the daughter of a king. When Miao Shan refused to marry because she wanted to devote herself to spiritual study, her father had her killed. In hell, she liberated a number of damned individuals. Then Buddha gave her a peach that granted her eternal life. Kwan Yin's name, when transcribed into English, can also be spelled Guanyin, Gwanyin, Kuan Yin, or Quan Yin. She is usually pictured sitting on a lotus blossom, dressed all in white. Sometimes she stands and holds a lotus in one hand. She may also carry a vase full of the dew of compassion. In some depictions, she holds a child as well, and in still other images, she rides a dragon. She can have two, four, six, or hundreds of arms. Childless women and newlyweds often appeal for her help in conceiving. In some traditions, she is associated with willow trees. Today she is honored throughout China and Japan and all over the world. She is also venerated in Vietnam and in many temples in various areas of the world, including Kuala Lumpur and Penang, Malaysia; Portland, Oregon, and San Jose, California; and in the provinces of British Columbia and Ontario, Canada. Her festival is celebrated on March 31.

> **❝** Cultivate the good. One can cultivate the good. If it were not possible, I would not ask you to do it. If this cultivation were to bring suffering, I would not ask you to do it. But as this cultivation brings benefits and happiness, I say, cultivate the good.
>
> —The Buddha **❞**

Exercise #1: Find a Friend and Change the World

Changing the world is always a little bit easier when we do it with a friend. And there seems to be no lack of ways—big and small—that we can make a difference in a loved one's life, the life of the community, or the life of the world. Start a Kwan Yin Bodhisattva club. Together, with at least one friend, meet regularly and come up with a list of ways you can be of service. Share in performing the tasks; taking turns depending on who is available, or simply so that everyone gets a chance to do something new. Here are some ideas:

- Volunteer to plant flowers for an elderly person who can't leave home very often anymore. Go back regularly to water the flowers, too! During your visits, turn an attentive eye to other things you could do easily that might be harder for your friend to accomplish. Ask if there are housekeeping chores you can do or errands you can run. Your elderly friend will appreciate the care and companionship.

- If you know a neighbor who is sick and has small children, offer your services to cook, clean, baby-sit, drive to the doctor—in short, to do whatever is needed.

- Offer to walk dogs or care for pets while owners are traveling—and at no charge!

- Use the special skills of each club member to teach or mentor another person. If you knit, teach a child. If you enjoy building things, build something for a family member or neighbor. If you are an investment whiz, offer club members advice on saving more and other sound strategies. If you paint, do a portrait for someone. Use what you enjoy and excel at to help someone else—and help each other, too.

- As a group, take a first aid or CPR course from your local volunteer fire department and let them know you're ready to help. Encourage others to do the same.

- Come up with a list of "daily service reminders" and vow to perform them faithfully whenever it's appropriate: Hold the door for someone else, take out your mother's trash, do the dishes for your sister without being asked, write personal thank-you notes for the gifts you receive, or simply tell someone you love and appreciate him or her.

There are as many ideas for your Kwan Yin club as there are women to join you and people to help! As your group grows, you may discover that your feelings of joy and inner peace grow as well. And you may make some new and lasting friendships along the way—both with other club members, and with the people who benefit from your efforts. After all, look at Princess Di and Mother Teresa! Whether you wear a royal tiara or a humble veil, friendship makes all things possible. Find a friend and set out together today to change the world for the better.

 Instant Goddess

Do you know the words to Beethoven's famous hymn, "Ode to Joy"? Whatever your religious beliefs, you'll find that this hymn speaks eloquently to the divine joy of living on this earth. Listen to the music (you'll know it when you hear it), and read along with the lyrics. Then walk outside, breathe deeply, and revel in the triumphant song of life!

Exercise #2: Gaia's World in a Box

Remember the Pandora's Box exercise that you did in Chapter 1? Doesn't it feel as if you did that exercise a long time ago? You have met many different Goddesses since that time, and you have explored the many and varied facets of your own inner Goddess. To help you consolidate what you have learned and to measure your progress on the Goddess path, you're going to make yourself another Goddess box.

According to some scholars, Pandora, the "giver of all," is also another name for Gaia. In stories that are older than the one in which Pandora releases evils into the world, she is truly the giver of all because she, like Gaia, is Mother Earth, the origin of all life. If you remember Gaia's story, she emerged from the shell of Nox's egg or she appeared out of chaos, and then she created the physical properties of the earth. In other words, she created herself, just the way you have been creating yourself while on the path to your inner Goddess, and just the way you will create, in a microcosmic form, when you make your new Goddess box.

As your first box did, your new box will reflect your outer self, the self that you show to the world, your way of dressing, talking, working, playing. Your box will also express the inner you—your private emotions, hopes, dreams, secrets, fantasies, and wishes for the future.

You will need the following:

- A white gift box about 6″ × 6″ × 6″
- Markers, pens, crayons, or colored pencils
- A glue stick
- Scissors
- Old magazines
- Yarn, feathers, beads, cloth scraps, polished stones, and other unique items that inspire you

Why not get together with some friends and make Goddess boxes together? Working alongside other women on such a project can be very educational. Everyone's box turns out to be so very different! Getting a group of friends together can also turn your box-making project into a celebration of your progress and an honoring of everyone's Goddess within.

When you're done working on your box, get out your Goddess journal. Place your new Goddess box on your altar beside the first box that you made. How are the two boxes similar? How are they different? In what ways do the differences in your two boxes indicate a changes within you? Take some time to think about both boxes and to reflect on your journey along the Goddess path of self-discovery.

When you feel ready, write a Goddess Prayer. Describe your altar. How has it changed and grown since you made it? Write about your progress. What have you learned about yourself? What behavioral shifts have you made? Feel free to page through your journal while you're writing. You may want to use words or phrases that you have already jotted down. Include information about your goals, hopes, and dreams for the future, as well. Where do you see yourself going next? How will your life continue to unfurl and express your Goddess within?

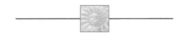

Have you noticed how much the Goddesses in this chapter have in common? Can you feel how they are all connected? Just the way you, as a woman, as a human being, and as a living creature of this earth, are connected to every other living thing, so the Goddesses, too, are connected to one another. And they are connected to you! You can see each Goddess as a manifestation of the Great Goddess, the sum total of all Goddess energy. She embodies all of the Goddess qualities you have learned about and more. Your inner Goddess is also a part of the Great Goddess. So, Goddess-to-Goddess, we are all divinely connected.

As the World card says, you have all the abilities and knowledge that you need. You are a self-actualized being. Like Gaia, you create and renew yourself, and you do so with the ever-present understanding that your actions affect all of earth's creatures. You also embody the pure essence of joy that is Oshun, and you share and spread that joy to all those you encounter. And you embody Kwan Yin's compassion and hold her example as a light in your heart. Is this the end of your Goddess journey or is it simply a new beginning? Let it be a great beginning!

A Who's Who of Goddesses

Amaterasu   The Shinto Goddess of the sun and guardian of the Japanese people, Amaterasu is worshipped as the Supreme Being. She is credited with inventing weaving and the cultivation of rice. She is celebrated every year on July 17 and also on December 21, the day of the winter solstice.

Aphrodite   She is the Greek Goddess of love, sex, and beauty. This beautiful woman was said to have been born from sea foam. Depictions of her often show her naked, stepping out of the sea or standing in a seashell.

Arachne   An ancient Greek Goddess associated with weaving, Arachne is thought by some to be mortal. An expert weaver, she challenged the Goddess Athena to a weaving competition. They both set to work, and Athena, enraged by the images of Zeus behaving badly in Arachne's tapestry, shamed Arachne. Athena was moved with pity when Arachne hanged herself; so Athena turned Arachne into a spider.

Artemis   The Greek Goddess of the moon, the hunt, and women, Artemis is a beautiful maiden. She is often depicted carrying bow and arrow and in the company of birds, deer, and lions. She is considered to be one of the virgin goddesses.

Atalanta   An ancient Greek Goddess of the hunt and the wild, Atalanta was renowned for her agility, swiftness, and knowledge of wild places. She agreed to marry only if her suitor could beat her in a footrace, and she remained undefeated for a long time. Some say that Atalanta is actually an aspect of Artemis, the maiden Goddess of the moon and the hunt, with whom she shares many traits.

Athena   The Greek Goddess of wisdom, she also is a warrior and rules over the city of Athens. She is associated with owls, olive trees, weaving, and the arts. She is said to have sprung full-formed from the head of Zeus, the lead deity in the Greek pantheon. She is another of the virgin goddesses.

Baba Yaga   A witch from Slavic folklore. Some scholars believe that Baba Yaga was originally a pagan Goddess of the forest, who embodied the Triple Goddess. She was maiden, mother, and crone all at once. She holds power over life and death and has often been seen as evil, although she can play a beneficent role in folktales. Deep in the forest, her house sits atop chicken legs, which enable it to move. In some tales, she is the keeper of day, sun, and night.

Bastet (or Bast)   She is the Egyptian Goddess of the sun and pleasure. She can be seen either as a woman with the head of a cat or as a woman with a lion's head. She is also a moon Goddess and is associated with music, dancing, and the pleasure that both of these arts bring.

Brigid   The Celtic Goddess of healing, fertility, and poetry, Brigid is also associated with fire, light, and inspiration. She sometimes takes triune form and thus is known as the Three Brigids. Her worship was only allowed to women. Eventually she was Christianized, and became known as Saint Brigid. Her feast day is celebrated on February 1.

Cerridwen   The Celtic Goddess of wisdom, poetry, the moon, and grain, Cerridwen is associated with magic and creativity. She also is a destroyer Goddess and is able to change her physical form at will. She was known as the White Lady of Inspiration and Death. She is often pictured as a crone stirring her pot of brew. Today she is much celebrated in Wiccan and Pagan circles.

Deer Woman   The Zuni Goddess associated with hunting, wild animals, and family, Deer Woman appears in many stories. In one of these stories, she marries a man. He criticizes her eating habits, so she leaves him.

Delphic Oracle Priestess   The shrine and the priestess of Apollo at Delphi, the Delphic Oracle was the site of many pilgrimages. Seekers of the truth came and questioned the priestess. To find their answers, she sat over a cleft in the rocks, breathed the steam that issued forth from the earth at that spot, and went into a trance. Because she was in touch with the divine, whatever the priestess said was thought to be the absolute and invariable truth.

Demeter The ancient Greek Goddess of the harvest and agriculture, Demeter is pictured as a mature woman. She is the mother of Persephone and thus is associated with the cycle of life and death. She and her daughter form a triad with the goddess Hecate, the crone.

Diana Diana is the Roman name for Artemis. *See* Artemis and Lucina-Diana-Hecate.

The Djanggawul Fertility and creator Goddesses from the Aboriginal people of Australia, the Djanggawul are two sisters (or sometimes two sisters and their brother). They arrived with their sacred objects in North Eastern Australia by boat, created all the physical features of the land, and gave birth to the first people. The sisters, who are also known as Dreamtime Daughters of the sun, gave each clan its sacred knowledge.

The Empress The third major Arcana card in the Tarot deck, the Empress represents the archetype of the Earth Mother. She is associated with fertility, growth, generosity, and healing. She is also associated with the planet Venus and demonstrates strong ties to the home. In a Tarot card reading, the Empress can indicate abundance, fertility, happiness, and prosperity.

Ennoia The Gnostic Goddess of thought and knowledge, Ennoia is one of the angels of thought who created all things. She can be described as the embodiment of wisdom. She also is said to be the mother of malevolent beings who pulled her down to earth where she causes women emotional pain and difficulties. She passed her knowledge of magic on to a Christian man who became one of the founders of the Gnostic sect.

Eve In the Bible, Eve tastes the fruit from the tree of knowledge and induces Adam to do the same. This action gets them both thrown out of the Garden of Eden. When Eve ate the apple, she ingested knowledge, which led to self-awareness, a loss of innocence, and self-consciousness.

The Fates The ancient Greek Goddesses who preside over the human life cycle, the Fates are known as the Moirae, which means "alloters." They dole out the length of thread that represents each human life. Clotho pulls the thread from the spool. Lachesis measures the thread, and Atropos cuts it. Some see the Fates as present at each new birth or beginning.

Freya The Teutonic Goddess of fertility, love, and sex, Freya wears a robe covered in feathers and a precious necklace that she obtained by sleeping with four dwarves. She rides in a wagon pulled by cats. Some say that Freya and Frigga are the same Goddess, but others see them as separate and distinct. Friday is her day, and the word *Friday* is derived from her name.

Gaia   The ancient Greek Goddess of the earth, Gaia is also the earth herself, a supreme being, and the creator of life. She was either self-created or emerged from the shell of Nox's egg, which was laid in the primordial chaos. She formed all the physical features of the landscape and may also have created the sky. She is the mother of Mnemosyne, the Goddess of memory and mother of the Muses. Gaia also is grandmother of Zeus, Hera, Demeter, Hestia, Hades, and Poseidon.

Greedy Woman   She is the Nigerian Goddess associated with agriculture and the necessity of human work. Because she took "too much," people ever since have had to work to gain food. Her story can be seen as a cautionary tale, but she also can be celebrated as a founder of human culture.

Halcyone   The daughter of the King of the Winds in ancient Greek legend, Halcyone married Ceyx, the King of Thessaly. After he was drowned at sea, the Gods sent her a vision to let her know the truth and transformed both lovers into birds. Halcyon has come to mean "calm and peaceful," and the "halcyon days" is a period of about two weeks around the time of the winter solstice when the weather is calm and the seas are tranquil.

Hathor   The Egyptian Queen of heaven, Hathor is associated with beauty, love, pleasure, motherhood, destruction, and the underworld. Typically she is depicted as a woman with a cow's head or as a cow. When in human form, she often wears a headdress bearing horns with a solar disc between them. She often carries a sacred rattle known as a sistrum.

Hecate   An ancient Greek Goddess associated with the moon and with the place where roads cross. *See* Lucina-Diana-Hecate.

The High Priestess   The second Major Arcana card in the Tarot deck, the High Priestess represents intuition, instincts, and hidden talents. Seated between two pillars of a temple, she is poised on the threshold between the world of flesh and the world of spirit. In a Tarot card reading, she turns up to remind you to trust your gut and look beneath the surface.

Iambe   An ancient Greek Goddess associated with happiness and poetry, Iambe cheered up Demeter when she was mourning her daughter Persephone. Iambe either recited poetry or told jokes and made Demeter laugh. Her laughter led to the thawing of the earth and to fertility, hence the association with laughter and fertility. Because of Iambe's abilities, she became Demeter's first priestess.

Inanna   The Queen of heaven in the ancient Sumerian tradition, Inanna is thought to be the first Great Goddess or Earth Mother. The Sumerians, who established one of history's earliest civilizations in the region that is now Iraq, honored Inanna as the Goddess of date groves, grain, love, and wine. She was also seen as Queen of Battles. The story of her trip to the underworld and her partnership with Dumuzi, the God of vegetation, are thought to explain the cycle of earth's seasons.

Isis   Isis is the Mother Goddess of ancient Egypt. She is associated with love, sex, the moon, fertility, magic, and rebirth. She is often depicted holding the infant Horus. According to one story, Isis once was mortal. She gained her powers from the sun God Ra after she had poisoned him.

Ix Chel   The Mayan Goddess of childbirth, sex, sorcery, healing, and weaving, Ix Chel is also associated with destructive floods, the moon, and night. Often she is seen as an older woman with claws and a headdress. Worshipped by weavers and by women to ensure a healthy pregnancy, Ix Chel's temple on the island of Cozumel, Mexico, was probably still in use into the 1500s.

Kali   The Hindu Goddess of destruction, death, earth, nature, and eternal time, Kali is often depicted as a naked wild woman with unruly hair and a protruding tongue. She wears a chain of skulls around her neck and stands on the body of her husband, Shiva. Kali sprang from the forehead of the Goddess Durga during a battle with a dangerous demon. Kali, a ruthless warrior, vanquished the demon and saved the gods from his army.

Kikimora   Despite the fact that many Russians describe her as a malevolent demon from the swamp, the Kikimora also is seen as a benevolent household spirit. One Russian artist describes two types of Kikimora—the evil swamp creature and the kind Kikimora, who is domestic. In her positive aspects, she may be persuaded to help around the house. She is also said to hide or break things and to keep children awake at night.

Kundalini   The sleeping energy that lies at the base of the spine, the Kundalini, in the Hindu tradition, is seen as a coiled snake of fire. She is found in all things. Awakened Kundalini energy rises up the spine and activates the body's chakras leading to *samadhi*, union with the divine.

Kwan Yin (or Quan Yin)   The mother of compassion in the Chinese Buddhist tradition, Kwan Yin, is also seen as the Goddess of mercy. She is associated with fertility and the protection of women and children. Her essence is perfect knowledge, and she is thought to be a future Buddha. She takes many physical forms, including that of a young woman sitting on a lotus, holding a vase full of the dew of compassion.

Lilith   Originally thought to have been a demon or a storm Goddess, Lilith has been reclaimed by feminist scholars. According to some stories, she was Adam's first wife and taught him wisdom. She left Adam and the garden of Eden, some say, because she refused to play a subservient role to her husband. She is now seen as representing knowledge, justice, freedom, and courage.

Lucina-Diana-Hecate   This triad is an example of the Triple Goddess from the Greek and Roman traditions. Lucina is a name used for both Juno, the supreme Goddess, and Diana, the Goddess of the moon and the hunt. Within this triad, Lucina represents birth. Diana is growth, and Hecate is death.

Mona Lisa   Probably the most famous painting in the world, the *Mona Lisa* which was painted by Leonardo Da Vinci in the early 1500s, hangs in the Louvre Museum in Paris. No one is absolutely sure who the sitter for this portrait was, but she is also known as *La Gioconda* in Italian, after one possible model. The life-like quality of the painting, the mystery surrounding the model's identity, and *Mona Lisa*'s smile, have all contributed to her enigma and her status in the public imagination.

Morgan Le Fay   A Goddess associated with water, magic, and healing from England and Wales, Morgan Le Fay is the queen of Avalon in Arthurian legend and is known as a sorceress. Although she is King Arthur's half-sister, she is also said to be his enemy. Despite this fact, she uses her special powers to heal him.

Morrigan   The British and Celtic Goddess of war and queen of ghosts, Morrigan, or the Morrigan as she often is called, may have been a sea Goddess and moon Goddess as well. Some people describe her as a fore-mother of Morgan Le Fay. She is associated with magic, and when called the Morrigan often takes triune form as Maiden, Mother, and Crone.

The Muses   The ancient Greek Goddesses of the arts, sciences, and inspiration, the Muses are the daughters of Zeus and Mnemosyne, the Goddess of memory. The Muses protect and inspire artists, and each Muse has her own specialty. They are Calliope (epic poetry), Clio (history), Erato (erotic poetry), Euterpe (lyric poetry), Melpomene (tragedy), Polyhymnia (sacred song and poetry), Terpsichore (dance), Thalia (comedy), and Urania (astronomy).

Nox   The ancient Greek Goddess of the night, Nox is a creator Goddess. Before the earth was born, Nox emerged from the primordial chaos and gave birth to Love. She is also the mother of Hypnos, the God of sleep, and is either the mother or grandmother of Morpheus, the God of dreams.

Oshun   One of the Orisha, or natural forces, from the religion of the Yoruba people of Nigeria, West Africa, Oshun is the essence of pure joy. She is associated with love, water, fertility, sensuality, and food. She is known as the mother of charity and is a healer. Personified, she is described either as a seductive young woman or as a dignified older woman. Despite the human characteristics she takes on in stories about her, her true nature is the energy of joy.

Oya   One of the Orisha, or natural forces, from the religion of the Yoruba people of Nigeria, West Africa, Oya is the energy of sudden change. She is associated with rainstorms, wind, the river Niger, and the Amazon. Although there are many stories in which Oya is personified and described as a tall woman who wears nine skirts, her energy is her most important aspect.

Pandora   An ancient Greek Goddess associated with earth, nature, and the evils of the world, Pandora was married to the God Epimethius. Although she had been warned not to, she opened the box that Zeus had given her and released evil into the world. Luckily, the box also contained hope. Some scholars believe that she is actually an incarnation of Gaia, Goddess of the earth.

Pele   The Hawaiian Goddess of fire, volcanoes, and dance, Pele is also a mother Goddess and thus is associated with sexual love and fertility. She is seen both as a crone and as a beautiful woman of childbearing age. In one story, she is said to marry the God of the ocean. When the two of them fight, her fire joins with his water to make the lava that pours from active volcanoes.

Persephone   Persephone is the Greek Goddess of fertility, spring, and the harvest. She is Demeter's daughter, and she is also the queen of death and the underworld. She spends the winter months in the underworld with her husband, Hades. She is also known as Kore, the maiden, and in this aspect is the Goddess of corn.

The Queens   From the Tarot deck, the Queen cards represent archetypes and are often used in readings to represent a woman over 40. The Queen of Wands represents ambition, growth, and leadership. The Queen of Cups stands for intuition. The Queen of Swords is representative of analytic thought and practical knowledge. The Queen of Pentacles rules over fertility of mind, body, and spirit.

The Red Shoes   The classic 1948 movie that tells the story of an aspiring ballet dancer, *The Red Shoes* has inspired generations of women to dance. Starring Moira Shearer as dancer Vicky Page, the film contains a 15-minute dance sequence of great power and beauty. The movie and the ballet within the movie speak to us about ambition, hard work, and a woman's conflict over career and family.

Sappho   An ancient Greek poet who lived on the Isle of Lesbos in the Aegean Sea, Sappho (630–612 B.C.E.) was dubbed the "tenth Muse" by the philosopher Plato. Although very little of her work has survived into the present day, today she still is considered to be one of the great poets because of her poetic innovation. Sappho often wrote about love, particularly her love for other women. She has served as inspiration for many lesbians and many poets.

Sarasvati   The Hindu Goddess of all the arts, Sarasvati also presides over knowledge, learning, and science. Known as the Goddess of speech and eloquence, she is honored in libraries as the patron of poets and writers, and because of her association with a river, is known as the Flowing One. She is the consort and Shakti of Brahma, the God of creation, and is pictured as a pale four-armed woman riding on a swan or seated on a lotus.

Shakti   In the Hindu tradition, Shakti is divine power or energy, which is seen as feminine. Each male God has a Shakti, who is considered to be his consort or wife. She is the driving force and active energy that activates him.

Sheherazade   The heroine from the literary classic *Arabian Nights*, or *Thousand and One Nights*, Sheherazade is the storyteller par excellence. First recorded in Arabic around the year 1000, the stories are held together by Sheherazade's own tale. Married to a king who has the habit of killing his brides on their wedding night, Sheherazade piques his curiosity with her verbal art and thus saves her own life. She teaches the king through her stories, and eventually they fall in love.

Shekinah   The manifestation of the divine presence on earth in Judaism, Shekinah, or the Shekinah, is the aspect of God that dwells among people. She represents pure compassion and, unlike the abstract God, she can be seen, heard, and felt. She is said to live wherever 10 people are assembled.

Sleeping Beauty   An archetypal character from European fairy tales, Sleeping Beauty was the much-wished-for daughter of the king and queen. The fairies blessed her with many talents, skills, and graces. One fairy, though, cursed her, and at the age of 16 the princess fell into a 100-year sleep from which she was awakened by a prince.

The Star   The seventeenth Major Arcana card in the Tarot deck, the Star represents hopes, dreams, and faith. The Star card portrays a woman pouring water both into a pond and onto the land of the shore. She evokes the connection between matter and spirit. In a Tarot card reading, the Star tells you that there is always hope and love and that your dreams can come true.

Tea Goddesses   The eighteenth-century chief priestess of the Daisho-ji women's temple in Kyoto, Japan, adopted the sencha-do form of the tea ceremony, which has its roots in Buddhist tradition, for use by her followers. We consider this priestess and her long line of followers to be tea Goddesses. In enacting the tea ceremony, the tea Goddesses exemplify the principle of harmony, respect, purity, and tranquility.

Saint Teresa of Avila   A Spanish Carmelite nun, Saint Teresa of Avila (1515–1582) was a reformer, the founder of a religious order, and the author of a number of influential books. She was subject to divine visions, one of which is depicted in the famous statue of her in Rome, which was carved by Giovanni Lorenzo Bernini (1598–1680). Saint Teresa was beatified in 1614, canonized as a saint in 1622, and given the title Doctor of the Church in 1970.

The Triple Goddess   A powerful archetype representing both the monthly cyclical nature of woman and the female life cycle, the Triple Goddess embodies the Maiden (youth), the Mother (full flowering of life), and the Crone (mature age). She is associated with the waxing, full, and waning moon. She is creator, protector, and destroyer. The Triple Goddess can appear as a triad of Goddesses all with different names, or she can be known under one name but with an emphasis on the representation of the three life stages.

Turtle Woman   The creator Goddess of the Arapaho people of the North American plains, Turtle Woman swam through the primordial waters until she found mud. Some people say that she swam for more than an entire day and almost died while on her quest. She brought the mud to the surface and created the world.

Uzume   The Shinto Goddess of mirth and dancing, Uzume is known in Japan as "Heavenly Alarming Female." She is also associated with fertility, shamanism, and physical ugliness. With her outrageous dancing, she lured the sun Goddess out of the cave in which she had been hiding. To this day, her dance, the karuga, is performed during religious festivals. She is also known as Ame-no-uzume.

Venus   The Roman Goddess of love, sex, and beauty, Venus is described in the same way as Aphrodite. *See* Aphrodite.

Venus of Willendorf   Uncovered in 1908 near Vienna, Austria, the Venus of Willendorf, a small limestone statue of a woman with a big belly and breasts, dates from 24,000 to 22,000 B.C.E. No one can say with certainty whether she was a representation of a Great Mother Goddess, a fertility charm, or child's toy. Nonetheless, she has become an icon of Paleolithic art and a symbol of both a woman's fertile power and of Goddess worship everywhere.

The women of Shakespeare   William Shakespeare (1564–1616), the English dramatist and poet, knew how to write roles for Goddesses! Like women traveling on the Goddess path, many of the women in Shakespeare's plays explore their own identities, learn about themselves, and try to determine who they truly are.

The World   The last Major Arcana card in the Tarot deck, the World is the card of attainment, integration of life-lessons, and self-actualization. The center of the World card shows a maiden dancing with the joy of understanding. In a Tarot reading, the World card tells you that you have all the talents and tools you need to move ahead, teach, travel, or start on a new path.

Yemaya   One of the Orisha, or natural forces, from the religion of the Yoruba people of Nigeria, West Africa, Yemaya (or Yemonja) is the essence of protective, nurturing energy. She is associated with water, oceans, fertility, childbirth, and motherhood. She has been called Mother Water and Star of the Sea. Sometime she is depicted as a mermaid. Although there are many stories in which Yemaya is personified, her energy is her most important aspect. It is usually seen as a mass of swirling color—blue, white, and silver.

Yoni Lotus   A Sanskrit term meaning "womb" or "abode," *yoni* is the word used to describe female genitalia in the Kama Sutra, a fourth-century Hindu text on sexuality. The yoni, which is often depicted as a lotus blossom and is the seat of fertility and creativity, is also the home of Shakti, the one universal power and energizing force. Both the yoni and the lotus symbolize life, death, and rebirth. The name Yoni Lotus honors that sacred connection.

The Zoryi   The Slavic Goddesses of morning, evening, and midnight, the Zoryi assist their father, the sun God, with his duties. The three sisters are also the guardians of the world, protecting it from the bear who lives in the Big Dipper. Zorya Utrennyaya is the aurora of the morning, or dawn; Zorya Vechernyaya is the aurora of the evening, or sunset; the Goddess of midnight's name has been lost.

A Goddess's Library: Books and Other Resources

Here is a listing, broken down by chapter topic, of other resources about the many Goddesses and the various topics covered in this book. You will find books, a few CDs, and a DVD. Enjoy exploring these resources as you continue to grow, learn, and express your own unique inner Goddess.

Chapter 1   Goddesses, Spirituality, and You

Adler, Margot. *Drawing Down the Moon: Witches, Druids, Goddess-Worshippers, and Other Pagans in American Today.* New York: Arkana, 1997.

Hamilton, Edith. *Mythology: Timeless Tales of Gods and Heroes.* New York: Mentor, 1969.

Robbins, Trina. *Eternally Bad: Goddesses with Attitude.* Berkeley, CA: Conari Press, 2001.

Sjoo, Monica, and Barbara Mor. *The Great Cosmic Mother*. San Francisco: HarperSanFrancisco, 1991.

Starhawk. *The Spiral Dance: The Rebirth of the Ancient Religion of the Great Goddess* (20th anniversary edition). San Francisco: HarperSanFrancisco, 1999.

Chapter 2   The Ages and Stages of Women

Angier, Natalie. *Woman: An Intimate Geography*. New York: Anchor Books, 2000.

Bolen, Jean Shinoda. *Goddesses in Every Woman*. New York: Harper & Row, 1984.

Edwards, Carolyn McVickar. *The Storyteller's Goddess: Tales of the Goddess and Her Wisdom from Around the World*. San Francisco: HarperSanFrancisco, 1991.

Graves, Robert. *The White Goddess*. New York: Noonday/FSG, 1948.

Woolger, Jennifer, and Roger Woolger. *The Goddess Within*. New York: Fawcett Columbine, 1989.

Chapter 3   Food: Nourishing Energy

Johnson, Cait. *Witch in the Kitchen: Magical Cooking for All Seasons*. Rochester, VT: Destiny Books, 2001.

Madison, Deborah. *Vegetarian Cooking for Everyone*. New York: Broadway Books, 1997.

Moore Lappé, Frances. *Diet for a Small Planet*. New York: Ballantine Books, 1982.

Robertson, Laurel, Carol Flinders, and Bronwen Godfrey. *Laurel's Kitchen: A Handbook for Vegetarian Cookery and Nutrition*. New York: Bantam, 1978.

Chapter 4   Drink: The River of Life

Carson, Rachel L. *The Sea Around Us* (Third Edition). New York: Oxford University Press, 1991.

Okakura, Kakuzo. *The Book of Tea*. New York: Dover Publications, 1966.

On the Wings of Song (artists) and Robert Gass, *From the Goddess*, Spring Hill Music, 1989. (This CD presents Z. Budapest's well-known chant "From the Goddess," interwoven with two other chants and sung by a 24-woman chorus.)

Chapter 5   Sleep: Inner Rejuvenation

Brown, Margaret Wise. *Goodnight Moon* (Reissue). New York: HarperCollins, 1991.

Faraday, Ann. *The Dream Game*. New York: Harper Paperbacks, 1974.

Long, Jill Murphy. *Permission to Nap: Taking Time to Restore Your Spirit*. Naperville, IL: Sourcebooks Trade, 2002.

Pliskin, Marci, and Shari L. Just. *The Complete Idiot's Guide to Interpreting Your Dreams*. New York: Alpha Books, 1998.

Chapter 6   Exercise: Moving in Harmony

Budilovsky, Joan, and Eve Adamson. *The Complete Idiot's Guide to Yoga*. Indianapolis: Alpha Books, 2001.

Judith, Anodea, and Selene Vega. *The Sevenfold Journey: Reclaiming Mind, Body, & Spirit Through the Chakras*. Santa Cruz, CA: Crossing Press, 1993.

The Red Shoes. Directed by Michael Powell and Emeric Pressberger. Criterion Collection (1948). (The DVD of this classic film brings Vicky Page's story and Moira Shearer's lovely dancing into your home.)

Roth, Gabrielle, with John Loudon. *Maps to Ecstasy: Teachings of an Urban Shaman*. Novato, CA: Nataraj Publishing, 1989.

Roth, Gabrielle, and The Mirrors. *Bones*. Red Bank, NJ: Raven Recording, 1989. This CD features music that is a calling to your inner dance, the dance around your bones.

Chapter 7   Play: Enjoying Life

Beckett, Sister Wendy. *Sister Wendy's Story of Painting* (Second Edition). New York: DK Publishing, 2000.

Edwards, Anne. *Maria Callas: An Intimate Biography*. New York: St. Martin's Press, 2001.

Keiler, Allan. Marian Anderson: *A Singer's Journey*. New York: Scribner, 2000.

Rogers, Richard, and Oscar Hammerstein. *Rodgers and Hammerstein's In My Own Little Corner*. Illustrated by Katherine Potter. New York: Simon & Schuster Books for Young Readers, 1995.

Vishnevskaya, Galina. *Galina: A Russian Story*. New York: Harcourt Brace Jovanovich, 1984.

Chapter 8   Sex: Sensually Spiritual

Bright, Susie. *Full Exposure: Opening Up to Sexual Creativity and Erotic Expression*. San Francisco: HarperSanFrancisco, 1999.

Dodson, Betty. *Sex for One: The Joy of Selfloving*. New York: Crown, 1996.

Ensler, Eve. *The Vagina Monologues: The V-Day Edition*. New York: Villard Books, 2000.

Wikoff, Johanina, and Deborah S. Romaine. *The Complete Idiot's Guide to the Kama Sutra*. Indianapolis: Alpha Books, 2000.

Chapter 9   Strength: Centering Power

Chödrön, Pema. *The Places That Scare You: A Guide to Fearlessness in Difficult Times*. Boston: Shambhala, 2001.

Kubler-Ross, Elisabeth. *On Death and Dying*. New York: Macmillan, 1969.

Neimark, Philip John. *The Way of the Orisa: Empowering Your Life Through the Ancient African Religion of Ifa*. San Francisco: Harper San Francisco, 1993.

Pinkola Estés, Clarissa. *Women Who Run with the Wolves: Myths and Stories of the Wild Woman Archetype*. New York: Ballantine Books, 1995.

Chapter 10   Creativity: Fertile Imagination

Cameron, Julia. *The Artist's Way: A Spiritual Path to Higher Creativity*. New York: Putnam, 1992.

Edwards, Betty. *Drawing on the Right Side of the Brain: A Course in Enhancing Creativity and Artistic Confidence* (Revised edition). Los Angeles: J.P. Tarcher, 1989.

Goldberg, Natalie. *Writing Down the Bones: Freeing the Writer Within*. Boston: Shambhala, 1986.

Rico, Gariele Lusser. *Writing the Natural Way: Using Right-Brain Techniques to Release Your Expressive Powers*. Los Angeles: J.P. Tarcher, 1983.

Warner, Sally. *Encouraging the Artist in Yourself*. New York: St. Martin's Press, 1991.

Chapter 11   Meditation: Calm and Aware

Coerr, Eleanor. *Sadako and the Thousand Paper Cranes* (Reissue). New York: Puffin, 1999.

Gawain, Shakti. *Creative Visualization*. Mill Valley, CA: Whatever Publishing, 1986.

Goldberg, Natalie. *Long Quiet Highway: Waking Up in America*. New York: Bantam, 1994.

Teresa of Avila. E. Allison Peters, tr. and ed. *Interior Castle*. New York: Image Books, 1972.

Chapter 12   Knowing: Your Inner Wisdom

Choquette, Sonia. *The Psychic Pathway: A Workbook for Reawakening the Voice of Your Soul*. New York: Crown, 1994.

Rosanoff, Nancy. *Intuition Workout: A Practical Guide to Discovering and Developing Your Inner Knowing*. Boulder Creek, CA: Aslan Publishing, 1988.

Weed, Susun S. *New Menopausal Years, The Wise Woman Way: Alternative Approaches for Women 30–90 (Wise Woman Herbal Series, Book 5)*. Woodstock, NY: Ash Tree Pub, 2001.

———. *Wise Woman Herbal for the Childbearing Years (Wise Woman Herbal Series, Book 1)*. Woodstock, NY: Ash Tree Pub, 1985.

Chapter 13   Action: Help Make the World a Better Place

Beethoven, Ludwig van. *Symphony No. 9/Karajan*, Berlin Philharmonic Orchestra, Polygram Records, 1996. (This CD contains the famous and powerful final chorus known as "Ode to Joy.")

Chearney, Lee Ann. *Visits: Caring for an Aging Parent, Reflections and Advice*. New York: Three Rivers Press, 1998.

Ingerman, Sandra. *Medicine for the Earth: How to Transform Personal and Environmental Toxins*. New York: Three Rivers Press, 2000.

Lovelock, James. *Healing Gaia: Practical Medicine for the Planet*. New York: Harmony Books, 1991.

Salzberg, Sharon. *Lovingkindness: The Revolutionary Art of Happiness*. Boston: Shambhala, 1997.

Goddess Index

Index

Goddesses, 7
    history of, 13-17, 115-117
Gods
    Brahma, 94
    Cronus, 194
    Domovoi, 107
    Dumuzi, 6
    Elegba, 198
    Hypnos, 79
    Morpheus, 79
    Obatala, 198
    Shakti of Brahma, 150
    Shiva, 94
    Uranus, 194
    Vishnu, 94
Gottlieb, Anne, 77
green tea, 60
Gwion, 64

H

hands collage, 33-34
hatha yoga, 96
healing powers, 186-187
Heavenly Alarming Female, 89
Helen of Troy, 119
herbs, 111
High Priestess, 185
history, 13-17, 115-117
hormone replacement therapy (HRT),
    30
household fun, 107-109
Howe, Marie, 153
*How to Read a Poem ... And Start a
    Poetry Circle*, 153
HRT (hormone replacement therapy),
    30
humility, knowledge and, 177-179
hunger, 37-38
Huong, Ho Xuan, 153

I

identity, 180, 182
    Romeo and Juliet, 181-182
    Shakespeare's heroines, 181-184
imagination, 147
    art, 149-152
    exercise, 157-158
    motherhood, 147-149
    poetry, 152-155
    writing, 155-157
in-vitro fertilization (IVF), 30
India, Kali, 17

Ingres, Jean-Auguste-Dominique, 45
inspiration, 164
    breathing exercise, 165
    Muses, 165
intuition, 184-185
IVF (in-vitro fertilization), 30

J

Japan, sencha-do tea ceremony, 59-60
jokes, 109-110
journals, 13
journeys, 191-193
joy
    emotions and, 198
    spiritual ecology, 197-199
Joyner, Florence Griffith, 86
Judaism, 16
Judeo-Christian tradition, 14
Jung, Carl Gustav, 5, 9, 148

K

Kama Sutra, 121, 123
Kataria, Dr. Madan, 111
Kersee, Jackie Joyner, 86
kindness, 199-202
Kirkland, Gelsey, 88
knowledge, 172, 174, 177
    balancing pride and humility,
        177-179
    Eve, 44
    food, 44-45, 49-51
    identity, 180-184
    intuition, 184-185
    perceptions of educated women,
        179-180
    witches, 186-187
Kundalini, 94
kykeon, 111

L

La, 9
La Joconde, 102
Lady Macbeth, 182-183
Lappé, Frances Moore, 197
laughing groups, 111-112
laws, Prohibition Act, 62
Leonore, 9
life cycle
    birth, 25-26, 55-56
    days, 28-30

petitionary prayer, 167
pets, 105
plays, *The Vagina Monologues*, 122
pleasure, 101
    dancing, 105-107
    household, 107-109
    jokes, 109-110
    laughing groups, 111-112
    music, 105-107
    paintings, 101-104
    poetry, 109-110
    sex, 120
    stand-up comedian acts, 112-114
Pliesetskaya, Maya, 88
poetry, 109-110, 152-155
    exercise, 158-159
    Sappho, 153-155
Polyhymnia, 165
prayer, compared to meditation, 167-168
pregnancy, 123-124.
    See also motherhood
pride, knowledge and, 177-179
Prohibition Act, 62
Puccini, Giacomo, 9

Q

Queen of Cups, 10
Queen of Pentacles, 10
Queen of Wands, 10
quizzes, Tarot cards, 10-11

R

Raktabija, 132
recipes, magic potions, 63-67
Reclaiming Collective, 15
The Red Shoes, 91-93
*A Return to Love: Reflections on a
    Course in Miracles*, 141
ritualistic prayer, 167
rituals
    alcohol, 61
    water, 59-60, 67-68
Rogers, Ginger, 89
Romeo and Juliet, 181-182
A Room of One's Own, 188
Roosevelt, Eleanor, 188
Rosalind, 183
Rubens, Peter Paul, 45
running, 86-88

S

Salzberg, Sharon, 200
samadhi, 94
Sasaki, Sadako, 169
Schwartz, Lillian F., 103
seasons, 21-22
self-empowerment, 141-142
self-expression
    poetry, 152-155
    story telling, 155-157
self-image, 44-45, 118-119
    creating, 18-20
self-preservation, Zuni, 47
sencha-do tea ceremony, 59-60
sex, 115
    partners, 121
        exercise describing ideal, 124-128
        practicing Shakti, 128-129
    pleasure, 120
    pregnancy, 123-124
    sexual responses, 120
    yoni, 121-123
Shakespeare, William, identity themes in
    plays, 181-184
Shakespeare in Love, 182
Shakti of Brahma, 150
Sheherazade (*Arabian Nights* character),
    155-156
shrieking, 171
Simos, Miriam, 15
sistrums, 105
six chakra exercise, 187-188
sleep, 71-72
    "beauty," 74-76
    dreams, 76-78, 80
        creating dream beds, 81-82
        Freud, Sigmund, 80
        Halcyone story, 78-79
        interpretations, 80-81
        investigating, 82-83
    Hypnos, 72
    requirements, 71, 73
    Sleeping Beauty, 74
    Sleeping Goddess of Malta, 73
Sosa, Mercedes, 32
The Spiral Dance, 15
spirituality, Goddess Force, 3-4
    as archetypes, 5
    as metaphors, 4
    dressing as, 5-6
Spring Essence, 153